A History of
British Baking

A History of British Baking

From Blood Bread to Bake-Off

Emma Kay

PEN & SWORD
HISTORY

First published in Great Britain in 2020 by
Pen & Sword History
An imprint of
Pen & Sword Books Ltd
Yorkshire – Philadelphia

ISBN 978 1 52675 748 7

Typeset by Mac Style
Printed and bound in the UK by TJ Books Limited,
Padstow, Cornwall.

Pen & Sword Books Limited incorporates the imprints of Atlas,
Archaeology, Aviation, Discovery, Family History, Fiction, History,
Maritime, Military, Military Classics, Politics, Select, Transport,
True Crime, Air World, Frontline Publishing, Leo Cooper, Remember
When, Seaforth Publishing, The Praetorian Press, Wharncliffe
Local History, Wharncliffe Transport, Wharncliffe True Crime
and White Owl.

For a complete list of Pen & Sword titles please contact

PEN & SWORD BOOKS LIMITED
47 Church Street, Barnsley, South Yorkshire, S70 2AS, England
E-mail: enquiries@pen-and-sword.co.uk
Website: www.pen-and-sword.co.uk

Or

PEN AND SWORD BOOKS
1950 Lawrence Rd, Havertown, PA 19083, USA
E-mail: Uspen-and-sword@casematepublishers.com
Website: www.penandswordbooks.com

Contents

Foreword

My history in baking

I have to admit, it's funny to be asked my opinion or feelings on the baking industry, because in my head I'm still a new boy, still learning the ropes as it were.

But in the twenty or so years I've been baking, I've picked up a few things.

That's why this book is an amazingly interesting read from cover to cover, written in the same passion and dedication to detail you need to be an actual baker, maybe Emma Kay has missed her calling in life.

Parts of this book really transfixed me, the history of baking is very close to my heart, as it has a depth of information on types, styles and methods; it really held my attention.

It looks at how bread really affected people and their own lives, how through new ideas bread shaped the word GREAT in **GREAT BRITAIN**.

This book is a must for anyone who finds history or baking fascinating. It looks at the true history of the daily loaf and analyses it in a way never done before. It shows just how the bread industry affected all aspects of the social scale, it will definitely help the reader to understand why the craft baking industry is so complex … well done Emma.

On top of that, as a baker myself, I loved the comments from other bakers, their view on the industry we love.

And this is my view:

1996 was the year I started full-time work in our small family bakery, which my dad had started from scratch.

My family (Swifts) had been baking since 1863, so as bakers we have a good understanding of what to do and why, our own history has been passed on to me from a very close relationship with my grandad who baked through the Second World War as a field-baker in Africa.

It was soon apparent to me that after sixteen years of living in the bakery, a few things had rubbed off on me; I was able to do things in my first year which were well beyond my experience.

As time rolled on and I got more involved in the baking and the running of our own little bakery, it became very obvious that I was part of an amazing industry, a small spoke in a much bigger wheel.

Now baking is not for everyone, well commercial baking anyway; we can all love baking at home and watch a certain TV programme, but in a small family bakery the hours are long (like, sixteen hours a day long), the job is hot, uncomfortable and very physical; add to that the pressure of making money into the equation and it becomes mentally challenging, and sometimes those are the biggest factors.

You have to push yourself all the time and in every way in baking, because at the end of the day the only thing that matters is the loaf; that one thing, big or small we as bakers strive for, that perfect loaf of bread.

Now all along this journey, I knew I was from baking stock, the stories from my family passed down to me were never too far away from my thoughts. The fact that so many bakers throughout time who had come before me, they took up the challenge of baking the daily bread, some had been successful and some lost their lives doing so, they also had a story to tell which was so fascinating to me.

In 2015 somehow I got a chance to tell that story.

I was one of the four bakers picked to experience working life as a Victorian Baker in the hit BBC2 series 'Victorian Bakers'.

Victorian Bakers (VB) was one of the highlights of my life so far, I got to meet amazing people, especially Duncan Glendinning and John Foster.

They are from opposite ends of the industry, but have the same passion for bread.

The biggest thing that VB showed me and all who work on the show, was that the internal and external focuses that put pressure upon bakers and the industry are as prevalent today as they were back then.

Ok, so today we don't kill bakers or customers with adulteration, but if you look closely at some working practices that go on, some craft bakers say it's just as bad.

There are also added pressures on the industry, not just the speed in which consumerism changes and in what direction it takes, but at the moment within the industry there is a movement which could see the craft side lost for ever.

But don't fear bread lovers, it's not all bad! The industry grows year on year offering new ideas and opportunities, not only for customers, but bakers alike.

To summarise, I love being a baker, I love my industry and the rich history it has.

It's now in a stronger position to go forward, but we must learn from the past; we need to help and nurture new bakers, to grow new ideas within our walls, to protect our values which we hold dear, or we will find the past will bite us back and we might lose what is most dear to us.

'GIVE US TODAY OUR DAILY BREAD'

This book is a must for anyone who loves baking, bread, and its history.

John Swift

Acknowledgements

This is the part of the book which always concerns me the most as I am cautious of trying not to leave anyone out. I spoke to many people, including those working in the baking trade while writing this book, but special thanks goes to Richard Marshall, Marshall's Bakery, Pewsey, Wiltshire; Caroline Walsh from Archipelago Bakery, Edinburgh; Edward Clark of Pastonacre, Cley next the Sea, Holt, Norfolk; Heidi Wall, Boutique Brownies, Chelmsford, Essex; Alison McTaggart, Bread On A Bike, Cambridge; Vitor Santos, The Celtic Bakers, London; Geoffrey Permain and Tony Greenwood. Thanks also to Henry Herbert of Hobbs House Bakery, Gloucestershire, and to John Swift of Swifts Bakery for agreeing to support this book. You are all baking legends.

I would like to thank Amy Yeates at The Federation of Bakers for taking time to answer my questions, along with Roy Clare for his lovely input, and Carolyn Findell for entrusting me with her family's very special collection. Also worth a big mention for providing useful images are John Graves on behalf of Chesham Society, and Curator of Chertsey Museum, Emma Warren.

On a personal note, my husband and young son have been so supportive as ever. I'm not sure what I would do without them. In particular thank you so much to Nick Kay for all his photographic skills, which always helps with making my work come to life.

I'm delighted to have written this book for Pen & Sword and would like to say thanks to my editors Laura Hirst, Karyn Burnham and Claire Hopkins for being so patient with me.

Introduction

Before even beginning to tackle the research for this book, several essential questions needed to be addressed, like, what exactly is British? And what exactly constitutes Baking? How far back should I investigate? What genuine impact has baking actually had on Britain as a nation, if any?

It turns out baking is as complex as the chicken and egg theory, as fundamental as night is to day. It is influential, innovative, contemporary and fast-moving, yet deeply ancient.

This is a book that primarily focuses on baking, within the context of bread, cakes and pastries. If you are seeking a narrative of baked meats and vegetables, then you may find little of substance here. This is mostly a content issue. A chronology of baking is a considerable task to condense into one book. As it is, I found myself frequently coming up against word counts, when I could have waxed lyrical for considerably longer on some subjects. I didn't want to wholly focus on the practicalities of baking, so rather than writing in-depth on the narrative of inventions that have enhanced the practice of baking, or enlighten readers about the scientific elements that constitute the perfect bake; while there are aspects of all these things, this book primarily seeks to uncover the numerous ambiguous effects of baking on society as a whole. The people, the transformations, the commercial and the domestic, the evolution of baking at the heart of dramas and conflict, while always seeking to unearth the origins of Britain's beloved dishes. From a research perspective it is very difficult to seesaw between one area of what traditionally constitutes baking and another, which is less straightforward. Some readers may also be looking for lots of facts and figures relating to baking legislation. Where I have endeavoured to argue as many of the most significant as possible, those seeking to be re-taught old school tutoring around related topics such as the Repeal of the Corn Laws may be disappointed, as I have deliberately not dwelt on the complexities of parliamentary debates and Britain's subsequent shift towards Free Trade.

What you will find in this book is a propensity towards the cultural and social elements of baking, relating to how the past continues to impact on present-day UK trends. How a wealth of nations influenced our baked goods and how Britain's own role in world politics ultimately motivated the way it bakes and what it eats.

Many of Britain's contemporary baked dishes are a confusing mix of cultural appropriations. The meringue, crème brûleé soufflé and many others besides all herald from France. It is also easy to confuse American dishes with British ones. It needs to be remembered that early settlers in America were largely British, as they were in Australia. So, when we think of macaroni cheese, or Mac & Cheese, as a classic American dish, it is of course a much older dish from Britain, who acquired it even earlier from the Italians. Whereas classics like the cheesecake and most puddings, including the cherished bread and butter, are adaptations and variations from early medieval dishes. Although, most of these were inherited from the French during the Norman invasions. While many of our earliest bakes, such as mince pies undoubtedly herald from Middle Eastern influences, and bread as we know it from the Romans.

Bread remains the most cost effective of foodstuffs and this is why it has been nurtured for so many centuries. Even as a half-starved student, which I have experienced several times over, I always felt that if I had enough money each week for a loaf of bread, I would be OK. Now, I tend to make a lot of my own bread and I still find myself mentally calculating every week, how much we need as a family for lunch boxes, breakfasts, snacks, mealtime accompaniments. It is integral to all of our daily lives, even for those with specialist diets, its properties once highly prized in an age of superstition and mysticism. There is an early seventeenth-century manuscript by Franciscus Jacobus which depicts a round piece of bread inscribed with a cure to kill worms. Perhaps this was the inspiration for the once well-regarded worm cakes that dominated the Victorian era.

It was thought that the chewing of bread promoted teething, and the crusts made a useful gum-stick. And that a poultice of bread and milk softened with salad oil could cure a viper bite.[1] Bread and other baked by-products have always played the nurturing, life sustaining role in Britain.

A Victorian breakfast for the labouring classes in Devon, Somerset, Dorset and Wiltshire was commonly tea-kettle broth, either made from milk, or bread, hot water, salt and pepper and a little fat or dairy. Bread and cakes were traditionally gifted to the poor for centuries, hardtack biscuits have sustained armies, while stodgy bread-based puddings bolstered the Industrial age.

Investigating the origins of individual baked goods for this book was a challenge. I deliberately omitted a few of the more popular ones to emphasise this point here in the introduction. Once you've fought your way through a minefield of Old English terms and phrases, taken into account the frequency of mis-spellings and variations of spellings, delved through archives – both British and global, that get older and older and include earlier versions that you had never thought possible, you can then start tackling the very nature of how recipes evolved, using a complex mix of pre-existing knowledge, speculation and new research. Take for example the humble Victoria sponge sandwich. One of the first references I came across was for a Victoria Cake in 1838, a year after the queen's accession. The original version bears little similarity with what we might recognise as a Victoria sponge sandwich today. In that the actual jam sandwich ensemble is obsolete. The recipe was published as a reader's letter in the *Magazine of Domestic Economy*:

Victoria Cake

Sir- I enclose a receipt for a cake which the confectioners have dignified with the name of the Victoria cake, which is greatly in request. I assure you it is excellent.

The yolks of twelve eggs, leaving out the whites of six; one pound of loaf sugar beat fine; the juice of one lemon, and the peels of two cut very fine; whisk these ingredients together for three quarters of an hour, then add twelve ounces of flour. This cake must be put into the oven immediately; an hour is sufficient to bake it.[2]

By 1846 Charles Francatelli, the queen's Head Chef, who one assumes would be an authority on this eponymous cake, adds butter to the list of ingredients above, together with almonds, cream and a variety of dried fruits. This cake was probably even more far removed, as it was intended to be a yeast-based Gugelhupf. Interestingly, Francatelli instructs that the cake be accompanied on the side by some diluted and warmed marmalade and some 'German custard sauce'. This may well have been the determiner for the cake's future reincarnation with a jam and cream filling.[3] In fact, it would be the year after Francatelli's book was first published, that the phrase Victoria Sandwich appears in the media, applied to jam or marmalade filled sponge cakes.

The Battenberg of the same era could be so named after either of the marriages of Queen Victoria's granddaughter, Princess Victoria to Prince Louis of Battenberg in 1884, or that of Prince Henry of Battenberg, who married Queen Victoria's youngest child, Princess Beatrice a year later. In terms of the latter, there were about a dozen cakes presented to the prince and princess on their wedding day, with two unique cakes made at Windsor castle placed on the royal tables. The 'presentation cakes'

Victoria Sponge Sandwich.
(*@ Emma Kay*)

were the creation of the Gunters, a family of leading society caterers
and confectioners of the time, with a long and distinguished heritage
in London. I cannot find any specific descriptions of these cakes that
liken them to the novelty 'coloured window' Battenberg variety. The
press reports from the wedding indicate that various cakes were given
as wedding gifts, so it may have been that a member of the Battenberg
house, gifted a national cake, which could have been one with coloured
squares encased in marzipan. However the cake evolved, it is clear that
its popularity was instantaneous, with advertisements in the media
immediately following the 1885 wedding announcing the sale of 'the
new Battenberg cake', which curiously was also frequently labelled
as being 'flavoured by fresh fruit'.[4] Sourcing Battenberg recipes from
the era is quite hard, but one that I did come by from 1912 suggests it
should be decorated with cherries and angelica, which may explain the
fruit element.[5] Battenberg is composed of a basic Genoese sponge, which
was frightfully popular during the nineteenth century, with the Italian
fashion for cooking prevalent across recipe books from as early as the late
1600s.

Italian influences in mind, that lovely, chewy, chocolatey, texture-rich
morsel, the Florentine, which has been a winner generally in our family
since at least the 1980s, has a heritage that is so complex and contentious
that I would not know where to begin. Is it Italian? French? Was it always
chocolate based? If so, it can only have a heritage equal to that of when
chocolate was introduced in confectionery work – so, not that long. A
Florentine was once known in Britain as a savoury dish of minced meats,
currants and spices, particularly popular during the 1600s. Gervaise
Markham's recipe of 1683 combines a curious mix of sweet paste and
veal kidneys, which actually adopts a very similar technique as to that
applied to the making of a contemporary chocolate Florentine. The veal
is cut small and mixed into a paste with herbs, currants, sugar, cinnamon,
bread crumbs and egg yolks. Flour mixed with melted butter and more
sugar is then added to this paste. After a bit more rolling and joining of
pastes in a dish, finally covered with egg-white wash and baked in an
oven.[6] The butter, sugar and flour paste combination with the addition of
chopped, dried fruit and meat, is undeniably related to the recipe I have
used for years, minus the carnivorous bits. The earliest version of this

recipe appears in Thomas Dawson's *A Good Huswifes Handmaide* 1594, but Markham's is slightly more detailed. The well-known nineteenth-century Swiss restauranteur of the Waldorf-Astoria, among other notable venues, Oscar Tschirky, capitalised on his position with the writing of a recipe book in 1896. The book includes a recipe for Florentine Meringues which involves a sheet of puff pastry being covered in jam, then covered in a layer of meringue and chopped almonds, before being baked.[7] Then there's Florentine eggs, a Florentine of tongues, Florentine Apple Pie. The word Florentine seems to have become a prefix to make a multitude of dishes sound more continental and therefore more interesting, by the following century. Then, I came across an old British recipe book dated circa mid-1600s, primarily written by Elizabeth Jacob, who included a recipe for 'Making Florentines' that reads as this:

Take mace, small Raysons, Ginger, eggs, Shugar, Saffron, Dates, make the paste with butter and eggs and bake it in a dish and cover it with fine paste above and beneath.[8]

An old recipe for Florentines without the meat, although it is encased in pastry. By the 1930s Florentines are being championed in the British press as 'The very latest thing', seemingly led by confection giant, Rowntree's.[9] This suggests chocolate Florentines are undoubtedly a more modern variation of an old theme, one that evolved in Italy, or from the confectionery authorities of France. Something with that name became popular in Britain as a savoury cousin during a time when the nation was being shaped and formed by a myriad of different global influences.

Someone, somewhere, mixed all of those influences up together, along with a few other existing sweet treats of old, to produce the Florentine we are most familiar with today. Often, it is that missing link that I will pursue. Who was that link? How did they get to that particular creation? What inspired them? But, with some dishes, you have to just admit defeat. The evidence may well be there to document the evolution of the chocolate Florentine, but it's compounded by the fact that it revolves around a famous city of the same name, a city which pops up in the archives in countless searches while having the added disadvantage of being associated with numerous other dishes of the same name.

Chocolate Florentines.
(*@ Emma Kay*)

Many of Britain's cakes and pastries are all a variation on a theme that began in the early medieval period, which is why this book doesn't keep addressing the plethora of different recipes that have emerged over the centuries.

The military perspective is an integral part of the baking dialogue and features with some significance in this book. On and off the front line. Not a great many people have influenced me over the years, but of the ones who have, Rear Admiral Roy Clare has remained a firm favourite. Having served in the Royal Navy for decades as man and boy, Roy has also steered Auckland War Memorial Museum and The National Maritime Museum, now part of Maritime Greenwich World Heritage Site, where I worked under his leadership as Director. He informed me that around the early 1970s the Royal Navy researched and developed a bread mix that could be used with salt water. It was intended for team members aboard the first fully crewed round-the-world yacht race. The Navy's entry was *Adventure*, a 55-ft sloop, which went on to win three of the four legs of the Whitbread Round the World Race, including the one Roy sailed as chief mate, from Rio to Portsmouth. Roy recalled that 'the bread was tasty, not salty, and lasted well. It was a popular accompaniment to the tinned Compo Rations that we had to survive on! And best of all – as fresh water was always scarce – it was baked "fresh from the sea"'.

Little nuggets such as this persuaded me to approach a range of bakers and former bakers when writing this book in order to better understand the key challenges and advantages of being a baker. There is this wide misconception today, I think, that everyone is at home baking their children's snacks, feeding their sourdough mixes and staging entertaining vintage tea parties. But I think the reality for most people is the bought-in frozen puff pastry, pre-packaged cakes, standard sliced white supermarket loaves, and the nearest they get to bread-making is by putting all the ingredients in a machine and flicking a switch. It's what we have been conditioned to do for decades. We live in a society where watching other people bake is preferable to actually having a go ourselves. The phenomenal popularity of the Great British Bake Off, has become something of an iconic obsession across the nation with the 2019 final watched by something like 6.9 million viewers. But I would really like to know what the percentage is of those who actually follow the recipes and bake themselves.

According to the Federation of Bakers, Britain eats the equivalent of 9 million large loaves every day. Some 80 per cent of this is manufactured by the large commercial bakeries, 17 per cent by in-store bakeries, and the remainder is provided by independent craft and high-street bakers.

There are numerous references and stories relating to most of the leading bakeries and bakers of Britain in this book. Many of which have survived decades, sometimes hundreds of years of change; adapting, innovating, expanding and increasing their markets. Most have adopted the mass-consumerist approach to baking, the Chorleywood and the Koenig modernisms. The three main bread manufacturers in Britain are Allied Bakeries, Hovis and Warburtons, accounting for almost three-quarters of the wrapped sliced bread market. So, are we really all at home lighting our ovens and watching the dough rise?

One of the objectives of this book is to inspire people to look at the past, in order to learn for the future. We live in a fast-paced world, with a great deal available at our finger-tips. Taking time out to make one humble loaf of bread, could help everyone connect a little more with their ancestors, while appreciating the simplicity of one of our oldest and most cherished arts. Below is a recipe for Allinson's classic wholemeal loaf. It's one I regularly bake, as it's relatively simple, quick and gets eaten in a day. The first loaf you bake doesn't need to be fancy or complicated and the more you do it, the more you might find you want to challenge yourself. Remember, making a sourdough starter means no more buying all that packet yeast! Give it a go. What's the worst that could happen…?

Classic Wholemeal loaf by Allinson's

Method:

1. MIX Mix the flours, yeast and salt in a big bowl. Mix together the melted butter, sugar and water, then mix in with a cutlery knife.
2. KNEAD Tip onto a lightly flour-dusted surface and knead for 10 minutes (or use the dough hook attachment on your mixer).
3. RISE Lightly grease the mixing bowl with some oil. Put the dough back in, cover the bowl with a clean tea towel and leave to rise until doubled in size.
4. SHAPE Knock back the dough by gently kneading just 5 times to get the air out. Mould into a smooth oval and lift into a lightly oiled 900g/2lb loaf tin.
5. PROVE Cover the dough again with a clean tea towel and leave to prove until doubled in size again. Preheat your oven to 200°C (fan 180°C, gas mark 6).
6. BAKE Lift the tin onto the middle oven shelf and bake for 35–40 minutes, until you can lift the bread loaf from the tin and when you tap the base it sounds hollow. Cool on a wire rack.

Ingredients:
- 400g Very Strong Wholemeal Flour (We like Allinson's)
- 100g Strong White Bread Flour (We like Allinson's)
- 1 Sachet Allinson's Easy Bake Yeast or Allinson's Time Saver Yeast
- 1½ tsp Salt
- 50g Butter (Melted)
- 1 tbsp Light Muscovado Sugar (We like Billington's)
- 300ml Warm Water

Equipment:
- 2lb Loaf Tin[10]

Chapter 1

Mastering the Masonry Oven
and Medieval Menus

Early Beginnings

Baking is as old as the human race and grains have been the most important source of food since the evolution of man. What is considered to be the world's oldest bread made from grains ground, sieved and kneaded, some 12,000 years before Christ and at least 4,000 years prior to the advent of agriculture, were recently discovered in a prehistoric oven unearthed in Jordan. Considering the dates of these primitive flatbreads, academics are now deliberating over bread being the determiner for agriculture, rather than the age-old consensus for it being the other way around.[1]

Early unleavened bread occurred, either naturally or by quirk of fortune, from grains being ground and mixed into a paste with water, then left on a hot stone to be toasted. No one quite understands how the

Unleavened Flat Breads. (@ *Emma Kay*)

addition of yeast and the leavening process began. Perhaps wild yeasts were spawned on dough that was abandoned or left overnight.[2]

As a food historian I am often asked where did this originate? How did this come about? Who made the first … whatever? A lot of the time the answer is consistently same – the Middle East. The Assyrians, people from Mesopotamia – arguably the first ever civilization, were baking dough in sealed pots of clay buried underground, quite possibly several hundred years before the Egyptians. Whatever the chain of events, it was the practices of these early civilizations, including the Egyptians, Greeks and Romans who refined the process of baking into what we have become to rely on so considerably today.

Remarkably, detailed numerical baking accounts from the reign of Seti I, the son of history's legendary pharaoh Ramesses I, have withstood centuries of evolution, offering a vestige of insight into baking at that time. According to these accounts the soldiers of the pharaoh received one large loaf of bread, possibly on a daily basis.[3] The accounts are complex and methodically divided into sections including lists of grain deliveries, individual baking activities, bread received from the bakery and monetary receipts. An average 168 loaves could be produced from three-and-a-half sacks of flour, with daily deliveries of these sacks ranging from 100 to 260. Each standard loaf weighed around thirteen-and-a-half *deben* (approximately 1kg). Not far off the size of a standard 800g loaf today.[4] The relationship between brewing and bread-making was intrinsic for the Egyptians, just as it always has been for most societies. Made from the same staple ingredients of wheat and barley, both needing to be milled and both requiring fermentation. The act of heating and cooking are also relevant to both processes. Querns and ovens were situated close to each other in ancient Egypt, in the same way that brewing and baking were almost always located on or adjacent to the same premises in Britain, right up until the twentieth century. There are three chronological kingdoms in Egyptian history: Old, Middle and New. By the time of the New Kingdom, between 1550–712 BC there were around forty types of bread being made in Egypt varying in shape and size from oval, round, concave and twisted all made from wheat (Emmer) barley and corn. Incredibly, a wall inscription found on the tomb of Ti in Saqqara, dating to the fifth century, mentions the importance attached to the sieving of flour, after being ground. It reads: 'Grind, grind well. I will grind with all my power. The servant is sieving the flour and I baked the cake myself.'[5]

The ancient Greeks took breadmaking to a whole other level, with as many as eighty different varieties being recorded and developed by professional bakers. These included flatbreads, which were predominantly made with barley and eaten together with a choice of vegetables, meat, fish and cheeses, often piled on top, a bit like assembling a pizza. Like the Egyptians, the Greeks also used wheat in bread production, the gluten from which would have given it a texture we are more familiar with today.[6] Other ancient communities like the Aztecs would have cultivated corn and Amaranth, a grain similar to something like quinoa to make bread. Having baked with it myself, for its non-gluten properties I can visualise why Amaranth became a popular grain to produce. It does have a slightly flowery, sweet aftertaste, but is far easier to manipulate than flours such as almond or arrowroot. Many East Asian communities also made do with gluten less grains, cultivating mostly rice and sorghum flours, or even ground wild seeds to bake with.

Invaders and Influencers

The culture that advanced Britain the most was undoubtedly the Romans. Following their invasion of 43 AD, clay became a popular vessel for baking. There is no one link to how this process was invented, or by whom. Mesopotamian communities were building full-scale kilns around 6,000 BC, while Indian tandoors have been used for at least 3,000 years. They are most commonly associated with Middle Eastern nomadic cultures; whose influence was significant across Europe during the Anglo-Saxon age. Even before the Romans invaded Britain, clay baking would invariably have been a common method of cooking, particularly in areas where this earthy matter was present. There is enough evidence of badly fired clay lumps scattered across numerous ancient sites to legitimise this. The clay itself would be gathered from nearby cliffs and moulded into sheets. Whatever required cooking would then be wrapped up like a parcel and once prepared, the item was dried and left to harden in its clay casing. It was then placed in a hearth and covered in hot embers to bake slowly. Once removed the clay could be cracked open to reveal the food within. Smaller items of meat would probably have been baked this way, with larger joints placed in an earth oven. An earth oven was basically a pit dug into the ground, allowing the heat to be trapped and food to be baked slowly. Although Plymouth boasts the title of the UK's oldest commercial bakery, Jackas, which has been trading since the 1500s, evidence of far earlier baking activity remains dotted around the country. On the site of a Parish Church in Chadwell, Essex, during the early part of the twentieth century, parts of a circular, domed oven were discovered with a diameter of around 5ft, and a flue about a foot shorter, thought to date from the third century.

Specific ovens were also built to dry corn for bread-making. When the M5 was being built an Iron Age T-shaped corn drying oven, which was partly constructed of limestone was discovered a few miles outside Cirencester.[7]

Archaeological evidence presented by the historian Dr Joan Frayn in 1978, identified five principal methods of Roman baking: baking in the ashes, baking in the *sub testu* (*sub* meaning underneath, *testu* meaning tasty) covering the food in an earthenware vessel, surrounded by hot ashes, similar to a 'chicken brick', and revived in the 1920s by the now iconic Pataki clay baker, manufactured by the Pataki Ceramic factory in Hungary. In Roman communities, this form of baking, along with

Clay Baking. (@ *Emma Kay*)

Contemporary Outdoor Wood Fire Baking. (@ *Emma Kay*)

the immersion in ashes was adopted by more rural, labouring Romans. The third method was the introduction of a small and stationary oven, built into a range and uncovered at the site of the ancient Roman town, Herculaneum. According to Frayn, the need to bake in larger quantities, fuelled the development of the *furnus*. This was similar to a contemporary pizza oven and inspired by the Roman *fornax* or corn dryer, used by commercial bakers. Finally, the *clibanus* and *thermospodium* evolved as types of portable ovens, taking influence from the original *testum*. These latter ovens, together with the *furnus* were arguably owned by more prosperous households.[8]

Ash cakes is the general term for anything that was baked in the ashes of a fire, christened *panis focacius* by the Romans, focacius meaning hearth and undoubtedly an early descendant of the Italian flat bread, focaccia. There is a 1946 recipe for ash cakes (or dampners as they are called in Australia) that was published in the Australian *Sydney Morning Herald* describing their simplicity. But the process would have been a lengthy one, from sourcing the grains to pounding, mixing and preparing them.

Take 1 lb of flour, water and a pinch of salt. Mix it into a stiff dough and knead for at least one hour, not continuously, but the longer it is kneaded the better the dampner. Press with the hands into a flat cake and cook it in at least a foot of hot ashes.[9]

By understanding how communities in Rome approached their day-to-day systems of baking, it's possible to determine how they might well have adopted the same practices in England. In the early days of the Roman Empire, some 329 bake-houses were said to have occupied the streets of Rome. It was common practice to send petty criminals or slaves to work in these bakeries, to undertake the hard labour involved with grinding the wheat.[10] Before commercialised baking cornered the market, *Puls* was the popular daily dish of choice for the Romans. It was a simple porridge consisting of cereals or legumes. *Puls* remained in use alongside the consumption of bread for some years, as a food primarily associated with the poorer classes. It was commonly used during sacrifices for its symbolic properties as a dish once considered essential to survival.[11]

Early recordings of domestic baking practices can be found in the writings of Pliny the Elder – a Roman author, philosopher and early army commander who wrote a famous text entitled *The Natural History*, completed around AD 77. The text provides vital social information about the Roman Empire, with Pliny describing women as the main bakers in the family. Bread was also predominantly of the sourdough variety, with grape juice often added to the leavening agent. This is a practice still applied today to some sourdough starters. Breads were also made in a variety of forms and from different grains. White raised bread was

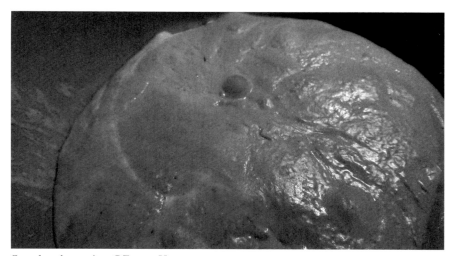

Sourdough proving @Emma Kay

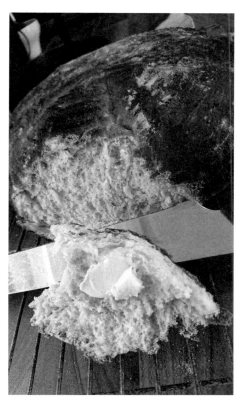

Sourdough Bread and Butter.
(*@Emma Kay*)

preferable to coarser unleavened brown breads, the latter historically always associated with the less elite of society. Domestic bread would have been baked in a *testum* (an earthenware pot) or *clibanus* (furnace kiln). The demise of these two forms of baking have been attributed to the rise in commercial baking, and the evolution of milling technology. Large slave and donkey powered mills meant more grain could be ground to yield more loaves.

Evidence to support the mass consumerism of baking during the Roman age is still visible, with places like Pompeii revealing over thirty-one commercial bakeries, including a very famous oven containing some eighty burnt loaves, abandoned and perfectly preserved after the fatal eruption in 79 AD. There are numerous connections to *pistores* (bakers) and *pistrinas* (a bakery and mill) throughout Roman literature. Roman Bakers could be identified by their frequent use of iconography; engraved on their tombs, shop signs and even on jewellery. Designs included symbolic single millstones as well as pictures of the donkey's that would turn those millstones.[12]

Unsurprisingly, bakers became heavily relied upon and were politically powerful contributors to Roman society, commanding increased salaries and greater protection. They would frequently strike, leading to riots and consumer discord. The Roman governing hierarchy worked diligently to enforce regulations ensuring bread production was protected with bakers and the state gradually securing a harmonious relationship. The status of bakers across the Roman Empire rose significantly over time.[13]

Bread is one of the most documented of Roman foods, with pastries not far behind. The pastry cooks or *pastillarium*; along with the *dulciarius*, a baker of sweetmeats, cakes and confectionery, were respected professions for Romans, with many types of these dishes consumed during festivities and pagan rituals.

The text *Apicius de re Coquinaria*, is a collection of Roman recipes dating to the first century AD, often associated with Marcus Gavius Apicius, of which very little is known. The book provides a wealth of ancient culinary details including that most timeworn of fare, the pie. Here is a recipe for cold asparagus pie, which turns out not to be as vegetarian friendly as first anticipated.

Asparagus Pie

Cold asparagus pie is made in this manner (1) Take well cleaned [cooked] asparagus, crush it in the mortar, dilute with water and presently strain it through the colander. Now trim, prepare [i.e. cook or roast] figpeckers (2) [and hold them in readiness]. (3) 3 scruples of pepper are crushed in the mortar, add broth, a glass of wine, put this in a saucepan with 3 ounces of oil, heat thoroughly. Meanwhile oil your pie mould, and with 6 eggs, flavored with œnogarum, and the asparagus preparation as described above; thicken the mixture on the hot ashes. thereupon arrange the figpeckers in the mould, cover them with this purée, bake the dish. [When cold, unmould it] sprinkle with pepper and serve.[14]

To translate – a figpecker is a small bird, while an œnogarum are pigs' livers stuffed with figs, and in case you were wondering about the scruples, these have nothing to do with doubting morality, rather they represent a Roman system of weight. If you consider there were around 750 scruples in one kilo, this might give you an indication of the weight required in this recipe.

The Roman way of cooking obviously differs hugely from the way we eat today, although we have continued to be influenced by their enduring impact over the centuries. The Romans were fascinated by food as an art form, often creating dishes made of one thing, to look like another. A revival of this can be seen in the Tudor and early modern periods, when extraordinary efforts were made by the wealthy to create decorative and ornate productions, like hunting scenes of spun sugar, or cheese boards of marzipan. Pies were baked with live birds and sometimes even people inside. A prominent court dwarf of the 1600s, Jeffrey Hudson who allegedly led an extraordinary life involving military action, incarceration by pirates and indentured slavery, along with all manner of other unspeakable misfortunes was, at the age of 7, encased in a large pie and presented as a gift to Queen Henrietta Maria of France; he emerged in front of her, to the Queen's absolute delight.[15] This homage to the frequently eccentric Roman era, an example of which is described by Roman courtier Petronius, who recounted one meal at the house of a man called Trimalchio, which included prunes stuck with thorns to replicate sea urchins, while a bowl resembling a duck surrounded by small fish, turned out to have been entirely sculptured from pork.[16] As the Romans travelled and invaded nation after nation, they became familiar with numerous exotic commodities from Asia and Africa; cultivating plants from far and wide across diverse foreign soils, a practice which would horticulturally benefit most of Europe.

The Roman scrutiny of herbs and spices created powerful tasting dishes, a trend that Britain adopted during the seventeenth, eighteenth and nineteenth centuries as trade, exploration and Empire provided a wealth of increased access to luxury culinary goods. This was a time when the nation began to cook with more complexity, reminiscent of the Roman recipes of centuries before. The Romans also adopted the use of hot, spicy sauces to experiment with flavour, while masking the stench and taint of rotting meat. This was a trick the English embraced in the medieval period, particularly in Tudor times. There is another theory suggesting that the use of spices can be attributed to the Greeks, who believed in balancing the properties of the body's four humours namely; black bile, yellow bile, phlegm and blood. It was essential to align the humours to create harmony. For example, black bile was representative of the spleen, phlegm with the brain, yellow bile with the gall bladder and blood with the heart. It was thought that by mixing cold and hot foods – both in terms of temperature and flavour, a person could maintain a balanced disposition, health and well-being.

As the process of cooking and baking has been influenced by the cross-cultures of the past, so too have the many words and phrases associated with baking: Artocopus. Bakare, Bachessor, Bagster, Baxter; Bollinger, Bullinger, Ballinger, Bellinger; Furnur', Furner, Furnagc, Fernier; Pain, Pannier, Pottinger; Pistor, Pestour, Pastelcr; Rybbare; Wastel, Wytbred; le Ovane, atte Novene are all good examples.[17]

Bullinger and Bollinger are possible derivatives of the old French word 'boulenger', meaning baker, with pain and pannier also deriving from French words. And *artocopus*, *pistor* and *pestour* are Latin terms for millers and bakers alike, whereas a *wastel* was a Germainc term for a kind of white bread. I'm sure on that basis *wytbred* is fairly self-explanatory. Any words beginning with 'Furn' or 'Fern' are undoubtedly related to furnace. I have been unable to trace the word *rybbare* but, *Novene* is commonly associated with the number nine in various European languages, so I'm a little perplexed by that one. *Ovane*, once again is fairly evident. *Bakare*, *Bachessor*, *Bagster*, *Baxter* were all generic old English words for a baker. Finally, a pottinger is a middle English phrase for a container that held a thick stew, or pottage. So, I'm thinking bread to soak up the meat, grains and vegetables, or even an association with bread trenchers. Thanks to influencers like the Romans, Anglo-Saxons and William The Conqueror, it never ceases to amaze me just how many words in the English language retain French, Latin, Germanic and Celtic origins and it's a little sad that we are only versed in the familiar baker and bakery today. In this age of 'artisan' products, I wonder if there will ever emerge a trend for becoming a baxter who makes wastel?

On the subject of language, it seems pertinent to mention the numerous terms for historical cakes, once known to Britons, but sadly are no longer evident today. *Strues* were a type of Roman pastry, positioned either in rows or piled up, during animal sacrifices and often made of honey and meal, while savoury cakes containing cheese, wine, milk, garlic and herbs were known as a *moretum*. A celebration cake, most associated with the summer solstice and shaped like a wheel was beautifully named a Summanalia, while sweet cake-breads called *Itrions*, containing honey, sesame and flowers conjure up images of rustic, delicate fare.[18]

During the seventeenth century, the English were captivated by cheesecake, with entire shops and street hawkers a plenty dedicated to the sale of these fatty and filling baked treats. It isn't difficult to make the connection between the cheesecakes we are familiar with now and those of 300 years ago and the Roman versions, represented here in this popular recipe for the libum, cake, extracted from the writings of Cato:

Libum (sweet cheesecake)

Ancient Roman Libum Recipe
Libum to be made as follows: two pounds cheese well crushed in a mortar; when it is well crushed, add in 1-pound bread-wheat flour or, if you want it to be lighter, just ½ a pound, to be mixed with the cheese. Add one egg and mix all together well. Make a loaf of this, with the leaves under it, and cook slowly in a hot fire under a brick.

If you fancy trying to replicate it at home, the following adapted version might help.

Modern Roman Libum Recipe (serves 4)
150g plain, all-purpose flour
225 g ricotta cheese
1 egg, beaten
bay leaves
110 ml clear honey

Sift the flour into a bowl. Beat the cheese until it's soft and stir it into the flour along with the egg. Form a soft dough and divide into 4. Mould each one into a bun and place them on a greased baking tray with a fresh bay leaf underneath. Heat the oven to 220° C. Cover the cakes with your brick and bake for 35–40 minutes until golden-brown. Warm the honey and place the warm cakes in it so that they absorb it. Allow to stand 30 minutes before serving.[19]

Unable to penetrate the borders of Scotland, Wales or Cornwall, the Germanic tribes, better known as the Anglo-Saxons, who inhabited Britain after the Romans during the fifth century mostly settled in England. They found themselves moving to areas near the sea or major rivers for access to trade and resources. The word 'cook', derives from the Anglo-Saxon word *cóc* and kitchen from *cycene*. Anglo-Saxons did not have a word for bread, choosing instead to use the word *half*, roughly translating as loaf.[20] Loaves, which would also include rolls, were often used as currency by tenants to their landlords, or by masters to their servants. Basic bread was frequently substituted with a special spiced variety on feast days.[21] Yeavering (or Ad Gefrin) in Northumberland is understood to be one of the most important locations relating to Anglo-Saxon heritage in the country. Kitchens or butcheries on this alleged former royal site, were found with two hearths containing vast quantities of bones, located in a sunken rectangular building. It has been speculated that the hearths may have been placed in damper and cooler conditions – hence the sunken building, to avoid the risk of fire.[22] Within the context of elite society, there is a great deal of evidence to suggest that cooking was becoming more specialised and carried out in new purpose-built buildings, such as those discovered in Yeavering. Towards the end of the Anglo-Saxon period watermills and ovens were also becoming more common, which meant the process of hand milling, a task that previously made bread production a painstaking process, was dwindling.[23] By the eleventh century there were over 5,000 watermills recorded in England.[24] The basic diet of most Anglo-Saxons was cereal based; brewed into beer, baked into bread or stewed up as a pottage.[25] The wheat they grew was more varied than that of today, including standard bread wheat, club wheat, spelt, emmer and einkorn.[26] The latter three are classed as Farro, or wheat that is incapable of being threshed. These are more likely to be added to soups or salad now, although there has been a bit of a spelt flour revival in recent years. In later Anglo-Saxon England standard bread wheat was being grown more than any other variety, and even the cultivation of barley was almost obsolete.[27] Perhaps this is another indication of bread-making becoming more sophisticated over time.

Leechdoms, Wortcunning and Starcraft provides a fascinating collection of documents from early England, translated and collated in the nineteenth century by Thomas Oswald Cockayne. To prevent vomiting, a cake was recommended. It was made up of finely sifted meal, mixed with cumin and 'seed of marche', which I think might have been a type of Italian lentil and then baked. To be truly effective this cake needed to be eaten together with soft eggs and a type of broth made from various nuts.[28]

Making bread in a brick oven. (*Wellcome Collection Creative Commons Attribution (CC BY 4.0)300*)

Other ancient cakes included Peri Didacheon – cheese mixed with boiling water and formed into little slabs, these were medicinal and placed over the eyes at night.[29] Anglo-Saxon specialist, Ann Hagen believes that meat was sometimes covered in a sort of flour and water paste prior to baking, allowing it to steam-bake, while oyster loaves (*osterhlafas*, meaning hard shelled creatures) were an Anglo-Saxon speciality, created by filling a hollowed out loaf with oysters before being baked.[30] Incidentally, I have come across later recipes for oyster loaves which show that they remained fashionable into the early 1700s at least.

Procopius of Caesarea was a noted sixth-century historian, whose works would have been known to some Anglo-Saxon communities. In his *Wars of Justinian*, Procopius talks about the importance of bread during wartime, but the bread he describes is more in the context of the hardtack ships' biscuits we are most familiar with in terms of the Tudor age of seafaring, before the emergence of canned foods. He wrote:

> The bread that soldiers are assigned to eat in camp must necessarily be put twice into the oven and be cooked so carefully as to last for a very long time and not spoil in a short time, and loaves cooked in this way necessarily weigh less. For this reason, when such bread is distributed to soldiers generally receive as their portion one-fourth more than the usual weight. Ioannes [commander of the auxillaries], therefore, calculating how he might reduce the amount of firewood used and have less to pay to the bakers in wages, and also how he might not lose in the weight of the bread, brought the still uncooked

dough to the public baths of Achilles, underneath which the fire is kept burning, and instructed his men to set it down there. When it only seemed to be cooked in some fashion or other, he threw it into bags, put it on the ships, and sent it off. When the fleet arrived at Methone, the loaves disintegrated and reverted to flour, not wholesome flour, however, but rotten, mouldy, and already giving out a heavy odour. The loaves were dispensed by measure to the soldiers by those to whom this office was assigned, and they made the distribution of the bread by *choinix* and *medimnos*. Feeding upon this in the summertime in a place where the climate is very hot, the soldiers became sick and not fewer than five hundred of them died.[31]

There are a few lessons to be learnt from this tragic story of Procopius. First, the ability to bake effectively and with some skill was just as important fifteen centuries ago as it is today. Second, it also opened my eyes to the historical roots of hardtack biscuits, which I had misguidedly always associated either with the Crusades and later, during the early years of the Royal Navy. Obviously, as Procopius' writings confirm, they go back much further than this and must have been integral to Anglo-Saxon society.

Magnus Nilsson is a contemporary, respected Nordic chef who advocates that his region has the most diverse and distinctive baking culture in the world, partly due to his theory that individuals baked in isolation thousands of years ago and rarely travelled. Recipes were not commonly shared, other than those passed down the family line and as a consequence he believes large numbers of traditional Nordic recipes and techniques remain undiscovered to this day. In the north of Sweden and Norway wheat was difficult to cultivate so barley, rye and oats were used for baking and producing a variety of unleavened flatbreads, while Iceland's sparse woodlands produced wood unsuitable for burning to bake; these communities were adept at making rye breads which would have been cooked in the ground in volcanic areas and steam-baked overnight. Seaweed, moss, dried fish and potatoes were all popular additions to Nordic breads and pastries which assisted with bulking out the finished product.

Blood-based breads were also common, with animals slaughtered and their blood used as a substitution for milk in baked goods. The

Swedish Bakery, Bageriet in London. (@ *Nick Kay*)

eighth-century Vikings who occupied Britain may well have introduced some of these techniques. Certainly, the drying and salting of fish was believed to have been a method of preservation that Britain's learned from its Viking invaders.[32] I have my own theories about Welsh laverbread being of Viking origin, as seaweed grew in such abundance in the Gower regions where, incidentally, small but significant numbers of Vikings settled in this otherwise largely uncolonized country. As well as adding it to bread as a supplement, Viking sailors frequently carried seaweed on their voyages and raids to prevent scurvy.[33] Although laverbread is not an actual bread, rather it is more of a puree of seaweed that would commonly have been eaten alongside seafood, on its own or on bread or toast. For this reason, and for its Nordic connections, as an alga that would undoubtedly have been added to bread at some stage, I have included a contemporary recipe here for a wholemeal laverbread courtesy of television chef Phil Vickery:

- 250g strong bread flour
- 100g wholemeal bread flour
- ½ tsp pouring salt
- 2 tbsp extra virgin olive oil
- 1 x 7g sachet quick acting dried yeast
- 350mls warm water, roughly
- ½ tsp castor sugar
- 1 tbsp any vinegar
- 75–80g laverbread
- Leave the flours in warm place overnight if that's possible.

- Pre heat the oven to 200°C, gas 7.
- Put the warm flour into a mixing bowl on a machine, add the salt, and olive oil, and then mix well.
- Next, add the yeast with ¾ of the water and ½ teaspoon of castor sugar.
- Add the laverbread to the flour, and mix for a minute or so.
- Mix well and then add the vinegar and the rest of the warm water until you end up with soft dough.
- Either knead in the machine or by hand for a good 4–5 minutes. It should be free from stickiness and leave the edges of the bowl.
- Place the dough back in the bowl and cover with cling film.
- Leave to prove in a warm place until the dough has doubled in size. This will take 25 minutes, approximately.
- When the dough is ready, turn out onto a lightly floured surface and gently 'knock back', this means to re-knead. But don't go mad, you just need to re-form lightly for 1–15 seconds that's all. Do not go mad, just massage out the air ready for moulding.
- Mould into a flattened loaf shape, making sure that the folds are underneath.
- Pop into a greased 2 lb loaf tin, dust with flour, cover with film and prove again to just under double the size.
- Carefully remove the cling film then slash the loaf top, right down the middle, with a very sharp knife, or a razor is the best for this.
- Place in the hot oven.
- Bake the bread until the crust is nicely browned, then take the loaf out of the tin, place it on a small wire rack on a baking sheet and put directly back into the oven. This will allow the crust to develop all around the loaf.
- When the loaf is cooked, remove from the oven and cool on a wire rack.
- Leave to cool completely before attempting to cut.[34]

Despite being unable to find a specific recipe for 'blood bread' in any old British cookery books, I did come across one in a nineteenth-century American publication *The Complete Bread, Cake and Cracker Baker*. Since many American settlers heralded from Britain or Europe, this is logically reflected in the baking techniques that Americans adopted in their new communities. The book simply stipulates preparing a recipe for 'ordinary wheat bread', 'using 20 per cent of uncoagulated blood from raw flesh, preferably beef. The writer emphasises that such a bread is highly nutritious in addition to containing the properties for preventing or curing scurvy. This type of bread, usually made with rye and known as 'Blutball' or 'Blutbrot' was also popular in parts of Germany during the early twentieth century.[35] Eliza Smith published a recipe for brown-bread pudding in her *Compleat Housewife* of 1730 which, among other ingredients you might find typical of this dish including bread, nutmeg and egg yolks, the addition of 'the blood of fowl' is perhaps more of a surprise element. Or perhaps not, when you consider it was a milk substitute to past Viking settlers.[36]

In many early Pagan rituals, blood and bread would be sacrificed to the gods, much like bread and wine are taken together in Christian ceremonies; such as the Eucharist, symbolic of the body and blood of Christ.

The Normans were simple eaters, but they did introduce Britain to a number of new culinary experiences including their ability to successfully breed rabbits and grow globe artichokes. Multiple early dishes eaten in Britain have a French provenance, many of which remained on the menu, or evolved into other familiar culinary incarnations. More of which will become apparent later in this book.

Globe artichokes or 'hartichoakes' have grown in kitchen gardens throughout Ireland since the Norman Conquest. A recipe using these artichokes in a pie taken from Birr Castle archives in County Offaly has survived since the 1600s and was updated in recent times by Lady Rosse of the Rosse family of Birr Castle.

Hartichoake Pie

Serves 8 to 10

2 cups/200g white flour, plus more for dusting.
½ tsp salt
¾ cup/190g cold butter, cut into small pieces, plus 4 tbsp butter, softened.

1 egg yolk beaten with 2 tbsp cold water, plus 4 egg yolks beaten
    with 1 tbsp water.
2 beef marrowbones
10 cooked small artichoke bottoms
Meat from 1 small cooked chicken. (1 to 1½ lb/500 to 750g) cut into
    1 inch/2.5cm pieces.
1 tbsp finely diced candied lemon peel
1 tbsp finely diced candied orange peel
½ tsp ground nutmeg
½ tsp ground mace
¼ tsp ground cloves
Pepper
1 cup/240ml dry white wine
2 tbsp sugar

Combine the flour and salt in a large bowl and rub in the ¾ cup/190g
of cold butter with your fingertips until the mixture resembles
coarse meal. Add the single beaten egg yolk and water, stir with a
fork, adding 1 to 3 tbsp more cold water as needed to form a dough
that can be gathered into a ball.

Turn the dough out onto a lightly floured board and shape it into
a disk. Wrap the dough in plastic wrap and chill for at least 1 hour
or as long as 24 hours before using.

Meanwhile, put the beef bones into a medium pot with salted
water to cover. Bring to a boil over high heat, then reduce the heat to
low and simmer until the marrow is set, 10 to 15 minutes, depending
on the size of the bones. Skim any foam that rises to the surface.
Drain the bones and set aside to cool slightly. Cut the marrow out
of each bone in one piece with a paring knife. Slice each piece of
marrow crosswise into ½ inch/1.25 cm thick rounds.

Generously grease a deep 6 cup/1.5 litre baking dish or casserole
with the remaining 4 tbsp of the butter. Arrange the artichoke
bottoms on the bottom of the baking dish in a single layer. Arrange
the chicken pieces over the artichokes. Sprinkle the candied lemon
peel, orange peel, nutmeg, mace and cloves over the chicken. Arrange
the pieces of marrow on top. Season to taste with salt and pepper.

Preheat the oven to 350 degrees Fahrenheit/175 degrees Celsius (Gas Mark 4).

Roll the dough out onto a floured board to a thickness of about ¼ inch/6mm. Cut a 1 inch/2.5cm hole out of the centre of the dough, discarding the cut of piece. Drape the dough over the filling in baking dish, centering the hole. Trim off the excess dough, leaving 1 inch/2.5cm overhanging the edge. Crimp the edge of the dough, sealing the crust to the baking dish. Brush the crust with some of the beaten egg yolk-water mixture. Set the remainder aside.

Bake the pie until the crust is golden brown and the filling is bubbling hot, 45–60 minutes. Remove the pie from the oven and allow to stand for 10 minutes.

Meanwhile, put remaining beaten egg yolk mixture, the white wine, and the sugar into a small saucepan and cook over low heat, stirring constantly until thickened, 3 to 4 minutes. (Do not allow to boil or it will curdle). Carefully pour the thickened sauce through the hole in the crust. Allow the pie to stand for about 10 minutes before serving.[37]

One of the most significant of the later Norman texts is the *Urbanus Magnus* (Civilised Man) These twelfth-century manuscript poems provide some evidence of the four humours, as mentioned earlier and their relationship to diet and cooking:

> Pork is nutritious, hare constipates,
> And lamb and mutton are good for the stomach.
> Meat from any sort of cattle causes flatulence.
> Suckling pigs abd lambs are exceedingly harmful.
> Salted meat is excellent, whether young or mature.
> Veal is very nutritious.
> Salted meat from an animal that is too old is drying.
> Boar dries the body and is more nourishing.[38]

The three principle methods of cooking in Britain during the twelfth century were roasting, baking and boiling. While roasting was thought to dry the food and boiling added moisture, baking was considered to achieve a bit of both. In terms of bread, the *Urbanus Magnus* stipulated that 'A fine baker's loaf should be sliced first and then bitten into'. It was permissible to cut bran bread once you had bitten into it and warm bread was always to be torn, rather than cut. The poems also adhere to the baking of figs, apples and pears in the ashes.[39]

There was no three-second rule allowed in early Britain. If you were unlucky enough to drop your bread on the floor, it was to be picked up, returned to the table and remain uneaten. Neither was it considered good etiquette to eat bread before the main dishes were served. A ritual which is quite the reverse today It was also thought to be uncouth to wipe any excess food up from the plate

From the book *Stands and Craftsmen* depicting early baking. (*Wellcome Collection Creative Commons Attribution* (*CC BY 4.0*)*300*)

using bread and any remaining bread from a meal was to be broken into crumbs and gifted to the poor.[40]

Assize and Guilds

As the Middle Ages progressed, so too did the legislation around baking – Every time you read anything related to the early history of baking, you will frequently be escorted down the route of the Assize of Bread and Ale, a thirteenth-century law which ensured every baker conformed to a specific weight, price and quality of bread and beer. It is the earliest of food regulations, an Act which continued to be enforced right up until the mid-1800s.

Bread-making was strictly policed for its precise shape and weight during the early medieval period, and there were harsh punishments inflicted onto those found to be selling baked goods outside of these regulations. An example of two such cases were put forward in 1316. The first was 'John in the Lane', a baker situated in Southwark who was found to be selling loaves that amounted to three shillings and five old pence short of the legal twenty-one shillings and eight pence in weight. The accused denied the offence and was put to trial. After further investigation the loaf in question was found to be clearly stamped with his seal and John was drawn on a hurdle through the streets of London as punishment. A second baker, was similarly accused four months later. Unfortunately, it was his third trial for the same crime and in addition to being drawn through the streets on a hurdle, he was permanently stripped of his occupation, 'trade of baker in the City'. Other punishments for under-weight bread being sold at regulated prices or trading adulterated baked goods in the medieval period included facing the pillory (put in the stocks to face public abuse).[41]

Baking regulations could often be complicated, seemingly irrelevant, but always for the benefit of hierarchy. Edward I decreed that all bakers living in the Bromley and Stratford areas of London had to sell their bread

in the markets of Bread Street. They were not allowed to sell from their own homes or their own bakeries. This is a very long street and can be best accessed today from Mansion House Tube station. It has become renowned in recent years with the addition of Gordon Ramsay's vibrant restaurant of the same name. Another unusual law of Edward's permitted London baker's to keep hogs in their houses, for personal consumption, as long as this practice was carried out in the suburbs. How this would have benefited bakers or baking is puzzling, although the fat from the meat certainly would have enhanced the bread.[42] Doubtless, in both these cases the king would have gained financially in some way.

Bread Street, scene of early bread trading laws and today, location of Gordon Ramsay's restaurant 'Bread Street Kitchen'. (@ *Nick Kay*)

The feudal lord or mayor controlled all of the milling activity of a town. Often people would have to carry corn for miles in treacherous conditions, frequently having to wait several days outside a mill, due to waters drying up and other delays with production, or the miller himself being absent. Even then the grain they received was likely to be substandard. Arguments and disputes were common both at mills and communal ovens. One such case involving hair-pulling and fisticuffs is recorded from the Court Rolls dating somewhere between 1150 and 1400, in William Maitland's *The Court-baron pub*:

> It fell out that on Monday next after S. Andrew that M. wife of the hayward and E. wife of a neighbour were baking at an oven, to wit that of N., and a dispute arose between them about the loss of a loaf taken from the oven, and the said old crones took to their fists and each other's hair and raised the hue; and their husbands hearing this ran up and made a great rout. Therefore, by award of the court the said women who made the rout and raised the hue are in mercy …
>
> And it is ordered that N. and E. (the husbands) do make fine for mercy at the next court.[43]

These disputes continued into subsequent centuries, with newspapers and journals littered with tales of disgruntled bakers, angry bread-less communities turning on the same disgruntled bakers, uprisings, conflicts and prosecutions galore, all in the name of bread.

In London during the early 1300s, brown-bread bakers considerably outnumbered white-bread makers, a trend which would alter over time. White flour was developed for the wealthier sectors of society to create a product that looked pure and superior in quality, opposed to the more rustic look of the darker bread flours. According to the English clergyman and biographer John Strype, the first records of white-bread bakers were officially recorded in 1155, despite the Company of White Bakers not officially forming until around the thirteenth or fourteenth century.[44] Queen Elizabeth I united the white and brown bakers' guilds sometime in the 1560s to establish the overall *Worshipful Company of Bakers*. Perhaps one aspect of the assize that has endured in the English language today is the phrase 'baker's dozen'. This is when the standard twelve units unofficially became thirteen for English bakers, thirteen loaves were sold for the same price as a dozen in order to avoid any penalties for selling below the legal weight. At some stage in the twelfth century the baker's dozen reverted to a different practice, that of bakers giving the hucksters or pedlars they supplied an additional sixpence at the start of each week and threepence at the end of the week as courtesy money, to compensate for any deficiencies. It was a short-lived custom and by the fourteenth century the system of the baker's dozen was firmly re-established.[45]

Surviving records relating to craft guilds from large towns and cities provide some insight into the organisation of medieval bakers. Only two companies were chartered prior to 1500 in the city of Chester. That is to say, they were granted exclusive rights and had investors or shareholders overseeing their best interests. One was the guild of fletchers and bowyers – bow and arrow makers. The other was the guild of bakers. These weren't considerable gangs of bread and pastry-makers either. In the 1490s the baker's guild consisted of just eighteen members. Interestingly, widows had permission to join this particular guild, possibly a consequence of losing their breadwinning master-baker husband, as membership was temporary. It was issued on the proviso that another male relative would

Bakers Hall, London. (@ *Nick Kay*)

take over the business, at which point the widow's membership would be revoked.[46]

Cities and larger towns also staged lavish annual pageants, with each guild having their own individual role to play. In Bristol the procession consisted of flowers, with silk flags and torch bearers.[47] Londoners were treated to pageants staged on the Thames, while in Chester the baker's guild regularly staged a re-enactment of the Last Supper, as they also did in York.[48]

Incidentally, the Craft Baker's Association was established in 1887 but was formerly known as the National Association of Master Bakers, with the Scottish Association forming a few years after this.

Superstition, Folklore and Custom

Bread and other baked goods were frequently included in ritualistic and superstitious practices, in tandem with white witchery throughout medieval Britain. The significance of bread has always exceeded its basic nutritional function. Historically, bread is both sacramental and generative.

Many medieval wedding festivities across the courts of Europe included hornpipers, drinking songs and a fool, along with a cup-bearer and cake-bearer. The former served the liquor, while the latter distributed cake. In pagan times, symbolic corn ears were worn by new brides to encourage healthy fertility. This tradition continued for years until small cakes were scattered over newly married couples as they left the church. Eventually the small cakes evolved into one large one sometime in the 1700s and I assume this is also linked to why we throw confetti.[49] Typically, wedding cakes were made according to the standard recipe for a 'Twelfth Cake' (which can be read all about

Wedding Cake from the 1930s.
(*Courtesy of Paul Bloxsome*)

later in this chapter) with the addition of slightly more dried fruit to make it more luxuriant. The oldest surviving complete wedding cake resides at the Willis Museum, Basingstoke, dating to 1898. It is a four-tier cake that visibly displays the scars of time, with a crack following a bomb blast during the Second World War, and an all-over brown hue, due to sugar seepage.

On the flip side of blissful union, there was also a ritual for getting rid of unwanted husbands. This involved the wife stripping naked, coating herself with honey and then rolling in grain. What was left was scraped off, ground and then milled backwards. The husband would be served a baked dish made with the resulting flour in the hope that it would dispose of him in some way. If the essence of added bodily fluids didn't do it, then perhaps they were relying on the fact that he might choke on a piece of poorly milled grain.[50]

It wasn't just superfluous husbands who needed to be mindful of what, or how, they ate. If you were a thief in the middle ages your accuser simply had to carve a series of letters on a piece of bread and then give it to the suspect to eat. If they were unable to swallow it, this would condemn them as guilty.[51]

Looking for a promotion? A way to increase your wealth or gain back greater control of your life? Before television advertisements provided a telephone number or web address to refer to, good old white magic offered an ancient spell, guaranteed to propel you into good fortune. It involved raising a candle to the fire after dark, writing your worldly desire on a piece of paper/vellum, including the name of someone influential who could help you achieve this success and the words HELIMAZ, FERIDOX and SOLADAR. Each word had to be rubbed with a ragged crust of bread. The paper then went through a process of being destroyed, soaked, rolled into a lump and thrown out of the house as far as possible.[52] Or perhaps you have it all and just need to shed a few pounds of weight to make life complete. Look no further than the moon, together with a few bits gathered from the larder. Once bathed in the glow of moonlight, the following incantation needed to be spoken:

> I make my vow to fast until
> This crescent Moon shines round and full;
> While she waxes let me wane:
> I must lose, that she may gain.

A series of victuals were then offered up to the moon as its light increased. These included silver milk and water (whatever that might involve) a transparent fish and bread (which had to be as white as snow or fine linen). Your desired dress/ trouser size would then be achieved, as long as you didn't eat all the fish and bread on the way home.[53]

Cutting a cross into dough before baking had little to do with letting the steam out, or any other purpose we may attribute it to today. Originally an indentation was made to ensure any evil spirits present would be released. Similarly bread-makers in Scotland once

Pendle Witches.

maintained that if the yeast failed to be added to dough within an hour of the sun rising, the result would lead to a hard and heavy bake.[54] At least there was some rationale to this belief, in terms of overnight proofing.

Although it's easy to deride these erroneous practices, in medieval Britain whole communities were often driven by superstition and folklore. In the 1970s, psychologist Linda Caporael proposed the notion that many of the women who were executed for their so-called 'bewitchment' during the Salem witch trials in America, were more than likely to have been suffering with the symptoms of ergotism, having researched the patterns of behaviour that were recorded and noting the agricultural systems which included the presence of rye grown just west of the village during a particularly warm and wet season.[55] Ergotism was a disease caused by eating bread made with mouldy grain. This was very common in the middle ages with symptoms including nausea, vomiting, muscle pain, irregular heart beat and at worst, visual impairment, convulsions and unconsciousness, leading to death. Is this a theory that could also be applied to the witch trials of Pendle in Lancashire? In his book *The Lancashire Witch Conspiracy*, John A. Clayton talks about the land all around the Pendle Way, producing wheat, corn, oats, rye and barley back in the sixteenth and seventeenth centuries.

There would have been mills and grain stores aplenty, ample opportunity for grain to become contaminated on a large scale. Could Ergotism have been responsible for other large-scale trials with witchcraft at the heart of them, such as the St Osyth Witches of Essex in 1582? In this particular case child witnesses were called upon to provide evidence against their family members. Thomas Rabbet, aged 8, declared that he had watched his mother feed the spirits she conjured up with white bread and beer.[56] Maybe she was hallucinating, or maybe she was actually trying to rebuke some form of diabolism.

Breads and cakes have always played a traditional role in giving thanks, promoting good luck or fending off evil. Ireland's Barmbrack or Bairin *breac* (speckled cake) is a sweet, fruit bread which is central to both the ancient custom of St Bridget's Eve and Irish Halloween traditions. It is a bread sometimes baked with trinkets inside. A thimble for spinsters or batchelors, a pea for poverty, a coin for wealth, a ring for marriage and so on. Spiced fruit breads didn't really become mainstream sellers until the sixteenth or seventeenth century, but undoubtedly they would have had an early presence in some societies, gained from the Eastern influences of the Crusades and new exploration, adding fruits and spices to the rich mix of British baking history. Even the presence of sugar in baking, which was imported from the Indies via Damascus, is mentioned in numerous recipes to be found in the ancient *Forme of Cury* of the twelfth century.

Halloween in Britain is of course central to the original Celtic pagan ceremony of Samhain (split between two worlds). A time when mortals can catch a glimpse of the afterlife. The Bara Brith is a fruit loaf very closely related to that of the Irish Barm-brack, but traditionally made without yeast and flavoured with tea; it was once a Christmas staple in Wales. Interestingly, 'Bara Brith' is defined in an *English and Welsh Dictionary* of 1828 as a multi-grain, or Maslin cake/bread, part wheat and rye. It is also described as a huge 'bun-loaf', made to a size to last over a fortnight in an 1878 edition of *Notes and Queries*.[57]

Bread balls were integral to the Samhain ritual. They were placed near five central candles representative of the goddess, hearth and season, and there needed to be as many bread balls as there were people present at the ceremony. Each person was then offered a piece of bread for sufficiency, some salt to dip it in for good health, and a sip of wine to maintain strength of spirit.[58]

Soul-cakes, sometimes called soul mass-cakes were made for All Hallows Eve and All Soul's Day, a pagan tradition which was legitimised around the ninth century, commemorating the dead. The cakes are redolent of the *shew bread* in a biblical or Jewish context, given as offerings to God. People from poorer communities would drift from parish to parish singing, or 'a-souling', to gain a soul-cake for their tunes. Traditionally these cakes were triangular in shape and made with aniseeds or oats.[59] In the 1700s it became customary for some counties, including Lancashire and Cheshire to hire 'Sin-Eaters', these men or women would eat off the corpses of the dead, thereby removing their sins in preparation for the afterlife. Sometimes this would include a mound of piled up soul-cakes.[60]

Lammas Bread, or loaf mass, was symbolic of the season's first grains. Lammas day, or Lughnasa (Lugh, being the goddess of light) is an Anglo-Saxon pagan tradition, which has all but disappeared in Britain now, although it was still recognised right up until the 1950s in some rural towns and villages. It once spawned long evening festivities, fairs, fetes and sacred celebrations marking the season around 1 August each year. In London there was a famous rowing match along the River Thames, which continued for some 200 years, from the Old Swan at London Bridge to the White Swan at Chelsea.[61] Perhaps more importantly, Lammas Day granted rights enabling 'commoners' to forage and hunt any of the lands to which they ordinarily were forbidden access.

Central to these festivities was a loaf blessing, placed on the altar in gratitude for the blessed harvest. The bread was made with one of the first sheaves of wheat to be cut down. When the festival was adopted by the Christian Church, this loaf was taken ceremoniously into the church where it was displayed for the congregation, similar to the one we might recognise at a harvest festival today.

Bread baked during yule time was also synonymous with magical powers. Scottish yule bread consisted of bannocks, which were traditionally, large, lardy round buns baked in a tin. On Twelfth Night one would be baked for every member of the household, their fate bound up in the baking process. For example, if the bannock that was allocated to you broke in the oven, you could be heading to an early grave that year.[62] One of the most ancient customs of this time of year was the Twelfth Night cake, or Twelfth cake. I have written many times about the customs surrounding Twelfth cake, but it was only when researching for this book that I discovered how important it was in theatrical circles. It was customary for all the cast to share in the cake, along with a glass of something cheering on Twelfth Night. The actor Robert Baddeley, who died of an epileptic seizure just before he was due to go on stage in 1794, bequeathed three guineas annually to cover the cost of a Twelfth cake to allow all the performers to continue celebrating this tradition each year at the Drury Lane Theatre.[63]

At one time Twelfth Night and Twelfth day represented more of a celebration than Christmas, with extravagant baking central to these festivities. Written in the 1600s, Robert May's *Accomplisht Cook* illustrates the bravado with honouring Twelfth Night, as he describes putting together a centrepiece consisting of a ship made from pastry, complete with flags and streamers. A variety of culinary objects were used to replicate objects, including eggshells filled with rose water, claret used as blood that oozed out of model knights astride horses – also made of pastry. There were pies dotted all around this military scene, made of 'course paste'. May instructs that some of these should be filled with live frogs, others with live birds, reminiscent of the exaggerated feasts of the Romans. The whole glorious, baked delight was designed for the guests in attendance to re-enact a battle using the objects provided, which would be followed by a fanfare of music and a sumptuous banquet.[64] It was probably the Victorians who ultimately did away with many of the old baking practices of Twelfth night, with their roast turkeys, cannon-ball shaped puddings and 'stir up Sunday' traditions.

It is important to remember that the medieval world was not somewhere that Christmas, as the Christian festival we know today, was celebrated. The early middle ages focused on Epiphany and festivities around Advent. Christmas became more of a public festival in the twelfth century, with the notion of gift giving and the wealthy bestowing the poor. Over the centuries the festival itself, including the food and drink consumed, has altered considerably.

Mince pies, or pyes, undeniably descend from Middle Eastern cuisine, originally containing a mixture of shredded meat, dried fruits and spices.

A combination introduced to Britain by the Crusaders returning from the Holy Land in the thirteenth century. It would have been essential to include cinnamon, cloves and nutmeg representing the three gifts offered to Christ by the three wise men. These pies did not become a staple of Christmas feasting until around the 1600s, and were of course considered taboo in the middle of the seventeenth century, in accordance with Cromwell's Puritan ideals. Often known as mutton, Christmas 'minch'd' or 'shrid pyes', they were served in an oval pastry 'coffyn' representing Jesus' crib, with the lid acting as his swaddling blanket.[65]

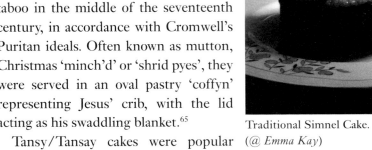

Traditional Simnel Cake.
(@ *Emma Kay*)

Tansy/Tansay cakes were popular at Easter according to John Russell in his *Book of Nurture* from the 1400s. He talks about their importance following Lent and the abundance of fish once consumed at a time when eating meat was forbidden. Tansy is a golden flowering plant originally coveted for its abilities to kill off worms in the gut. Many people would have consumed fish worms during Lent, and the tansy cakes were thought to counteract these nasty parasitic creatures. It was also a plant that helped with flatulence. Russell quotes another writer's recipe for the cakes which includes tansy, milk, cream, eggs, grated bread and nutmeg. These ingredients were heated until they were thick, and then baked into cakes.[66]

Easter is of course synonymous with hot cross buns and the heavily laden symbolism of simnel cake. The cake as we recognise it today was more of a Mothering Sunday cake until the latter part of the nineteenth century. The marzipan balls representing the apostles of Christ were also much more of a twentieth-century incarnation. The cake is a descendant of an older simnel bread, one that harkens back to at least the eleventh century. Samuel Jeake mentions a 'Simnel Cake or Bisket-Bread made from some butter and spice'in the 1600s.[67] There are ecclesiastical records citing the distribution of 'Simnels' on specific saints' days, dating to the eleventh century,[68] and a 'simnel loaf' appears in the calendar of close rolls, for Edward II in 1317.[69]

In a document titled *London Tradesmen and their Creditors*, published in 1332, it is evident that simnel bread was also sometimes known as *demeine* bread, which derives from *Panis Dominicus*, or 'the lord's bread'.[70] From this reference it is possible to verify the link between the simnel cake we know today and its significance to Christian festivals, such as Lent and Easter.[71] Throughout history, royalty consistently altered the goalposts of baking, usually for financial or politically economic reasons. It is thought that the word simnel may be a derivative of the Latin *simila*, or fine flour. Perhaps, the flour used to make the simnel bread was of a higher quality, which is why Henry V introduced the Act, to minimise its use. The hot cross bun label is also an eighteenth- or nineteenth-century contrivance, consumed traditionally on Good Friday. Its origins, however, are firmly entrenched in early British history. The once Roman and then Anglo-Saxon female deity, *Eastre*, was worshipped in the month of April and when this pagan festival was adopted by the church to become Easter, early Christian worshippers chose to inherit the custom of offering the goddess small cakes. These eventually took the form of buns, which they marked with the Christian symbol of the cross in order to protect themselves from any enchantment or evil forces previously associated with the old heathen ways.[72] These little buns, or *bouns*, retained their superstitious qualities. In rural communities some families kept them in their homes as symbols of good luck to prevent sickness and disease and as deterrents against fire or lightning.[73]

I found an advertisement for a Good Friday 'cros-bun distributor' in a 1791 edition of *The British Mercury*, suggesting they had become synonymous with this name by the 1700s, together with the musical quote made famous by the nineteenth-century poet Eliza Cook, but written by the English composer Luffman Atterbury in the mid-1760s.

One a penny, two a penny, hot Cros-buns;
If you've no daughters, give them to your sons; And if you've no
    kind of pretty little elves,
Why then good faith, e'en eat them all yourselves.

The earliest reference I can find of this ditty is in a 1767 edition of the *Leeds Intelligencer*.

The harmony was said to have been inspired by the cries of the street hawkers touting their buns on Good Friday. Some authors reference the

Notice of Hot Cross
Bun Traders from
the Surrey Herald.
(*Courtesy of Chertsey
Museum*)

> HOT CROSS BUNS.—The Chertsey bakers have decided that in consequence of the shortness of staffs hot cross buns will not be delivered on Good Friday. Hence we presume that they must be fetched !

first citation of this traders' chant appearing in a volume of the satirical *Poor Robin's Almanac*, dating a little earlier in 1753.

Below are two recipes, a basic sweet bun from the 1700s and an early twentieth-century hot cross bun.

To make Buns

Take to three pounds of flour well dry'd before the fire, two pounds and a half of butter, a pound of sugar, and two ounces of Carraway-comfits; melt your butter in warm water upon the fire, with six spoonful's of rose-water, a few more carraway-seeds, if you please and a pint of new barm; knead all these together, and set your buns into the oven, after white bread is drawn.[74]

Hot Cross Buns

You will need: Twelve oz. plain flour. Four oz. cornflour. Three-quarters oz. yeast. One and half oz. sugar. Half pint milk. Two oz. lard. Two oz. butter or margarine. Two oz. currants. One teaspoonful mixed spice. One teaspoonful salt. Sift the flour, cornflour, salt and spice together. Rub in the fat, add currants and put in warm place. Cream the yeast with sugar, add the milk (just warm) and leave to stand for ten minutes. Make a hole in the centre of the flour, turn in the milk and mix thoroughly. Beat for few minutes. Cover with a cloth and put in a warm place to rise for about an hour. Turn on floured board and knead slightly. Form into twelve buns and put on a floured baking tin. Mark deeply with cross and put in a warm place to for twenty minutes. Bake for about twenty minutes in a moderately hot oven.[75]

Distributing bread and cakes to the poor during religious and festive days in the middle ages was a custom carried out in most parishes across the country. There are too many to mention here, but one I particularly like is a tradition that prevailed until 1645 in Twickenham church on Easter day; two large cakes were divided among the young, with the aim of scrabbling to grab as much as you could. One can imagine the chaos and mess that would ensue, so unsurprisingly, perhaps, it was a tradition banned on the basis of causing 'great disorder'.[76]

Early Literary references

As a historian, my sources of research often revert back to literary references. Journals, diaries, novels, plays and general dialogues of the period are always going to offer up little gems of first-hand insight. *Piers Plowman* is a twelfth-century poem, considered to be one of the most important literary works of the Middle Ages. It is a dreamy narrative journey into Christian life; both mythical and satirical, it is thought to have been written by William Langland, a man from Hereford or Worcestershire, who may have had a connection to the clergy. It mentions items like 'hauer cakes', which were basic oat cakes and bean and bran bread, either fed to horses or used to sustain poorer communities.

> 'I've no money', said Piers, 'for chickens or geese or pork. All I've got is a couple of fresh cheeses, a tiny amount of curds and cream, an oat-cake and a couple of loaves for my children, baked from bean-flour and bran.'[77]

I appreciate he wasn't a British explorer, but Marco Polo's travels throughout Asia during the thirteenth century provide a wealth of information on the baking practices of societies in far-off lands, much the same as Drake or Raleigh would have come across. In Fanfur, an ancient kingdom now known as Indonesia, communities produced a bread from the sago palm, taken from the pith of the trunk. This substance was placed in tubs of water and stirred until the impurities rose to the top, leaving a starchy residue which was moulded into cakes and baked. Marco Polo compared it to the taste and texture of barley bread, and he even reputedly took some home with him back to Venice. Although what state it would have been in is anyone's guess. He also mentions the bread made in regions of the Persian Gulf being hard to digest, with a bitter, unpalatable taste. A consequence of the salty, tainted local waters.

The anonymous romantic Arthurian story of *Sir Gawain and the Green Knight* written in the late fourteenth century mentions fish baked in parcels of bread and spiced cakes, served with mulled wine. Perhaps the most famous text of all, the Bible is a good place to interpret even earlier references to the symbolism in baking. In the book of Genesis, the chief cupbearer and baker offend the King of Egypt and are imprisoned. They both dream that night in their cells; the cupbearer of plentiful grapes growing on a vine and the baker of baskets of baked bread on his head, being eaten by a bird. Joseph interprets their dreams as positive for the cupbearer, but symbolic of a public beheading for the baker. The Pharaoh later dreams about seven good grains of corn being eaten by seven frail grains of corn, which Joseph interprets as the famine of Egypt. The Israelites fled Egypt without any yeast to rise their bread, indicative of the unleavened bread of the Jewish community. It is also stipulates in Leviticus, that God himself must only ever be presented with yeast-free bread. Leavened bread was considered sinful. The bread prepared for God had to be made with olive oil and most crucially of all, salt. In the book of Matthew, we find one of the most quoted references of all from the Bible, when Jesus feeds a crowd of 5,000 people waiting to be healed with just five loaves and two fishes.

Cakes composed of squashed figs, raisins and dates are referenced throughout the Bible. Bear in mind that although it was written in several Testaments, the Bible was compiled around 3,000 years ago. One of my favourite accolades to baking has to be the parable which is written in Matthew 13:33: 'The kingdom of heaven is like yeast that a woman took and mixed into about sixty pounds of flour until it worked all through the dough.' Heaven is all about women and dough. Of course, it is!

Christ's own body is always represented by bread; his blood, as wine. Whether you hold with Christianity or not, the Bible reiterates to its readers again and again about the importance of bread, as a basic necessity of life, something integral to our very souls.

Jumping forward, an old 'A' Level, or GCE curriculum favourite of mine, Geoffrey Chaucer is perhaps the best writer to provide us with an insight into baking during the medieval period. The Miller in his Prologue to *The Canterbury Tales*, is a shady and bullish character who makes his living from grinding grain and defrauding his customers. There are numerous references to 'pyes' in Chaucer's works, often 'mete' pies. These weren't meat, but pies that were designed to encompass an entire meal; the contents eaten and the pie casing discarded. He refers to bakers, or 'bakere's' of the time as important members of the community, a distinct profession who had started to form significant and powerful guilds in England around this time. Chaucer acknowledges that bread played a fundamental role in the medieval diet and mentions the distinction between types of grain. How barley bread was considered inferior and vulgar at the time, compared to the finer white loaves. How brown bread also was usually reserved for the lower classes of society.

> Milk and broun breed, in which she foond no lak
> *The Nun's Priest's Tale*

> Lat hem be breed of pured whete seed,
> And lat us wyves hoten barly-breed;
> And yet with barly-breed, Mark telle kan,
> Oure Lord Jhesu refresshed many a man
> *The Wife of Bath's Tale*[78]

Writing in the tenth century, the English abbot Ælfric provided the most prolific literary works of this period. Teacher, scholar and devoted monk, his '*Colloquy*', written with the intention of helping students to learn Latin, offers some interesting insights into Anglo-Saxon baking. Bread was traded as payment for essentials such as rent, and its role was central to any dining table, rich or poor. Ælfric describes the lives of tradesmen such as cooks, lawyers, fishermen and bakers as harsh. He writes:

Teacher: What do you say, baker, how does your skill benefit us, or can we lead our live without it?

Baker: You can live for some time without my craft, but you cannot live well for a long time without it. For without my craft the whole table would appear bare, and without bread all your food would become vomit. I put new heart into man, I see the strength of men and not even small children would with to shun me.

Farmers, or ploughmen as they were known, worked in extremely difficult conditions to cultivate grain for bread. The lawyer in Ælfric's

Colloquy reinforces this by declaring 'the plough feeds us all'. While the ploughman confirms:

> Master, I have to work so very hard. I go out at the crack of dawn to drive the oxen to the field and yoke them to the plough. For not even in the bitter winter would I dare to stay at home for fear of my lord; but, when I have yoked up the oxen and fastened the plough and the ploughshare to the plough, then I must plough a whole field or more for the whole day.[79]

Finally, The early Irish Law book *Bretha im Fhuillema Gell* (Judgements concerning pledge interests) states that the following are all part of the *batterie de cuisine* and essential to the process of baking: The griddle (*lann*) the griddle slice (*lainnin*) the grain measurer (*airmed*) bucket (*sithal*) kneading trough (*losat*) and the sieve or *criathar*. These baking tools were such highly prized, valued commodities in every household, that if they were damaged, lost or stolen, it is likely tough penalties would be enforced.[80]

Early Medieval Top Ten

The Middle Ages was a transition period following the decline of the Roman Empire and the Saxon and Norman invasions; a nation socially,

Medieval hand-raised pear pies @Emma Kay

culturally and emotionally driven by a vast mix of Christian and pagan ideologies. Although superstitious and primitive in many ways, the world was beginning to open up courtesy of early exploration, new systems of government were finding their feet and glimmers of progress and modernisation were on the horizon.

Unquestionably baking remained at the heart of this complex society. There are many baked dishes from early Britain that are noteworthy of showcasing. The first of which is very symbolic of the era – the pie. Once completely raised by hand, without a mould or dish, its casing discarded in favour of the contents only.

One:

> Pye or pies
> Flesh pies of capon or of fessand
>
> To mak pyes of flesche of capon or of fessand tak
> good beef pork vele and venison hew it smalle do ther
> to pork of peper clowes maces guinger and mynced
> dates and raissins of corans mete it with malmsey or
> vergius and cast in saffron and salt and luk it be welle
> sessoned then couch it in a large coffyne and couch in
> the capon or fessand hole and if ye wille smyt them in
> peces and colour them with saffron and put in it other
> wild foule if ye wille and plant ther in hard yolks of
> egges and strawe on clowes maces dates mynced
> raissins of corrans quybibes then close them up and
> bak them and serue them.[81]

In case you were wondering about the 'fessand', this was the word used for pheasant in early England.

Two: Flaumpeyns
'Flampoyne' or flampoint/flaumpeyn was a shallow tart decorated with pointed pieces of pastry. This one is taken from the *Forme of cury* dated 1390 and is filled with cheese and minced pork.

Flaumpeyns

Take clene pork and boile it tendre. þenne hewe it small and bray it smal in a morter. take fyges and boile hem tendre in smale ale. and bray hem and tendre chese þerwith. þenne waisthe hem in water & þene lyes (1) hem alle togider wit Ayrenn, þenne take powdour of pepper. or els powdour marchannt & ayrenn and a porcioun of safroun and salt. þenne take blank sugur. eyrenn & flour & make a past wit a roller, þene make þerof smale pelettes (2). & fry hem broun in clene grece & set hem asyde. þenne make of þat ooþer deel (3) of þat past long coffyns (4) & do þat comade (5) þerin. and close hem faire with a countoer (6) & pynche hem smale about. þanne kyt aboue foure oþer sex wayes, þanne take euy (7) of þat kuttyng up, & þenne colour it wit zolkes of Ayrenn, and plannt hem thick, into the flaumpeyns above þat þou kuttest hem & set hem in an ovene and lat hem bake eselich (8). and þanne serue hem forth.

(1) lyer. mix. (2) Pelettes. *Pelotys* Ms. (ed.) No. 16. Balls, pellets, from Fr. *pelote*. (3) deel. deal, i.e. part, half. (4) Coffyns. Pies without lids. (5) comade. Qu. (6) coutour. coverture, a lid. (7) euy. every. (8) eselich. easily, gently.[82]

Three: Dariols
‘Dariols’ or Daryols/Daryoles were simple, baked custards. This recipe is taken from a book dated 1420, originally from the Harleian Collection now housed at the British Library. It was transcribed in the nineteenth century and again in the late twentieth century.

Daryoles.—Take wyne & Fressche broþe, Clowes, Maces, & Marow, & pouder of Gyngere, & Safroun, & let al boyle to-gederys, & put þer-to creme, (& ȝif it be clowtys, draw it þorwe a straynoure,) & ȝolkys of Eyroun, & melle hem to-gederys, & pore þe licoure þat þe Marow was soþyn yn þer-to; þan make fayre cofyns of fayre past, & put þe Marow þer-yn, & mynce datys, & strawberys in tyme of ȝere, & put þe cofyns [leaf 38.] in þe ovyn, & late hem harde a lytel; þan take hem owt, & put þe licoure þer-to, & late hem bake, & serue forth.[83]

Very roughly translated:

Take wine and fresh broth, cloves, mace and marrow, ginger and saffron then boil altogether together with cream. Strain off the hard spices like the cloves. Mix together with egg yolks. Meanwhile make a batch of pastry cases and add dates and strawberries. Or whatever you have at that time of year. Then place the cases with the fruit in the oven to harden. (Or as we would say today, bake blind). Once done, take them out and fill the cases with the liquid, returning them to the oven to continue baking. Then serve.

Four: Baked Lampreys
Baked fish pies were a big part of Lenten traditions. This may have evolved from the process of storing, distributing and preserving fish which was placed in stoneware pots, together with a lot of fat and spices to help the contents travel well, or last for up to a few weeks. Lampreys from the Severn river in Gloucestershire, a particular favourite of Henry III, were transported all over the country in cold butter-sealed pies.[84] The following recipe, taken from the early English cookbook *Liber Cure Cocorum*, represents just one variant of this extremely popular medieval baked dish:

For lamprays bakun

Fyrst scalde þy lamprays fayre and wele,
As I tolde byfore, so have þou cele;
Soþun, rere a cofyne of flowre so fre,
Rolle in þo lampray, as hit may be;
Take mynsud onyons þer to, gode wonne,
But fyrst take powder of peper, anon
Of maces, cloves and graynys also,
And dates al hole þou take þerto,
Poure rede wyne þerto þou schalle,
Coloure hit with safrone and closen alle.
In myddes þo lydde an tuel þou make,
Set hit in þo ovyn for to bake;
Ʒete take hit oute, fede hit with wyne,
Lay on þo tuel a past fulle fyne,
And bake hit forthe, as I þe kenne,
To serve in sale before gode menne.

If you're struggling, here is the translated version:

For baked lampreys

> First scald your lampreys fair and well,
> As I told before, so have you bliss;
> Then, raise a coffin of flour so free,
> Roll in the lamprey, as it may be;
> Take minced onions thereto, [a] good quantity,
> But first take powder of pepper, anon
> Of maces, cloves and grains [of paradise] also,
> And dates all whole you take thereto,
> Pour red wine thereto you shall,
> Color it with saffron and close all.
> In [the] middle [of] the lid an opening you make,
> Set it in the oven for to bake;
> Carefully take it out, feed it with wine,
> Lay on the opening a very fine paste,
> And bake it forth, as I teach you,
> To serve in hall before good men.[85]

Baker's Kitchen in France. Wellcome Collection Creative Commons Attribution. (*CC BY 4.0*)*300*)

Five: Pain Perdu

'Payne puredew', or payn pur-dew/pain perdu, meaning lost bread, was a popular dish made from frying slices of white bread dipped in egg. Yes, that's right – French bread, French toast, eggy bread has a provenance that stretches back to medieval times. It was brought from France to England during the Norman conquest, also gaining the nickname of The Poor Knights of Windsor.[86]

This recipe is circa 1490

Payne Puredew. Recipe shyves of whyte brede & toste þam; þan take þe ʒolkes of egges & swyng þam, & turn þe brede þerin, & fry it in grece or buttur, & serof it forth.[87]

Six: Rice Pudding

Rice pudding was often served following a major feast or banquet.

I have read numerous accounts regarding the popularity of rice in England in the 1500s. But I think it more likely that it was a commodity available to nobility from at least the twelfth century. C. Anne Wilson, in her *Food and Drink of Britain*, notes that the Countess of Leicester and her household got through one 110 lb of rice in just four months between Christmas and April in 1265.[88] It's quite possible that rice was procured from Spain in the Middle Ages, a cereal grain planted there during the Muslim conquests. Rice pottages were a favoured dish for Lent and somewhere along the way, the common pudding traditionally boiled in any form of animal gut, turned into the platter pudding which was baked in the oven and sometimes referred to as a pudding/poddyng pie.

Baked milky dishes were also commonly known as white-pot, containing milk, eggs, spices, bread and a little butter. Rice could be added to make a baked rice pudding. *Liber Cure Cocorum* contains an early fifteenth-century recipe, ancestor to its baked successor noted by Hannah Glasse in 1747.

Ryse

Take ryse and wasshe and grynde hem smalle,
Temper hom up fayre and grynd hom wele;
Temper hom up with wyne so clene,
Drau3e hom thorowghe a steynour clene,
Boyle hom and seson hom with sugar schene;
Fors hit with fryude almonds gode,
Pen hase pou done, syr, by po rode.[89]

To make a rice white pot

BOIL a pound of rice in two quarts of new milk, till it is tender and thick, beat it in a mortar with a quarter of a pound of sweet almonds blanched; then boil two quarts of cream, with a few crumbs of white bread, and two or three blades of mace. Mix it all with eight eggs and a little rose water, and sweeten to your taste. Cut some candied orange and citron peels thin, and lay it in. It must be put into a slow oyen.[90]

Seven: Trenchers

Trenchers were bread used as plates, commonplace in grander households from the twelfth century, before being replaced with wood and then pewter sometime in the 1500s.

In John Russell's *Boke of Nurture*, written circa 1460, he provides a great deal of advice about the use of and etiquette involved with trenchers. According to Russell, trenchers should be made from bread that is four days old, and there were special 'trencher knives', only to be used for the purpose of cutting trenchers out of loaves. A 'trencher salt' was initially a small hollowed out cavity in the trencher itself, containing salt to season the contents. This was later replaced with a wooden or silver trencher salt. The remains of the trencher were often used as food for dogs or other animals on the property.[91]

Eight: Rafioles or Rissoles

'Rafioles', or rasiowls/rasyols, were meatballs made of pork and baked in a crust, the foremother of the popular rissole.

Take swyne lyvors and seeth hem wel. Take brede and grate it. And take Zolkes of ayren (eggs) and make hit sowple, (supple) and do thereto a lytull of lard carnon lyche a dee (cut like dice) chese gratyd and whyte grece, (lard) powdor-douce and of gynger and wynde (roll) it to balles as grete as apples. Take the calle of the swyne and cast evere (each) by hymself thereinne. Make a crust in a trape (pan) and lay the balles thereinne and bake it and whan they buth ynowz (enough) put thereinne a layor (mixture) of ayren (egg)s with powdor fort and safron and serve it forth.[92]

The phrase 'powdor-douce' was common to the Middle Ages. It simply referred to a mixture of sweet spices, which might include; cinnamon, nutmeg, ginger and even sugar.

Nine: Manchet
Manchet/manchette or pain de main was an early specialist bread, made of the best quality flour, the recipe for which altered slightly depending on the region.

The first citation I have been able to find for manchet is in the *Forme of Cury* from the 1300s. However, recipes appear much later. This one from 1594 is taken from Thomas Dawson's *The Good Huswifes Handmaide for the Kitchin*

The making of fine Manchet

Take halfe a bushell of fine flower twise boulted,
and a gallon of faire luke warm water, almost a
handful of white salt, and almost a pinte of yest,
then temper all these together, without any more
liquor, as hard as ye can handle it: then let it lie
halfe an hower, then take it vp, and make your
Manchetts, and let them stande almost an hower in
the ouen. Memorandum, that of euery bushell of
meale may be made fiue and twentie caste of bread,
and euerie loafe to way a pounde beyside the
chesill.[93]

Ten: Rastons

Rastons were small loaves fortified with eggs and sugar. The following recipe from the 1400s describes how, when baked, the top was removed and some of the bread scooped out. This was then mixed with butter and filled back into the bread shell. The lid of the bread was replaced and the whole thing re-baked.

Rastons.—Take fayre Flowre, & þe whyte of Eyroun, & þe ȝolke, a lytel; þan take Warme Berme, & putte al þes to-gederys, & bete hem to-gederys with þin hond tyl it be schort & þikke y-now, & caste Sugre y-now þer-to, & þenne lat reste a whyle; þan kaste in a fayre place in þe oven,

Medieval Bread Oven in Wales. (@ *Emma Kay*)

& late bake y-now; & þen with a knyf cutte yt round a-boue in maner of a crowne, & kepe þe cruste þat þou kyttyst; & þan pyke al þe cromys withynne to-gederys, an pike hem smal with þin knyf, & saue þe sydys & al þe[94]

Chapter 2

Of Pies and Puddings –
Tudor and Stuart Baking

Royal Baking

N ever has a period in history been quite so distinctive in terms of class and royalty. Shifts in political power, the dissolution of the monasteries, a Commonwealth government, aspirational landed gentry with money to burn, and towards the end of the 1600s a new royal household who set the trends and influenced society significantly, both domestically and commercially. In the royal household between 1660 and 1805 the 'Pastry' consisted of an entire department dedicated to providing baked meats, tarts, pies and some of the many sauces required for mealtimes. In 1660 this included of a staff including a clerk, a sergeant, yeoman, grooms and some child labour. A few years later the office merged with the bakehouse, poultry, scullery and woodyard. The pastry division had become obsolete by the 1800s, replaced by one pastry cook and several assistants. Either baking just got easier with the arrival of new labour-saving devices, negating the need for so many staff, or it simply became less rich and abundant. Personally, I think it would have been a combination of both.

Royalty in Britain has always lavished in its exorbitance, food being no exception. That aside, medieval Britain was also fiercely devoted to its fasting practices. Christian abstinence rituals and the avoidance of meat on designated days, meant that it was customary to eat more fish in the later middle ages. The British commercial fish trade grew and evolved significantly throughout this period and Richard III would have consumed a great deal of freshwater fish. The University of Leicester and other archaeological and scientific experts have wasted no time in using evidence gathered from Richard's remains to assist with investigating all manner of information pertaining to his diet, health and wellbeing. His levels of nitrogen alone dictate that Richard's nutritional intake was

Fifteenth-Century
Banquet. (*Wellcome
Collection Creative
Commons Attribution
(CC BY 4.0)300*)

A Rich Banquet : c. 1460

The walls are hung with tapestry representing a battle scene; over the master of the
house is a canopy and behind him a wicker fire-screen. The carver has a towel over his
shoulder; above him is the steward with his rod of office

consistent with what to expect from an aristocrat living in the fifteenth century. Bread, ale, meat, fish, wine and spices. In particular, large quantities of fish, with higher levels than average of 'marine components' identified in his diet.[1]

Small round pastry tarts called chewettes, (not to be confused with the brand of lurid coloured sweets made famous in the twentieth century) were very popular during the 1400s. Often minced-meat based, they were filled with all manner of ingredients. The 1468 *Noble Boke Off Cookry* contains a lovely recipe for chewettes that could be eaten on 'fishe daies' and may well have been enjoyed by Richard III himself.

> To mak chewettes on fische dais tak molet freshe
> samon or bace rawe clef them frome the bone and
> chope them in peces and couche them in coffins put
> eles ther to and othere metes as ye did be for and mak

> a ceripe of thik almond mylk all saue the juce of eggs
> then set the coffins in the ovon and fille them fulle of
> good ceripe and ye may fry the fische and serue it
> furthe.[2]

Henry VI's 1429 coronation feast is testament to the enduring luxuries that baking offered early royalty. Staged in Westminster Hall, the first of three courses included a 'Viande royale planted with lozenges of gold, and a custard royal with a leopard of gold sitting thereon'. Lozenges, or 'loseyns', were exceedingly popular during this period. Essentially little lozenge-shaped parcels of cheese, wine and spices encased in a sort of bread pasta casing rolled thinly and boiled, they appear in all manner of texts of the time and are often interpreted differently by food historians, either as a confection, some sort of early lasagne dish or as fried delicacy. The following recipe comes directly from the early mediaeval *Forme of Curye*.

> Take gode broth and do in an erthen pot, take flour of payndemayn and
> make per of past with water. and make per of thynne foyles as paper
> with a roller, drye it harde and seep hyt in broth take Chese ruayn
> grated and lay it in disshes with powdour douce. and lay per on
> loseyns isode as hoole as pou mizt. and above powdour and chese,
> and so twyse or thryse, & serue it forth.[3]

The 'payndemayn' is the bread which, when mixed with additional flour and water, needed to be rolled out as thin as foils of paper, dried hard, filled with the cheesy, spicy, broth and boiled.

An 'enhackled' Peacock was presented for the second course. This term refers to the skin head and feathers of the bird being removed carefully prior to cooking. It would then have been re-dressed and served up to make it look as if it was a live creature. The third dish was a baked dish. A large piece of meat which was quartered red and white to resemble a shield. Possibly Henry's coat of arms or a symbol of his reign over both France and England. This was also set with gilt lozenges and borage flowers, which would have been bright blue and star shaped.[4] Quite the show.

By the time we get to Henry VIII, baking in the royal household had reached monstrous proportions. Over a period of forty-two days in 1512, accounts place the total cost of goods produced by the bakehouse and pastry for Henry VIII's royal court at £11 18s 8½d. That equates to a staggering £7,911.76, for just pies, tarts, bread and other baked goods covering a timescale of just over one month.[5]

A pasty was a dish-less pie, first recorded around 1300. Venison pasties were the most popular, often with the whole joint of deer encased in pastry. Pepys made them famous, and Henry VIII enjoyed them probably a bit too much. In 1541, six venison pasties were sent to Hampton Court Palace and were consumed by the next day; the king communicated to one of his courtiers, Charles de Marillac, that they were 'marvellously good'.[6] His predecessor Henry III was clearly also a pasty fan. He granted a charter to the town of Great Yarmouth in 1208, with an obligation to annually deliver twenty-four pasties, containing 100 herring to his residence whenever he was visiting.[7] I wonder whether any of the royal family today takes advantage of this whenever touring Yarmouth? Although, having never tasted a herring pasty, I'm not sure how nice it would actually be, let alone having to eat twenty-four of them if you were a bit undecided.

We know medieval pasties must have sometimes been of considerable size, as the accounts of John Menyman for his Michaelmas festivities of 1478 demonstrate, with 'three pecks of flour bought for the venison pasty'. A peck today would be equivalent to around two dry gallons, so that's a whopping six dry gallons, or forty-eight dry pints of flour required for one pasty. It was also seasoned with ½ lb of pepper.[8]

In the Middle Ages it was common to bake capons or beef in a pasty, as well as herrings. Pastelers prepared pasties and pies to sell and there were four Master Pastelers operating in London in 1379. Their lesser ranking baking colleagues were all party to some major criticism that year for selling 'stinking' pasties, which often contained 'garbage' (another term for giblets). Beef was often substituted for venison with rabbit and geese thrown in as general fillers. On King Richard II's orders, the four Master Pastelers were entrusted with authorising and policing new laws regarding the contents of pasties, including:

that no one of the said trade shall bake rabbits in pasties for sale, on pain of paying, the first time, if found guilty thereof, 6*s*.8*d*., to the use of the Chamber, and of going bodily to prison, at the will of the Mayor; the second time, 13*s*. 4*d*. to the use of the Chamber, and of going etc.; and the third time, 20*s*. to the use of the Chamber, and of going etc.

Also,—that no one of the said trade shall buy of any cook of Bredestret, or, at the hostels of the great lords, of the cooks of such lords, any garbage from capons, hens, or geese, to bake in a pasty, and sell, under the same penalty.

Also,—that no one shall bake beef in a pasty for sale, and sell it as venison, under the same penalty.

Also,—that no one of the said trade shall bake either whole geese in a pasty, halves of geese, or quarters of geese, for sale, on the pain aforesaid.[9]

I'm thinking the number of 'also's here was a deliberate attempt to emphasise a point. It seems they were quite insistent about the need to regulate the contents of these baked savouries.

During Elizabeth I's reign the country faced the highest bread prices of the century. There was a ban on all grain exports and new measures were introduced to improve agriculture.

Foods and continental diets from overseas were scrutinised and documented with great enthusiasm during the reigns of both Elizabeth I and her father Henry, and in the Elizabethan court, baking-related tasks were run meticulously, alongside all the other day-to-day activities. The bakehouse had its own department with responsibility for buying all the necessary grain. The 'baking house' was a separate preparation area, just for cooking breads, while the 'pastry' was designated to the baking of meats. Bread was then stored in the pantry, while wafers even had their own 'wafery', which is perhaps an indication of the quantity consumed.[10] The commonest form of baked dish was the pie; where meat, vegetables, fish, poultry or fruit were stuffed into a 'coffyn' lid of pastry to seal the contents, which was originally discarded as soon as the dish was served. This is a recipe for veal pie, published during Elizabeth's reign.

> To make a veale pie.
> Let your Veale boyle a good while, and
> when it is boyled, mince it by it selfe,
> and the white, by it selfe, and season it with
> salt and pepper, cinamon and ginger, and
> suger, and cloues and mace, and you muste
> haue prunes and raisons, dates & currantes
> on the top.[11]

It was said that Queen Elizabeth I was particularly fond of bread, choosing to eat manchet (the best quality leavened bread of medieval Britain, made from stoneground wheat sifted several times) together with soup, when under great stress.

Potatoes arrived in England towards the end of the 1500s. The privateer and alleged favourite of the queen, Sir Walter Raleigh, is frequently quoted as being the first person to plant and cultivate them at his home in Ireland. Whether it was Raleigh who actually introduced potatoes to Europe remains contentious. The botanist John Parkinson's makes an early reference to baking potatoes in his *Paradisus Terrestris* of 1629; at this time potatoes were becoming more commonplace in Britain, either for roasting in the embers or cooked in sack (canarian wine, which later became known as sherry). But they were also baked with marrowbone, sugar and a variety of spices. All relatively new and luxury commodities in England and a far cry from our rather less impressive bean or cheese fillings of today.

The diarist John Evelyn noted in 1699:

> Potato. The ſmall green Fruit (when about the ſize of the Wild Cherry) being pickled, is an agreeable Sallet. (salad) But the Root being roaſted under the Embers, or otherwiſe, open'd with a Knife, the Pulp is butter'd in the Skin, of which it will take up a good Quantity, and is ſeaſoned with a little Salt and Pepper. Some eat them with Sugar together in the Skin, which has a pleaſant Crimpneſs. They are alſo ſtew'd and bak'd in Pyes, &c.[12]

Born in 1540, Lady Katherine Grey was the granddaughter of Henry VIII's sister Mary. Her life appears to have been fraught with traumas

– divorce, clandestine relationships, giving birth in the Tower, incurring the wrath of Queen Elizabeth I, basically blowing her chances of ever becoming a prospective successor to the throne. She died young at the age of 27 from consumption and a copy of her death-bed statement in ink on velum was found and documented, together with a number of medicinal and culinary recipes. Dated 1567, the manuscripts are edited with notes, possibly annotated by more than one person, and have been catalogued by the University of Pennsylvania.

One of the recipes is an early instruction for making cake. What I like most about this recipe is the advice on removing the cakes from the oven before they brown, to ensure they remain moist and soft. It has been a technique of mine for many years to always remove cakes just before they are cooked. My theory being that they continue the cooking process for a few minutes if left in their tins. Whoever wrote this provided a rare insightful gem on baking, at a time when few useful instructions accompanied recipes. Note that despite the inclusion of flower and butter, the omission of eggs does not make this a sponge cake, which would not materialise for another few years. I imagine this cake would have been a little bit like a sweet rich brioche.

Instructiones to make Cakes

Fyrst take a qyarte of fyne flower a pound of Sugar ij of
Cloves fyne beaten and thereunto put a pound of swete butter &
   the[n]
worcke yt to gether untyll suche tyme as you shall thincke yt
well-wrought & so make yt in cakes & put yt in to the oven
wher manchets or cakes hathe bene baked imedyatelye after the
same ys drawen, And you must note that to the baking of fyne
cakes a temperate heate must be in the oven & you must not
suffer them to stande in the oven tyll they be broune because
they wyll harden and wax broune when they be broune after they
   hav[e]
stand a whyle.[13]

Mary of Guise, who would later become Scotland's regent in the absence of monarchy for some six years, distributed bread to black immigrants on a daily basis at Stirling Castle for a whole year throughout 1549.[14] Mary was the mother of Mary Queen of Scots – she, who is so often associated with shortbread, but more of that later.

By the 1600s, and the onset of a new Stuart dynasty, most larger establishments would have had kitchens that maintained both a stove and a bee-hive oven. The oven being central to most of the activity and the extent to which bread once supplemented everyday diets is palpable from reading Charles I daily intake, consisting of a breakfast including two kinds of bread, mutton, chicken and beer. For dinner, three kinds of bread were consumed along with a choice of ten meats and poultry, a sweet desert and beer or wine. Supper was similar, with more bread and beer available to snack on between meals.[15] Even Charles' last meal was bread and wine as he awaited his fatal journey to the scaffold outside the Banqueting House in the Palace of Whitehall.[16] His Puritanical successor, Oliver Cromwell, effectively banned the festival of Christmas in the mid-seventeenth century. Although there was no specific Christmas cake, there was boiled pottage, which later morphed into the solid Christmas pudding we are familiar with now and there would undoubtedly have been the customary Twelfth, or Twelfth Night cake. Here is James Jenk's recipe for Twelfth cake from 1769. Jenks was an Irish cook and it's interesting that he titles his recipe here as a Rich Cake, noting that it's called a Twelfth cake in London. Suggesting that this name did not extend to Ireland. It is also, understandably, very reminiscent of the Christmas cake recipes of today.

Twelfth Cake

Take six pounds of the best fresh butter; work it to cream with your hands: then throw in by degrees three pounds of double refined sugar well beat and sifted: mix them well together: then work in three pounds of blanched almonds: and having beaten four pounds of eggs, and strained them through a sieve, put them in, beat them all together till they are thick and look white. Then add half a pint of French brandy, half a pint of sack; a small quantity of ginger, and about two ounces of mace, cloves, and cinnamon, each, and three large nutmegs, all beaten in a mortar as fine as possible. Then shake in gradually four pounds of well dried and sifted flour: and when the oven is well prepared, and a tin hoop to bake it in, stir into this mixture (as you put it into the hoop) seven pounds of currants clean washed and rubbed, and such a quantity of candied orange, lemon and citron, in equal proportions as shall be thought convenient. The oven must be quick and the cake will take at least four hours to bake it: *Or* you may make two or more cakes out of these ingredients. During the whole time of mixing these ingredients, you must beat it with your hands, and the currants must be dried before the fire and put into the cake warm. This is called a twelfth cake at London.

In order to ice it beat up the whites of twenty-four eggs with a pound of double refined sugar beaten and sifted very fine, till it looks very white and grows thick. Spread this with a feather or a fine brush over the top of the cake after it is taken out of the tin hoop: and set it thus iced before a clear fire, at a proper distance and keep turning it round for fear of discolouring it. But the best way is to harden this ice in an oven for about an hour.[17]

Mince pies, that other Christmas favourite, would also have been taboo. Below is a recipe from one of the most significant recipe writers of the 1600s, Gervase Markham.

Take a Legge of Mutton, and cut the best of the flesh from the bone, and parboyl it well then put to it three pound of the best Mutton suet & shred it very small; then spread it abroad, and fashion it with Salt Cloves and Mace: then put in good store of Currants, great Raisins and Prunes clean washed and picked a few Dates sliced, and some Orenge-pils sliced; then being all well mixt together, put it into a coffin, or into divers coffins, and so bake them and when they are served up, open the lids and strow store of Sugar on the top of the meat and upon the lid. And in this sort, you may also bake Beef or Veal, onely the Beef would not be parboyld, and the Veal will ask a double quantity of Suet.[18]

It is difficult to determine when they stopped using meat in mince pie recipes. Eliza Acton's 1845 *Modern Cookery for Private Families* includes the use of Ox Tongue, but by the end of the nineteenth-century suet definitely began replacing the actual lumps of meat.

We know that hard biscuits, similar to those taken to sea were convenient sources of food in the military and this would have been no different during the English Civil War. Cooked at a high temperature very slowly, a mixture of flour, water and salt could sustain long journeys. Fighting for the Parliamentary cause, Colonel Edward Popham's regiment in 1643 survived on a daily ration of 10½ ounces of biscuits, subsidised with a few peas, water and around 5 ounces of cheese or meat. In contrast, the cavalier army reputedly had daily rations which included 2 lbs of bread, 1 lb of meat and two bottles of beer. Bread was baked in garrisons, mostly at the one based in Oxford, which was then distributed out to all the surrounding units. Some more remote units, like Devonshire, had to make their own bread and employed four bakers to do the job.[19] Bread was often difficult to source during the Civil War, with soldiers frequently scrounging provisions on a daily basis. The diaries of the Royalist Richard Coe mentions a food run at Bagshot where they acquired mutton, veal, lamb and some venison in abundance, but were unable to obtain any bread or beer. One account of a victory gained at Taunton in 1644 noted roundheads pausing their fighting to raid homes for edibles. Seizing their opportunity to strike distracted soldiers, the Royalist opposition were also known to have had a habit of dispatching their unassuming enemies as their mouths were full of bread.[20]

On occasion, as with the Siege of Worcester in 1646, when the whole city was effectively shut down by the Royalists, grinding grain and finding the manpower to produce bread was difficult. With few horses left in the city to power the mill, other sources of flour to make bread had to be sourced. A local baker named Smith was approached, but refused to help the Cavalier cause. When threatened with being thrown over the city walls, he relented and reluctantly baked bread for the troops.[21] Similarly, at the siege of Brampton Bryan castle, all the bread had to be made from grain ground down in a hand mill, making the process both very difficult and lengthy. With one soldier noting, 'our provisions were very scarce'.[22]

The Twelfth cake, along with mince pies and pottage, seen as wickedly extravagant by Cromwell's army, would not be revived again until the

Restoration, when King Charles II, a man allegedly very devoted to his gingerbread, revitalized the spirit of Christmas in all its glory.

How to make course Ginger-bread

> To make course Ginger-bread, take a quart of Honey, and set it on the coals and refine it: then take a penny-worth of Ginger, as much Pepper, as much Licoras, and quarter of a pound of Aniseeds, and a penny-worth of Saunders: all these must be beaten and searsed, and so put into the Hony; then put in a quarter of a pint of Claret wine, or old Ale: then take three penny manchets finely grated, and strew it among the rest, and stir it till it come to a stiff paste, and then make into Cakes, and dry them gently.[23]

Archimagirus Anglo-Gallicus (English-French Chef) of 1658 is a collection of recipes compiled by the Frenchman, Sir Theodore Mayerne, who was a knight and physician to King Charles II. The volume represents a documented shift in medicinal recipes becoming more culinary, with greater emphasis placed on the importance of food following the restoration. The opening note to the reader is testament to this:

> The great Author of this small Enchiridion [manual] shewes you the Excellency of Kitchin-physick, beyond all Gally pots, and their Adherents. He doth in this book teach you, *Ex parvis componore magna*, to improve a Porters dinner into a Dish fit for a Princes Table, to make badde meat good, and good meat better. This Book is a Save-all; It Suffers nothing to be left. It will teach you to keep good houses, by keeping good things in them.[24]

Just as the French were heavily influencing culinary trends in Britain during the Renaissance, so too were the Italians. Naples biskets were terribly popular at the time, as was the trend for 'biskets' generally. Naples bisks were similar to savoy biscuits or ladyfingers, also an eighteenth-century favourite, varying marginally in terms of the ingredients. Visualise a slightly cruder version of today's sponge trifle fingers, to get a good idea of what they may have looked like. Or try this royal recipe from Theodore Mayerne's *Archimagirus Anglo-Gallicus.*

To make Naples bisket

Take Almonds and Pineapple seeds; and kernels of Musk-millions, fine searced sugar, as much as all the seeds do weigh, then take a little fine basket flour, or else rice flower, and as much of the white of an egge as will moisten it and a little quantity of musk, a spoonful of sweet cream; beat all this well together in a morter, then lay it upon a pye-plate upon wafers, like lozinges, to bake it.[25]

Prior to the impending coronation of William and Mary, a very important document was published, which offers information relating to baking in Britain towards the latter part of the seventeenth century. *Academy of Armory*, written by Randle Holme, is much more than a record of heraldry, as you might at first expect. It is a more generic manual, listing the instruments and terms associated with a wide variety of trades and sciences, baking being one of them. Holme teaches us that there were numerous types of bread consumed at this time, including Horse bread, which was a much older bread dating to at least the twelfth century

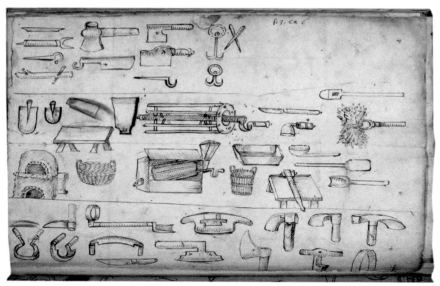

Drawings from Randle Holme III's manuscripts for the *Academy of Armoury* showing dough drough, peels, brake, bread oven, baskets and so on. (*Courtesy of The British Library*)

(and one, incidentally, not covered by the laws of the assize) made from beans and peas; Mackeron, a sweet bread made into rolls; Bisket bread, consisting of fine flour, eggs and sugar; Cracknel bread, kneaded together with saffron and currants; Iannock bread, which was a sourdough made from oats, alongside the more recognisable French, brown and white breads. The tools of the baker are also listed in a rather haphazard manner. It seems there were separate *peels* or *shod peels* for bread and cake to place baked goods in and out of the hot oven. These looked like a spade, with an iron paddle and a wooden staff. The *Dough scrane* or *Gralter* was a device used to scrape the dough away from the sides of the wooden *kneading trough*, which resembled an oversized child's crib. This was where all the flour, any leavening products, salt and water would be mixed and kneaded together. From the trough, the dough would transfer to a *Brake*, described as 'a thick plank set upon four or more strong feet'. Here the dough would be beaten some more and then moulded into shapes. Freshly milled flour was stored in an *Ark* and transferred to the trough using a shovel.

Holme mentions the importance of 'custard fillers', which were simple wooden dishes on the end of a wooden staff, then placed in the oven to

Victorian Dough Trough and Dough Cutter. (@ *Nick Kay*)

bake custards. The *Braide* or *Braed* was a long and broad board with a hole at one end, designed for cooks or other household domestics to transport all unbaked products to the oven. An array of 'bread baskets', or *wislkets*, made of twigs bound together would store the loaves themselves.[26]

The last of the Stuart monarchs, Queen Anne came to the throne at a time of tremendous political upheaval and her limited abilities at leadership left the country at the mercy of ministers and courtiers. Throughout this period there are numerous references to carrot cake, once also known as Queen Anne's Cake, from the alleged association with Queen Anne's lace; a type of 'wild carrot', which is actually more of a flower than a vegetable. The name is attributed to both Queen Anne and her great grandmother, Anne of Denmark.

Robert Smith, one time cook for Anne's predecessor King William, documented his recipe for carrot cake, which was at the time more of a baked carrot pudding. Queen Anne way well have indulged in this very same recipe:

To make a Carrot Pudding

Take a large Carrot, boil it tender, then set it to be cold, and grate it thro' a Sieve very fine; then put in half a Pound of melted Butter beaten together with eight Eggs, (leave out half the Whites) with three spoonfuls of Sack, and one spoonful of Orange flower Water, half a Pint of good Cream, a Nutmeg, Bread grated, a little Salt, and make it of a moderate thickness, and give it the fame Baking as a Custard.[27]

Queen Anne's biscuits were also fashionable during the eighteenth and nineteenth centuries. They contained a great deal of flour, with flour biscuits once considered to be useful at alleviating epilepsy. Not that the queen suffered from this, she would more likely have required treatments for her ongoing gout. Here is Mary Eaton's recipe for Queen Anne's Biscuits. They are very rich, which one might expect.

Queen Anne's Biscuits

A pound of flour well dried, half a pound of fine sugar powdered and sifted, a pound of currants well washed and picked, and a half pound of butter. Rub the butter into the flour, then mix in the sugar and currants; add ten spoonfuls of cream, the yolks of three eggs, three spoonfuls of sack, and a little mace finely pounded. When the paste is well worked up, set it in a dish before the fire till it be thoroughly warm. Make it up into cakes, place them on a tin well buttered, prick them full of holes on the top, and bake them in a quick oven.[28]

With Queen Anne being fond of her food and drink, it is alleged that her cook, Joseph Centlivre, was instructed to bake special pies for each new month of the year, commencing with a January oyster pie.[29] Incidentally, Centlivre married the well-known writer and actress Susanna Freeman in 1707. The *Literary Encyclopaedia of 2001* heralds Susanna Centlivre as 'the most successful female playwright of the eighteenth century'.[30] The Centlivre's had a happy marriage, living at Buckingham Court with Joseph going on to cook for George I. The Centlivre family had a heritage of court life, with Joseph probably being the father of another Joseph Centlivre, recorded as a 'child of the chapel' between 1710 and 1715, in addition to being a relative of Edward Centlivre, a former 'child of the royal kitchen' between 1708 and 1714. I can find no reference to Susannah having children herself, so I am both sceptical and intrigued by this information.[31]

Local laws

The courts were always preoccupied with minor offences during the medieval period, particularly where baking and brewing was concerned. Apart from the universal Assize, it seems that each town had different baking laws. Baking was one of the leading occupations in most communities up until the 1800s, with bakers also paying some of the highest taxes. In 1524, there were sixteen full-time and nine part-time bakers employed in Oxford, with an assessed combined wealth of £206. In comparison, the town's sixteen carpenters grossed an assessed wealth of just £64.[32]

There were ongoing conflicts from county to county owing to stringent restrictions and numerous examples of towns and cities dissatisfied with their enforced milling, baking and distribution arrangements. This frequently incited rebellion and noncompliance. In Chester in particular the bakers fought hard for their rights. In 1557 they defied the terms of the assize, set down tools and refused to bake. The mayor was forced to open up trade to others, but also briefly shut down the local baker's guild as punishment. This continued for another thirty years, until permission was granted for anyone to sell bread on the city's two market days. Despite all trade restricted to the corn market alone, local bakers were often caught intercepting supplies en route to Chester. They also disliked having to use the designated royal mills to grind their grain. This flouting of the rules led to armed conflict between the millers and the bakers. In the fourteenth century some twelve bakers worked in the city, decreasing to just six at one stage before rising dramatically to twenty bakeries by the 1500s, perhaps another indication of the ongoing discontent in this period.[33]

In Buckingham in 1552, it became forbidden for anyone to bake any form of 'kake' containing butter after Shrove Tuesday. Penalties of up to 20*d* were put in place, to deter law breakers, and in Northampton substantial fees were frequently collected between 1285 and 1300 on the basis of selling unsealed or badly baked bread.[34] A new 'Bakers' Book', which, up until the middle of the twentieth century at least, continued to survive in the town of Stratford-upon-Avon, was issued in 1598 with numerous clauses enforcing the need for baking, above all other trades, to be tightly controlled by the Corporation. If you were a local baker, you could only own one bakery and no one was permitted to lease the business from you for any purpose.[35] In sixteenth-century Leicester there were five ovens belonging to the king and it was strictly forbidden to build any new ovens, with baking and selling coming under exacting jurisdiction throughout the city.[36] One of the strangest of these local laws was the one stipulated in Guildford, forbidding bakers to buy corn before 11'oclock in the morning. Perhaps the town had a history of sly early-morning contraband-corn trading.[37] While in Manchester, single women during the 1500s were not permitted to bake, brew or trade for themselves. They weren't even allowed to keep their own property, which wasn't uncommon at the time.[38] If you were unlucky enough to have been a member of the company of bakers in Salisbury in the 1600s, you were forbidden to make any kind of sweet or specialist cakes, other than at Christmas, Easter or for funerals. Neither were you allowed to trade in the market or pay local innkeepers to sell your goods.[39]

There were successive crop failures between 1594 and 1597, producing a shortage of grain and subsequent bloody food riots throughout the nation. The people of the North-East in particular were said to be starving and dying in the streets from hunger. The death rate rose by 6 per cent nationwide between 1596 and 1598.[40] The bitter years of failing harvests was compounded with a scourge of Bubonic plague, striking London the hardest between 1563 and 1593. Restrictions were even harsher during these times; maltsters would be searched and any stored barley found in their possession would be confiscated by the authorities, with the maltsters themselves forced to sell their grain in the market places to continue to meet the demand for bread during times of adversity.[41]

It appears that in Melton Mowbray, yes, they of the famed pork pie, the town successfully withheld the right to carry out their own methods of bakery, as the Manor oven, a central building with a diameter of 14ft remained unused. Matthew Lamb, the town's feudal lord in the mid-1700s failed to persuade the residents to comply with his law and they constructed a new, bigger communal oven to suit their purposes.[42] The majority of people couldn't afford a domestic oven and the structure of most basic dwellings were not able to support proper cooking facilities. While the communal oven was a convenient necessity, it also provided the lord of the manor with a good regular income from renting out both the oven and mill.

Pen, Plague & Pyre

Kickshaws were popular little appetisers, small parcels filled with meat or sweet jams, resembling the Indian samosa, or Chinese fortune cookie. The word is said to be a misspelling of the French phrase *quelque chose* (something) an anomaly that probably originated during the early seventeenth-century to denote little dainty morsels from overseas. The word Kickshaw was often incorporated into the theatrical and artistic world during the Stuart era, as a xenophobic term used to deride foreigners and immigrants on stage.[43] A writer known to reference food a great deal for the stage was William Shakespeare. There are too many altogether to include with some references more conspicuous than others, as in *Troilus and Cressida*:

> Pandarus. He that will have a cake out of the wheat must tarry the grinding.
> Troilus. Have I not tarried?
> Pandarus. Ay, the grinding; but you must tarry the bolting.
> Troilus. Have I not tarried?
> Pandarus. Ay, the bolting, but you must tarry the leavening.
> Troilus. Still have I tarried.
> Pandarus. Ay, to the leavening; but here's yet in the word 'hereafter' the kneading, the making of the cake, the heating of the oven and the baking; nay, you must stay the cooling too, or you may chance to burn your lips.[44]

As a craft, baking was once a very lengthy process and Shakespeare applies it here in *Troilus and Cressida* as a metaphor for patience, to take stock and adopt the necessary steps methodically. Perhaps this is best exemplified in Markham's instructions documented in *The English Huswife* of 1615:

Kickshaws. (@ Emma Kay)

To bake the best cheat bread, which is also simply of wheat only, you shall, after your meal is dressed and bolted through a more coarse bolter than was used for your manchets, and put also into a clean tub, trough or kimnel, take a sour leven, that is a piece of such like leaven saved from your former batch, and well filled with salt, and so laid up to sour, and this sour leven you shall break in small pieces into warm water, and then strain it, which done make a deep hollow hole in the midst of your flour, and therein pour your strained liquor, then with your hand mix some part of the flour therewith, till all the liquor be as thick as pancake better, then cover it all over with meal, and so let it lie all that night, then next morning stir it, and all the rest of the meal well together, and with a little more warm water, barm, and salt to season it with, bring it to a perfect leaven, stiff and firm; then knead it, break it, and tread it… and so mould it up in reasonable big loaves, and then bake it with indifferent good heat.[45]

Possibly Shakespeare's most gruesome play, *Titus Andronicus*, contains one of the most distasteful pie eating scenes in dramatic history. That, together with the 1970s classic Theatre of Blood, in which actor Robert Morley unknowingly consumes his own beloved dogs in a pie. In Shakespeare's play, the character Lavinia is raped by brothers Chiron and Demetrius, her tongue cut out and her hands cut off, leaving her unable to communicate. However, she manages to draw the crime out in the sand. Her father Titus avenges his daughter by murdering both brothers, then has them made into pies, which he feeds to their mother and father as he watches.

> Why, there they are, both baked in this pie;
> Whereof their mother daintily hath fed,
> Eating the flesh that she herself hath bred.
> 'Tis true, 'tis true, witness my knive's sharp point.[46]

This dramatisation must have been very sensational to audiences of the sixteenth century, despite their familiarity with death, disease and public execution. It also stands as a reminder of how easy it once was to disguise the contents of pies, a notion captured throughout the centuries with fictional characters like Sweeney Todd, and of course in Shakespeare's day it was still highly fashionable to place live birds in pies for the delight and amusement of guests. We are all acquainted with the tune of *Sing a Song of Sixpence*.

John Evelyn was a seventeenth-century English diarist and prolific author who wrote on diverse subjects, including cookery. His *Discourse of Sallets* published in 1699 combined cooking with his favourite subject, horticulture. It is considered to be the first recorded book dedicated to making salads.

Such was the popularity and desire to increase one's knowledge about continental methods of baking during the 1600s, that John Evelyn read excerpts on the art of French breadmaking from Nicolas de Bonnefons' *Les Delices de la campagne* (1654) out to the Royal Society in 1666. He then published this same essay under the title *Panificium*, or 'The

Four and Twenty Blackbirds Baked in a Pie, John Doyle 1836. (*Wellcome Collection Creative Commons Attribution* (*CC BY 4.0*) *300*)

several manners of making bread in France, etc'. But he never credited Bonnefons who worked in the French royal household and wrote a couple of very popular books.[47] There is indeed a chapter in *Les Delices De La Campagne*, a copy of which can be accessed from the Library of Congress, called 'Du Pain'. The opening paragraph roughly translates as – 'The most necessary of all foods that the divine goodness has created for the maintenance of the life of man, is bread. His blessing is so much on this nourishment, that we never tire of it.' Evelyn's *Panificium* includes much of Bonnefons advice, waxing lyrical about the many and varied properties of bread and its components, including plagiarised recipes. Here is Evelyn's translation of Bonnefons *Pain Benit O Brioche*

Pain Benit O Brioche

Take a bushel of the finest wheat flower, of which mix a quarter with leaven, yeast, and hot water, let this rise in a tray or bowl, first warmed and well covered, if it be in winter: while this is set to rise take the three other parts of your flower, and temper them with water as hot as your hand can suffer, and put in a quarter of a pound of salt, a pound of fresh butter and a new fresh curd cheese; two hours after, mix these with the leavened dough and work them together; then lay it together to rise again in the tray, knead it again on a table, spreading and working it exceedingly; then make it up upon a large peel, and let it stand a while: when it is ready to set into the oven (but first varnish it over with an egg) stop and govern the heat…When the batch is ready to draw, set it on a peel or wicker hurdle, to keep it from breaking because it is exceeding brittle. The varnish is made with the yolk of fresh eggs, beaten without water; some to spare cost add honey, but that obliges you to slacken the oven.[48]

Pain Benit O Brioche would have been used specifically during church services in France in the seventeenth and eighteenth centuries. Not for communion, but as a charitable gift from a member of the congregation to gift to other members of the community.

Evelyn's peer, Samuel Pepys mentions cheesecake a great deal in his diaries. Often eaten when dining out at inns, along with custards and tarts. The closest pastry relative to the 'cheesecake' eaten by

Pepys would be the Yorkshire Curd Tart. A lovely surviving regional dish that was baked for special occasions using the surplus fresh curds from cheese-making. By the 1700s lemon became a popular addition to cheese-cakes, mixed with the curds, eggs and sometimes ground rice to produce what we recognise today as lemon curd. This probably evolved a century later into the lemon meringue pie. Exactly when cheese-cakes began to be made incorporating a biscuit base is difficult to determine, but the use of extra cream and eggs as a substitute for the curd, was introduced during the eighteenth century with the addition of crushed, or grated biscuits, a practice that was commonplace by the next century. Certainly, by the mid-eighteenth century the cheese curd mix was adapted and many recipes included crushed meringues (mackeroons) crushed almonds or Naples biscuits. At some stage the crunchy element was removed from the egg and curd mix and used to replace the traditional pastry case.

Kenelm Digby's cheesecake recipe, published in *The Closet of Sir Kenelm Digby Knight Opened*, probably best describes the type of cheesecakes Pepys may have frequently indulged in:

Contemporary
Cheesecake.
(@ *Emma Kay*)

To make cheese-cakes

Take twelve quarts of Milk warm from the Cow, turn it with a good spoonful of Runnet. Break it well, and put it into a large strainer, in which rowl it up and down, that all the Whey may run out into a little tub; when all that will be run out, wring out more. Then break the curds well; then wring it again, and more whey will come. Thus, break and wring till no more come. Then work the Curds exceedingly with your hand in a tray, till they become a short uniform Paste. Then put to it the yolks of eight new laid Eggs, and two whites, and a pound of butter. Work all this long together.

In the long working (at the several times) consisteth the making them good. Then season them to your taste with Sugar finely beaten; and put in some Cloves and Mace in subtile powder. Then lay them thick in Coffins of fine Paste, and bake them.[49]

Egg beaters, old and vintage. (@ *Nick Kay*)

It's worth taking a moment here to consider the introduction of meringues to British baking. The word itself is often linked to the Swiss municipality of Meiringen, although there is little direct evidence to support this. Meringue does not appear in print in relation to confection until the 1690s in French chef Massialot's book *The Court and Country Cook*. The French word Meringue has no known origin, although I have found the word *meringhe* in early Dutch texts of the 1500s. The combination of whipped and baked egg whites and sugar/honey, with various other additions, such as nuts to make macaroons (also a word garnered from the French and Italians) is a time-honoured one in Britain, long before the word we now associate it with. Eggs were still whisked using bunches of twigs during this period, so it would have been no mean feat, getting them up to meringue standard.

Here is Massialot's seventeenth-century recipe, translated for the British market in 1702:

Dry Meringues

Having caus'd the Whites of four new laid Eggs to be whipt as before till they rise up to a Snow, let four Spoonfuls of very dry Powder-sugar be put into it and well temper'd with a Spoon: Then let all be set over a gentle Fire, to be dried a little at two several times and add some Pistachoes that are pounded and dried a little in the Stove. Afterwards they are to be dress'd as the others and bak'd in the Oven somewhat leisurely, with a little Fire underneath and more on the top: When they are sufficiently done and very dry let them be taken out and cut off with a Knife: Lastly as soon as they are somewhat cold let them be laid upon Paper and set into the Stove to be kept dry.[50]

Pepys writes about his wife spending a day making Christmas pies and he is sent out to purchase a baking pan, costing him sixteen shillings. This was a considerable sum in 1662, worth around £90 today.[51] This evidence of the expenses incurred with home baking during the seventeenth century is indicative of the number of people who continued to use their local bakeries and communal ovens. The English nursery rhyme 'Pat-a-cake, pat-a-cake, baker's man', is commonly associated with this era.

Taking your uncooked pie or pastry to the communal oven meant patting, pricking and marking for the purposes of identification.

Cloth merchant and author Henry Machyn discusses the lavish post funeral dining rituals, following the death of one of his colleagues, in a diary entry from the sixteenth century. The second course (following a whole host of roasted meats) consisted of tarts, bread, wine, ale and beer, followed by French wine, a box of wafers and the Hippocras, or spiced wine. It was common practice to indulge in wafers and sweetmeats at the end of a meal, with a glass of Hippocras in affluent households or notable occasions.[52] Machyn also references spice-bread a great deal, which was probably the French pain d'épices, popular in England at the time and still eaten around the Festive holiday season in France. Pain d'épices is a loaf traditionally made from barley meal which blends aromatic spices like nutmeg, ginger and cinnamon with honey; it is similar to gingerbread. One of Antonin Careme's most famous apprentices, Jules Gouffe, included a recipe for pain d'épices in his *Book of Preserves* of 1869. It does not contain ginger, but they are certainly spice fuelled little brick-shaped cakes.

Pain d' epices

Melt ½ lb of honey and ½ lb of treacle in a copper sugar boiler;
Sift 1 lb of rye flour on to a pasteboard, make a hollow in the centre, and put in:

the melted honey and treacle,
¼ oz of ground cloves,
1 oz of ground cinnamon
Mix, and add:
½ oz of carbonate of soda dissolved in a little water,
a few grains of carbonate of ammonia also dissolved in water;
Work the paste thoroughly by pulling it apart and folding it over and over;
and put it in a basin to rest for eight days;

Oil some brick shaped wooden frames; place them on some floured baking sheets; put the paste into them, and bake the *pain d epices* in a moderate oven. 2 oz of well washed and dried currants may he added to every pound of the paste, or the same quantity of stoned raisins may be added, if preferred.[53]

One of the grimmest events of the Stuart era was the great bubonic plague that wiped out around a quarter of the population of London. A good second-hand account of the plague exists in Daniel Defoe's *A Journal of the Plague Year*, published in 1722 and initialled H.F., it is understood to represent the journals of Defoe's uncle Henry. The journal informs us that it was common for people visiting the bakehouses in London during the plague years to return with the sickness. Stopping at other shops, inns or the physician en route to get their bread or pies baked. The germs they carried were passed on to others and vice versa.[54] Nonetheless, the community ovens across the city remained open and trading, this was a stipulation of the Lord Mayor, who decreed that any baker seen not to be providing a service would automatically lose their privilege of Freeman of the City of London.[55] Presumably because people had to eat no matter what the circumstances. Communities living in the settlements around

THE GREAT PLAGUE: SCENES IN THE STREETS OF LONDON. (See p. 816.)

Two Men Discovering a Woman Dead in the Street During the Great Plague. (*Wellcome Collection Creative Commons Attribution (CC BY 4.0)*)

London, were too afraid to enter the city for provisions and suffered significantly as a consequence. Defoe informs us that these groups of people were sustained by wealthier, philanthropic citizens who had meat, cheese and milk sent out to them. The corn that was supplied could not be ground and there was nowhere to bake bread products. Initially people ate the corn raw, which must have been pretty undigestible, until they managed to find a mill near Woodford (now a district of Redbridge) where they were able to process grain and bake biscuits by constructing a makeshift hollow dry hearth.[56]

A letter from Pepys to lady Carteret written on 4 September, 1665 from Woolwich London provides a glimpse of the city during the Plague:

> I having stayed in the city till about 7400 died in one week, and of them above 6000 of the plague, and little noise heard day nor night but tolling of bells; till I could walk Lumber-Street and not meet twenty persons from one end to the other, and not fifty upon the Exchange; till whole families, ten and twelve together, have been swept away; till my very physician, Dr Burnet, who undertook to secure me against any infection, having survived the month of his own being shut up, died himself of the plague; till the nights, though much lengthened, are grown too short to conceal the burials of those that died the day before, people being thereby constrained to borrow daylight for that service. The butcheries are everywhere visited, this brewer is shut up, and his baker dead with his whole family.[57]

Sadly, things would only get worse for disease-ridden Londoners, as a new terrible disaster was about to sweep its way through the capital. A great deal has been speculated about the Great Fire of London, which is thought to have started in the early hours of Sunday morning on 2 September, 1666 at the bakery of Thomas Farriner in Pudding Lane (today EC3). Around a third of the city was destroyed as a consequence and resulted in some 100,000 people being made homeless. The fire spread rapidly following a long, hot and dry summer, combined with a surrounding location full of warehouses containing numerous combustible materials and a strong easterly wind.[58] Little information exists about Farriner himself, except that he was apprenticed to one Thomas Dodson in 1629, was married in

Pudding Lane, London. (@ *Nick Kay*)

1637 to Hanna Mathewes and had established his business in Pudding
Lane, where he lived in a substantial property in the adjacent Fish Yard
by 1666. Active in his community, Farriner served as an overseer of the
poor, supplied biscuits to the Navy and held the title of 'Conduct of the
King's Bakehouse'. Following the fire, he resumed his trade, dying four
years later, remaining resolute with regard to accusations of negligence.
According to Farriner he extinguished the fire in his oven around 10 pm
on the Saturday evening. Checked it again at midnight, raked the coals
and closed all the oven doors and surrounding doors and windows to
minimise the risk of draughts.[59] As there was no formal conviction or
clear evidence to legitimately link Farriner with the fire at the time, the
legacy of its origins left communities suspicious, fuelling ignorance and
distrust.

   During the seventeenth century London was home to a significant surge
of migrant settlers. Lascars, Dutch, French, black slaves, Chinese and
many other overseas refugees and victims of early Empire. A great deal of
these migrants, who were left without anywhere to live after the fire, were
forced to return to their home countries. Some of those who remained
became the victims of hate campaigns, public beatings, imprisonment, ill-
treatment, disrespect and worse. If you were considered to be a foreigner,

NEAR THIS SITE STOOD THE SHOP
BELONGING TO THOMAS FARYNER.
THE KING'S BAKER. IN WHICH THE
GREAT FIRE OF SEPTEMBER 1666 BEGAN.

PRESENTED BY
THE WORSHIPFUL COMPANY OF BAKERS
TO MARK THE 500th ANNIVERSARY OF
THEIR CHARTER GRANTED BY
KING HENRY VII IN 1486

Plaque commemorating the Fire of London. (@ *Nick Kay*)

you were blacklisted as a firestarter. One Dutch baker in Westminster was dragged into the street and beaten to near death by an angry mob. His house and business destroyed.[60]

Fashions and trends

It was during the seventeenth century that pastry making really became fashionable. Bakers invented new techniques and began being creative with elaborate designs and challenging creations. Puff pastry; the invention of the French, became de rigueur, particularly as all high-profile grand houses employed talented French or Italian pastry chefs.

Edward Kidder was a celebrated cook of the seventeenth and eighteenth century, and a man who really knew his pastry. As well as writing the definitive guide to pastry making, he also ran a training school, located in Queen Street, East Central London, where he taught every afternoon from Monday to Saturday. Here is his recipe for puff pastry:

Lay down a pound of flower, break it into two ounces of butter and 2 eggs; then make it into paste with cold water, then work the other part of the pound of butter to the stiffness of your paste; then roul out yor paste into a Square Sheet: stick it all over with bitts of butter, flower it, and roul it up like a collar, double it up at both ends that they meet in the middle, roul it out again as aforesaid, till all the pound of butter is in.[61]

If you're curious to know what Kidder looked like, his portrait can be found in the collections of The National Portrait Gallery, London.

Traditional pastry-making continued to expand, with pies and pasties a plenty. Pasties were popular parcels in the Tudor and Stuart eras. Despite their well-known relationship with Cornwall, pasties, as previously noted, had a long association of being enjoyed by the nobility in towns and cities throughout Britain. Tin mines, coal fields and pits were well established in mining towns by the Elizabethan era and the pasty became a firm favourite for people who worked in these fields. Although it is difficult to accurately date each individual regional pasty, in the north, miners took the Lancashire, or collier's foot (so named after its shape) to work with them. Essentially a meal of meat and vegetables wrapped in pastry, it would have sustained them for the day. Similarly, the Oggie, also confusingly linked to the Devonshire and Cornish Teddy or Tiddy Oggie, were popular across Wales and its mining communities in the seventeenth, eighteenth and nineteenth centuries. Some say the true Cornish version should contain a pilchard,[62] while it is understood that the 'Teddy', represents the potato and the 'Oggie' is the meat, either pig or cow.[63] I have also read that 'Tiddy Oggies' were a favoured snack aboard ships of war much later in the twentieth century. An even older version, called a Hoggan, which was a flatbread filled with

St. Mary's Bakery, Paignton Devon, established 1890 and seller of pasties. (@ *Nick Kay*)

meat and, most importantly, joined up together in the middle, rather than being sealed and crimped along the side, which would just make it a regular pasty apparently.[64] The Hoggan has a more legitimate connection to Cornwall, as a 'tinner's pasty'.[65] Personally, I think the whole pasty debate is impossible to clarify and that they evolved at similar times for a similar purpose across the UK. What is more interesting is the knowledge that it has always been a dish which straddles class.

There was also the fried variety of pasty, which has not retained its popularity in quite the same way in Britain, although the culinary world across continents contains an abundance of fried meat or vegetable parcels: Indian samosas, Chinese spring rolls, the battered pies of Northern Ireland, Thailand's crispy dumplings. Far too many to mention in detail and I'm sure their provenance goes much further back than that of the English fried pasty. Here is Kenelm Digby's seventeenth-century recipe for spinage pasties.

Excellent marrow-spinage-pasties

Take Spinage, and chop it a little; then boil it, till it be tender. In the meantime, make the best rich light Crust you can, and roul it out, and put a little of your Spinage into it, and Currants and Sugar, and store of lumps of Marrow; Clap the Past over this to make little Pasties deep within, and fry them with clarified Butter.[66]

While researching another of those classic British baked goodies, I was surprised to find that the word scone, in the context of a cake, was in use as early as 1480. A man named Frank Mathewe, listed in the petty customs accounts for that year, was documented as having a small wooden chest containing 400 spice cakes and 500 'scone Jesus'. Frank Mathewe was a baker who had stamped his 500 scones with the figure of Christ, which was a common practice in the fifteenth century when you made bread products from the finest high-quality flour, or pandemain.[67]

The earliest record I can find for a printed scone recipe is 1669 is 'Mrs Fellard's scone cake', which appears in a folio of miscellaneous recipes to be found in the Wellcome Library archives. The recipe-writer's handwriting is extremely difficult to interpret, but from what

Fruit Scones. (@ *Emma Kay*)

I could translate she instructs to incorporate very fine flour, what looks like currants, but is written 'carrance', which need to be 'well juiced and dried', good eggs, sugar, a pint of good ale yeast and a quart of good rich cream. I can then decipher that the 'liquor', or liquid, was added to the flour and left to sit by the fire for half an hour, before ensuring the 'oven is hot' and 'mix altogether very well', finally adding the 'carrance'. She/he then suggests putting the mixture in a 'hoope', which was probably an old metal cake hoop, acting as a mould to form cakes. The hoop sat on a baking tray and the mixture was poured into it before being baked. Again, the text becomes a bit illegible, but from what I can make out the writer instructs to beat together four egg whites and sugar, presumably to wash over the top of the scone prior to baking.

The recipe continues, and as they so often did back in the seventeenth and eighteenth centuries, suggests 'another way', or an alternative version. This is where it gets very interesting, as Mrs Fellard's scone cake appears to have a savoury alternative, one which includes bacon and half a pint of 'gravey'.[68] Similar, in fact, to what Americans term 'biscuits and gravy'. I have always understood that the scone, or at least the very early concept of what became a scone, originated in Scotland, once better known as a girdle (and I'm not referring to undergarments). The generic term for any type of cake cooked on a cast iron girdle over the fire. They

Cheese Scones baking in an outdoor wood-fired oven. (@ *Emma Kay*)

were probably also made with oats and would have been a large, flat shape. Although there is no way of authenticating its provenance. Incidentally Culross in Perth received royal patents from both James VI and Charles II to bake oatmeal cakes and the town's mine was, for many years, active in providing materials to manufacture the girdles necessary to bake with.

Welsh cakes were cooked in this way and closely resemble the modern-day scone as we know it. At some stage, someone must have adapted the girdle version for the oven. The word possibly derives from a European term like *schoonbrood*, the Dutch for 'clean bread', or the medieval village of Scone in Scotland. Mrs Fellard's recipe, together with the knowledge we have about the 'scone Jesus' dating to the fifteenth century, suggests that early scones were not just prepared with oats over the fire, they were baked cakey, bread products made in the oven. It also ascertains that scones didn't have to be sweet. Perhaps this is why we have inherited the cheese scone and its other savoury adaptions today.

The word cake, 'cakys', or other variations, can be found in the oldest of recipe books. It is a Scandinavian word which Britain probably inherited from the Vikings. Simply translated it means flat, small roll or paste of some kind. Marchpane or marzipan was sometimes called sugar-cakes in the 1600s. The earliest reference I can find for a sponge cake as we know it today, incorporating flour, eggs and butter, appears in *The Good Huswifes*

Jewell of 1596, written by Thomas Dawson, but first published over ten years before this version. Some literature claims that sponge cakes were the invention of the 1600s, but this publication informs us otherwise:

To make fine Cakes.

> Take fine flowre and good Samaske wa-
> ter you must haue no other liquour but
> that, then take sweet butter, two or three
> yolkes of egges and a good quantity of Su-
> ger, and a fewe cloues, and mace, as your
> Cookes mouth shall serue him, and a lyttle
> saffron, and a little Gods good about a spon-
> full if you put in too much they shall arise,
> cutte them in squares lyke vnto trenchers,
> and pricke them well, and let your ouen be
> well swept and lay them vppon papers and
> so set them into the ouen, do not burne them
> if they be three or foure dayes olde they bee
> the better.[69]

Contemporary popular
Pineapple Upside Down
Cake. (@ *Emma Kay*)

One of the most popular sponge cakes of the 1800s, despite its earlier heritage of the century before, was undoubtedly the staple pound cake. As the name implies, it contained one pound each of flour, butter, eggs and sugar. It found greater fame in America, with earlier recipes using cornmeal flour. Over time the cake included numerous variations with the addition of vanilla, almonds or as Hannah Glasse suggests in 1747, clean, washed currants.

Tarts and Custards or crustardes were hugely popular in the Tudor and Stuart age. Tarts or tartes, both sweet and savoury, often included eggs and cream mixed together, with either fruits or cheese and vegetables, sometimes meat and fish. This recipe for the base of the tart is taken from *A Propre new booke of Cokery*.

To make shorte paest for tart.
Take fine floure and a curtesy of faire water and a disshe of swete butter and a litle saffron and the yolkes of two egges and make it thin and tender as ye maie.

Basically, it translates to this:

Combine flour & saffron. Combine the flour and butter, add the egg yolks and enough water to allow the pastry to come together into a ball. Roll out into thin sheets of pastry and use as required.

'curtesy' probably just means the proper or right amount.[70]

A Propre new booke of Cokery, published in 1545 lists ten separate recipes for tarts, including ones that contain meddlers and gooseberries and savoury spinach and cheese tarts. These are very reminiscent of the French quiche or Italian torta and appeared on the menu for royal feasts and festivals as early as the fourteenth century in Britain, but they really came into their own during the Tudor age. Certainly, the famous medieval Italian culinary text, *Libro de arte coquinaria*, contains similar dishes. It raises the question of which country first influenced the other. As exploration and travel were so extensive throughout Europe at this time, it is a thankless task trying to pinpoint the exact origins of the baked custard or tart. Although I wouldn't mind having a go. As more

Fruit Custards
(@ *Emma Kay*)

sophisticated pastry-making became commonplace, numerous British regional variations began to emerge, ones that remain well known today. For instance, what is the difference between an Eccles cake and a Chorley cake, other than that one uses shortcrust pastry, the other puff pastry? Banbury cakes are also a variation of this curranty, sugary pastry delight, but have the oldest patronage. Written anonymously under the initials W.M., the *Compleat Cook* contains the following recipe for Banbury cakes. It is attributed to the Countess of Rutland, having been served at her daughter's wedding:

> Take a peck of fine flower, and halfe an ounce of large Mace, halfe an ounce of Nutmegs, and halfe an ounce of Cinnamon, your Cinnamon and Nutmegs must be sifted through a Searce, two pounds of Butter, halfe a score of Eggs, put out four of the whites of them, something above a pint of good Ale-yeast, beate your Eggs very well and straine them with your yeast, and a little warme water into your flowre, and stirre them together, then put your butter cold

in little Lumpes: The water you knead withall must be scalding hot, if you will make it good past, the which having done, lay the past to rise in a warme Cloth a quarter of an hour, or thereupon; Then put in ten pounds of Currans, and a little Muske and Ambergreece dissolved in Rosewater; your Currans must be made very dry, or else they will make your Cake heavy, strew as much Sugar finely beaten among the Currans, as you shall think the water hath taken away the sweetnesse from them; Break your past into little pieces, into a kimnell or such like thing, and lay a Layer of past broken into little pieces, and a Layer of Currans, untill your Currans are all put in, mingle the past and the Currans very well, but take heed of breaking the Currans, you must take out a piece of past after it hath risen in a warme cloth before you put in the currans to cover the top, and the bottom, you must roule the cover something thin, and the bottom likewise, and wet it with Rosewater, and close them at the bottom of the side, or the middle which you like best, prick the top and the sides with a small long Pin, when your Cake is ready to go into the Oven, cut it in the midst of the side roundabout with a knife an inch deep, if your Cake be of a peck of Meale, it must stand two hours in the Oven, your Oven must be as hot as for Manchet.[71]

One reason for these variations may be attributed to the increase in published material and levels of literacy, which provided the public with greater access to recipes on how to prepare and make popular dishes. The Tudor and Stuart age produced a wealth of inspirational cookery writers and recipe books. It was also a time when cooks who had worked for nobility began sharing the secrets of their aristocratic and royal households. Edward Kidder, John Nott, Thomas Dawson, Hugh Plat, John Murrell, Sir Kenelm Digby Knight, Gervaise Markham, Robert May, Hannah Woolley, Hannah Bisaker and Mary Eales were among the main contributors.

There are too many variations of the pork pie to mention here, but the trend to keep producing the hearty, raised hot-water crust pies of early Britain continued well into the following centuries. One unusual pie originating in Leicestershire, fashioned in the manner of a pig and stuffed with mincemeat, The Checky Pig, appears to have been completely eradicated from the archives. I can only find a couple of references remaining, one of which was provided by Dorothy Hartley writing in the 1950s, who alludes to its demise back then. A recipe for Checky Pigs was published in 1931 in the *West London Observer*, in an aim to appeal for readers to come forward with historical regional recipes:

Checky Pigs

Rub 5 oz. butter and 2 oz. of lard into 1lb.of flour. Add 3 tablespoons of Ideal milk diluted in ¼ pint water, and mix into a moderately stiff paste. Cut into the shapes of pigs, lay a little mincemeat on half the shapes, and seal with remain half. Bake for about ¼ hour.[72]

The hardtack ships' biscuits discussed in the previous chapter were one type of useful travelling snack, but by the 1600s the bis cotus, bisket, biskettes, biskettella, bisquet and finally biscuit, despite being a Roman concept, was undoubtedly made popular in Britain during the Middle Ages; one of the many French acquisitions from the days of Norman occupation. Hugh Plat, in his *Delightes for Ladies*, provides a number of biscuit recipes, including one for 'bisket bread, otherwise called French bisket' and some early posset recipes. Posset, being a spiced medieval milk and ale beverage, often included grated biscuit. Biscuits could also be stand-alone elaborate creations. Jumbolls/Jumbles, also known as 'knot biscuits', functioned as both an excellent travelling biscuit and provided a skilled and aesthetically pleasing addition to any banquet.

Chocolate Biscuits (@ *Emma Kay*)

They were so called after the fashion for knot gardens which evolved during the reign of Elizabeth I.

To make Jumbolls

> Take half a pound of Almonds being beaten to a paste with a short cake being grated, and 2 eggs, 2 ounces of carroway seeds, being beaten, and the juice of a Lemmon: and being brought into paste, roule it into round strings: then cast it into knots, and so bake it in an oven and when they are baked, ice them with Rose-water and Sugar, and the white of an egge being beaten together, then take a feather and gild them, and put them again into the oven, and let them stand in a little while, and they will be iced cleane over with a white ice: and so boxe them up, and you may keep them all the yeare.[73]

As Plat mentions, the density and longevity of Jumbles meant they travelled well and widely. There are variant recipes with different names to be found across Europe, the United States and Australia.

A wealth of breads could be found in the English language from the seventeenth and eighteenth century which are no longer current. These include: Angel bread, or Manna, a flaky thin bake with Jewish origins and associated with purity. I also found a recipe for Angel bread in an early manuscript, describing it as a remedy for consumption. Cheet, or cheat/chett bread (it has many variables) was bread made with a lower quality of flour. So christened, because if you had purchased a manchet, but actually received an inferior cheet loaf, you had obviously been cheated.

Rumpy Bread or Rumple Bread was a round loaf with shallow cuts all over, producing a criss-cross, chequered look. Wastel Bread is ancient and linked to the old Saxon Wassil bowl tradition – waes-hael (health to you) a custom of carrying a bowl with hot ale, or mulled cider, from house to house that continued with enthusiasm in Britain into the Victorian period and beyond in some smaller rural communities. Cakes or fine white bread were soaked in the wassel, hence wastel bread.

In the transactions of the Royal Society, a Mr Samuel Dale, writing in 1693, discusses how a shortage of all types of corn drove people to turn to making turnip bread. He provided the following recipe:

Take turnips, peel and boil them until they become soft and tender, then press strongly out the juice, chop them small, and mix them with an equal quantity of wheaten meal, add salt and barm, with a sufficient quantity of water, and knead it up as other dough or paste, let it stand a little time to ferment or rise, then order and bake it as common bread.[74]

This was probably a cousin of that faithful old staple, potato bread. Basically, when times were hard, famines prevailed or conflict interfered, just about anything could be formed into bread.

Finally, and perhaps one of the oldest and most frequently of baked treats, gingerbread, is a name that is as synonymous with medieval England as apples are to cider. It emerged from Germany and Sweden and initially came in a myriad of forms. Fine gingerbread was an amalgam of ground almonds, a sort of fortified Marchpane. Other gingerbreads contained flour and treacle, a little like parkin. It was frequently moulded into fancy shapes.

I have a small collection of wooden and wax springelers used for this purpose. Gingerbread street-sellers and the cakey biscuits presented at

Victorian and Vintage Gingerbread and Biscuit Moulds. (@ *Emma Kay*)

fairs and fetes were commonplace, making it a product less likely to be made in the home for domestic consumption. The Calendar of Letter books for London informs us that it cost 1/4*d* for one bushel (around ½ gram) of gingerbread in 1315.[75] That's somewhere in the region of 45p in today's money, which is a little on the steep side, and perhaps suggests it wasn't quite such a mainstream commodity in the twelfth century.

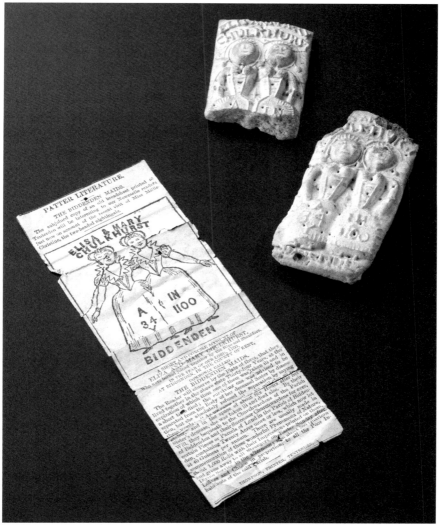

Early biscuit moulds detailing the Biddenden Maids, folklore characters. (*Wellcome Collection Creative Commons Attribution (CC BY 4.0) 300-1*)

Ormskirk in Lancashire has a long history of gingerbread production, a product in such demand that it was exported overseas in the nineteenth century.[76] Just a little further up the road in the Lake District, you can still sample the unique qualities of Victorian Grasmere gingerbread, made famous by local creative baker, Sarah Nelson for its chewy, spicy and biscuit-cake consistency. I have eaten my fair share and can vouch for its deliciousness.

In the 1700s you could find gingerbread for sale on the 'bum' or 'scavenger' boats, used to ferry supplies back and forth across the Thames, and many of the hawkers and street vendors of the eighteenth and nineteenth century acquired a type of celebrity status, more of which you can read about in the next chapter. For centuries gingerbread was THE dominant commercial sugary treat. In a market-place saturated with cakes and biscuits of every type, it seems a shame that today we tend to only indulge in it now at Christmas.

Immigrants and Emigrants

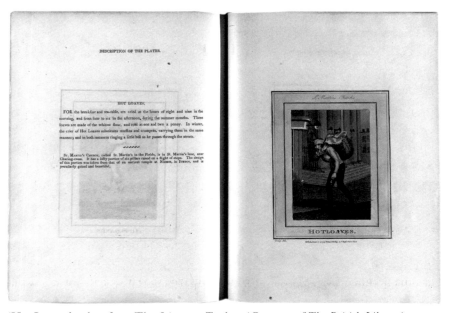

'Hot Loaves', taken from The *Itinerant Traders. (Courtesy of The British Library)*

In London there was fierce social debate in the late 1700s about 'foreign bakers', particularly those from Germany, who often produced bread that catered to the migrant communities. Bread that was made with milk, baked with a crusty consistency and designed to 'tempt the eye and appetite'. It was understood that these types of bread used double the quantities of flour and violated the assize laws, in addition to generating more profits for the baker. Magistrates in Bow-street served foreign bakers with a notice, threatening them with eviction from the country, if they continued to make and sell continental breads.[77]

The Old Post Office Bakery, London's Oldest Organic Bakery, which is also German.

German migrant bakers were not just bread-makers, a large population of German migrants living in London in both the eighteenth and nineteenth centuries were sugar-bakers. As the East India Company pillaged West Indian colonies for its raw sugar, it needed a way of processing it to turn it into powder. This meant diluting, boiling and baking. German immigrants were recruited in their hundreds to undertake this task, earning between £30 and £50 a year, or around £4,000 in today's currency. A sizeable wage then. Communities of German workers grew all around Whitechapel, the East and Mile End, districts surrounded by the docks where the sugar landed.[78]

Sourcing direct references for migrants working in the baking trade in early and medieval Britain is challenging. Made harder by the fact that 'foreign bakers' were those classified as not being local to the town, city or village they were trading in. Robert the Black Baker is listed as a miller living in London as early as the thirteenth century. He was drawn on hurdles through the city of London as punishment, possibly for flouting the assize laws.[79] Henry Bourchier, the fifth earl of Bath and great-grandson of Edward III employed 'James the blackamoor' as his cook in Devon from 1640 to 1646.[80] While Samuel Pepys, a man who profited significantly from the slave trade, had a cook, Edna Watson, whom he nicknamed 'Doll' and was among several slaves of African descent who worked in his household.[81] Pepys mentions her rarely and there is no real record of her baking skills, other than to say that 'she dresses our meat well'.

Despite a description of the food markets in Port Royal, Jamaica, in 1687 exhibiting a wealth of 'cheese-cakes, custard, tarts, etc. which are here made as curious as those sold by our pastry cooks in London'. It was also noted that the only thing you could not buy was bread. Whether the writer meant the type of European bread he was familiar with, or no bread at all is unclear, but cassava bread would probably have been the bread most likely to have been manufactured by bakers working in Jamaica during English occupation.[82] Although it is certainly not a bread that left any significant impression on British culture.

Chinese, Japanese and Lascar sailors were employed by the East India Company working on the Oriental routes out of the Port of London. And African cooks worked on British warships and merchant vessels. Many of these communities settled in the East End of London where burgeoning Chinese grocers and restaurants also acted as fronts for hidden opium dens. There was racial tension and prejudice in areas of segregated communities housing migrants such as East London, which was not only a place for workers to dwell and new trades to thrive, but an area affected by poverty, unemployment and crime. *The Public Advertiser* (1786) appealed to its readers 'to consider their [lascars] hard fate, and to provide for their relief'. The article announced that Mr Brown, a baker in Wigmore Street, Cavendish Square, was issued with the task of ensuring a quarter of a loaf of bread was distributed to 'every black in distress'.[83] By the end of the eighteenth century more unskilled workmen and their families from countries including Russia, Poland, Germany and Italy moved into the Kings Cross area of London, but many also arrived with great skills. The sanctuary provided to Huguenots in Britain escaping persecution from France in the 1600s also added to the rich mix of early immigrant communities. Letters of denization and acts of naturalisation were stringently documented from the fourteenth century

Contemporary
German Bakery,
Konditor, London.
(*@ Nick Kay*)

and it is possible to capture a snapshot of bakers who brought their trade
to England as early as the 1500s. Thomas Accourte was a baker from
Normandy who came to England around 1514; he married an English
woman and they had four children. Fraunces Atyna from France arrived
in England in 1504 and was still listed as a baker forty years later. Frauncys
Bellett also migrated from his birth place of Normandy in 1504 and was
living and working as a baker in Dorset.[84] The legacy of these early skilled
migrant workers continues to burn brightly across London and some of
Britain's larger port cities today.

In Wilton, Wiltshire, a significant Jewish community had been
established since the twelfth century. There were fourteen bakers listed in
the town during the thirteenth century, whether any of these were Jewish

is undetermined, but there are more legitimate historical links regarding Jewish bakers in Devon and Cornwall. There were four predominant Jewish communities in the South West of England in the 1700s, all of them took responsibility for organising festival activities. Passover, the first of the annual calendar of festivals requires matzo, a sacred unleavened bread which traditionally requires a turnaround time of 18 minutes before the flour comes into contact with the water. Matzo/Matzah, Matza preparation has the added disadvantage of having to dispose all the crumbs from the previous dough, lest they leaven the following batch. For the Jewish communities of Devon and Cornwall this was no easy task, considering the scale of matzo required. As a consequence, the Honorary Officers of the Plymouth Congregation had to ensure that there was an ongoing supply of flour along with appropriate and kosher utensils and a special oven was built for this purpose in 1779. By the early 1800s a system had been established in which the baking took place in the synagogue over a two-day period. All members of the congregation who sat in the seats on the right had to help with the baking on the first day, while all those seated on the left assisted on day two. Anyone who wanted matzo but declined to help with this task was expected to pay a penalty of £2 6*d* per pound of bread. In 1803 the system broke down and matzo supplies were ordered from London. However, the 200-mile journey

Matzah, baked to an original Egyptian Roqaq recipe. (@ *Nick Kay*)

for half-a-ton of delicate matzo proved too hazardous and by 1805 the congregation were once again baking it all themselves. This time a team of three men took on the task, a baking relationship that lasted some thirty years. The last records pertaining to the communal matzo baking in the Plymouth Congregation Minute books were filed in 1884, when the congregation itself purchased extra matzo for the poorer members of the community.[85] Some academics allude to the ancient Egyptian recipe of *Raqaq* or *Roqaq*, still made in traditional clay ovens in Egypt, as being the closest equivalent to the Matzah baked by the Israelites, before the Exodus.

Roqaq

Ingredients:
3 cups wheat flour
Pinch of salt
1 cup water

Method:
1. Add salt to flour. Add water and knead until a dough forms.
2. Cut dough into orange-sized pieces
3. Roll out dough balls with rolling pin into large thin circles.
4. Bake in a hot oven for 2 minutes for soft roqaq or 5 minutes for crunchier roqaq.[86]

Investigating activities both home and abroad, is an essential part of understanding the history of Britain's baking past. At the height of the Stuart period, thousands of British citizens chose to embark on lives in the new worlds of America and Australia, or had the misfortune of ending up non-voluntarily migrating, courtesy of the justice system.

The first colony in America was established in 1607 in Jamestown, Virginia, and by 1650 England's presence was a dominant force along the Atlantic coast. Wheat simply could not be cultivated and colonists substituted it for corn in their baking, a practice that they learnt from Native Americans. The typical British rural loaf combining wheat and rye, became rye and corn meal, a mixture termed 'rye n injun'. This would have been a dense loaf, lacking in any gluten. On the rare occasions that wheat flour was available, a little would be added to this basic mix, making what was known as 'thirded bread'. The recipe books brought from England had to be adapted significantly, until American women began to write their own. Amelia Simmons book *American Cookery* is considered one of the first published works of early American cuisine circulated in 1796.

Many of Amelia's uniquely 'American' recipes include those using indigenous foods. Cornmeal to make 'Johnnycakes', a flat-bread that some attribute to New England and 'Indian Slapjacks', a type of pancake. Better known as 'flapjack' today. Although, there is evidence to suggest that the origins of the word flapjack can be traced back at least to 1500s England, a term you can find quoted by Shakespeare:

> Come, thou shant go home, and we'll have flesh for holidays, fish for fasting-days, and moreo'er puddings and flap-jacks, and thou shalt be welcome.[87]

I have been unable to source any medieval flapjack recipes, although I discovered in the writings of John Taylor from 1610 a reference that, together with Shakespeare's citation substantiates their early existence:

> He is an English man, and English dyet will serue his turne. If the Norfolk Dumplin, and the Deuonshire White-pot, be at variance, he will atone them, the Bag-puadings of Gloucester shire, the Blacke-puddings of Worcester shire, the Pan puddings of Shropshire, the White puddings of Somersetshire, the Hasty-puddings of Hamshire, and the Pudding-pyes of any shire, all is one to him, nothing comes amisse, a contented mind is worth all, and let any thing come in the shape of fodder, or eating stuffe, it is welcome, whe|ther it bee Sawsedge, or Custard, or Eg-pye, or Cheese-cake, or Plawne, or Foole, or Froyze, or Tanzy, or Pancake, or Fritter, or Flap-iacke, or Posset, Galley-mawfrey, Mackeroone, Kickshaw, or Tantablin...[88]

It's possible that flapjacks or flap-jackes may have gone out of fashion, only to be revived and reinvented centuries later. In James Jennings *Observations on some of the dialects in the West of England* (1825) he notes

Oat Flapjacks. (@ *Emma Kay*)

that a flapjack is 'a fried cake made of batter, apples, &c. Or a fritter'.[89] Like Amelia Simmons' American version, the flapjack wasn't originally a baked creation at all. I have also read that it was known in some counties in England as an Apple-Jack or an Apple-Twelin. It is difficult to determine when Flapjacks began to be baked in the oven and when they became oatmeal based. There is a brief reference to baked flapjacks in the *Taunton Courier and Western Advertiser*, 1925. An oat version of flapjacks appeared at the end of the Second World War, oats making a good alternative to baking with flour, which was still in short supply. Perhaps this is around the time the transition from fried batter pancake to baked oatcake occurred. 'Matriarch of the kitchen' Marguerite Patten also noted that flapjacks were popular during the early part of the twentieth century and it is her recipe that I have included here:

Flapjacks

85g butter margarine or lard
2 tablespoons golden syrup
50g soft brown sugar
175g rolled oats

Preheat the oven to 180 degrees Celsius/350 Fahrenheit/Gas Mark 4/160 degrees Celsius with a fan.

Grease and flour an 18 to 20 cm/7 to 8-inch square tin.

Put the fat, syrup and sugar into a saucepan and melt over a low heat. Remove from the heat and stir in the rolled oats. Spoon into the tin and smooth flat on top. Bake for approximately 25 minutes or until evenly golden brown. Allow to cool for 2 to 3 minutes then cut into 12 to 16 portions. Leave for another 10 to 15 minutes then carefully lift out of the tin on to a wire cooling tray. When quite cold put into an airtight tin.[90]

The American explorers Lewis and Clark talk at length in their journals about Native American practices, which would almost certainly have been adopted by early British settlers. The native flowering herb quawmash was found in abundance in the Rocky Mountains and used for baking in a landscape that afforded little else back then. A fire of dry wood would be set on a pile of stones and left to continue burning until the stones became really hot. A layer of earth and then grass was placed over these stones and the roots of the quawmash on top of this. Further grass was added and water poured over to create steam, which was encased quickly with more dry wood. Everything was then left to bake for around twelve hours. A process reminiscent of the earliest of baking practices. Once cooked the roots became edible and apparently tasted a lot like roasted onions. Bread and cakes were also made from the roots following a second process in which the baked roots were pounded between two stones until a rough dough formed. This dough was then rolled in grass and shaped into cakes around ¾ of an inch thick. Once dried in the sun or from the smoke of the fire, they were then ready to be eaten. These little baked and steamed breads of dried roots were known for their longevity, as long as they were kept moisture free.[91]

In 1607, the journals of early British settler Master George Percy observed the Native American way of baking as:

I saw Bread made by their women, which doe all their drugerie. The men takes their pleasure in hunting and their warrres, which they are in continually, one Kingdome against another. The manner of baking bread is thus. After they pound their wheat into flower, with hot water they make it into paste, and worke it into round balls and Cakes, then they put it into a pot of seething water: when it is sod throughly, they lay it on a smooth stone, there they harden it as well as in an Oven.[92]

The transition from Percy's observations to the writings of Martha Ballard (née Moore) a second-generation frontier-woman, born in America to European settlers in Oxford, Massachusetts, is striking. Martha maintained a diary of her work as a midwife, a career that saw her deliver over 816 babies between 1785 and 1812. Her diary entries include a summary of her daily chores, including baking. It is clear that a lot more bread by this time was being made with wheat, although corn was still the predominant grain. She notes on 22 August 1794 that, 'he went [Cyrus, her eldest son] to mill to Varsalboro with two Bushels of wheat of our own raising. It made Beautiful flower'. The diary makes fascinating reading for anyone studying that period of history, or wanting to know more about cooking at that time. Martha regularly baked pumpkin and apple pies and 'mins' pies around Christmas.[93]

Within the context of 300 years or so, Britain learned to enhance its baking, gaining from the wisdoms of Europe and the New Worlds, from conflicts and Imperial power; experimenting, evolving, creating. The exciting transition of Tudor and Stuart Britain from a burgeoning nation surfing the dark ages, to global immersion, is carved into the country's baking heritage. Despite Britain's rapid advancement and appropriation of lands and people creating numerous and wonderous influences, it is all blighted by the savagery and egotism with which it executed this transformation. A transformation that would continue to rage into the succeeding centuries.

Chapter 3

Gorging Georgians to Excessive Empire

T he excesses of the Georgian period, with access to increasing trade links and new markets, made the eighteenth century a veritable feast of baking opportunities. It also made bakers greedy, leading to the mass adulteration of flour. The subsequent loss of life this caused was significant enough to alter legislation.

Sugar was readily accessible, along with a choice of spices, increasing the number and variety of numerous fancy baked dishes, pastries and biscuits but, at the cost of slavery and the seedier transactions of the East India Company.

During the Napoleonic Wars, which took up a great deal of the first quarter of the nineteenth century, bakers a struggled to manage increasing fluctuations in the cost of yeast, salt, candles and so on. In Worcester three bakers closed over a period of four years, with two or three failing in Exeter. Thirty bakehouses were listed as financially 'broken' in Leicester, and four out of their seven village bakeries shut down in Wilton near Salisbury, while two of its four bakehouses ceased trading in Wheatley near Oxford.[1]

Advances in technology as a consequence of industrialisation meant that by the Victorian period, baking was a slightly easier task. Commercially, this is when many of the big-name bakeries appeared, such as Hovis, Joseph Rank, McDougall's and the Aerated Bread Company.

Sugar was now a regular commodity and much cheaper to come by. The Victorians mimicked their Tudor fore-bakers and produced many wonderful confections and sweet treats for the growing consumer market; the rise of the covered shop, the fashion for high tea and the popularity for picnic sandwiches, among other trends. All with baked goods at the heart of them.

Tariffs on imported cereal grains throughout much of the nineteenth century in order to favour domestic producers and landowners, led to an increase in the cost of basic products like bread at a time when poor harvests and famines meant corn, wheat and barley were already at a premium.

Hazards, crimes and colonies

In the time before health and safety concerns, media exploited injustices and the right to be treated without discrimination, there was a great deal of room for unnecessary illness, pain and suffering and the practice of baking was not immune to this. There was also a lot less awareness of the dangers of wild flora and fauna. Remember, for centuries society relied heavily on nature both for it's essential healing properties and as a basic source of food.

The ryegrass, known as darnel, often grows alongside areas of wheat production, in fact it is so similar that is was at one stage known as 'false wheat'. Darnel turns black when it is ripe, while wheat appears brown. Darnel can be very dangerous as it is easily infected by a type of fungus that can be fatal if eaten. It most certainly would have been eaten during the seventeenth and eighteenth centuries, but with dire consequences.[2] *The Dictionarium Domesticum of 1736* warns of bread made with darnel as likely to procure headaches and make the 'eyes dazzle'. While spelt was considered hard to digest. There was a case in Roscrea, Ireland, on Christmas day 1853, when several families, totalling thirty-nine people altogether, were poisoned by darnel flour which had found its way into their bread. They were all struck down with a variety of frightening symptoms including giddiness, violent tremors, impaired vision, coldness of the skin and partial paralysis.[3] Thankfully they all recovered, but it must be one of the largest domestic examples of mass poisoning via darnel.

There are numerous accidental and murderous deaths recorded in the media from dodgy pie fillings in the eighteenth and nineteenth century; unsurprisingly perhaps, considering the ease with which poisonous substances could be introduced, not to mention the possibilities of contamination with the amount of rancid ingredients and poor hygiene that existed during this period. Of course, I need not remind readers of the fateful antics of Sweeney Todd. But they weren't all psychopaths.

Seemingly innocent herbalist and hawker John Hilliard was accused of manslaughter in 1846 when he was found guilty of making and selling fruit pies containing *atropa belladonna*, or deadly nightshade. A beer-shop owner and a 3-year-old boy both died, while a handful of other consumers fell seriously ill. Hilliard maintained that the fruit was whortleberries and harmless, until the judge suggested that he finish the pie that was presented as evidence, an offer which he swiftly declined.[4]

If you think about it, primitive bakeries were ideal locations to commit crimes, often dark and full of equipment that had the potential to do some lethal damage in the wrong hands; unsociable hours, below street level and underground meant no one could hear you scream.

As well as bodies actually bieng shoved into bakehouse ovens in order to dispose of the evidence, frequent murders were reported to have taken place while in the process of baking; Josiah Hubbard, for example, had his skull bashed in by his nephew while they were working in their bakehouse near Lutterworth, Leicester.[5] Philip Schmidt was stabbed and shot in his bakehouse by fellow baker Karl Meiss, who then committed suicide immediately afterwards,[6] and Thomas Furlonger was found dead in Neville's Bakery, Brixton, having been robbed and killed with an iron bar. His fellow baking colleague, Daniel Stew, was indicted for his murder.[7]

The Old Bailey proceedings are bursting with crimes involving bakers and baking goods. Some men, like John Thompson, a baker who was convicted of stealing a bread peal, shovel and brass skillet from another baker in 1685, got off lightly – in this case with a fine of 10*d*.[8] Or Richard Kelly, a baker to the Right Honourable Charles Earl of Westmorland, who stole two silver plates from his master in 1691, which he then melted down to sell on more readily. His sentence was to be branded with a hot iron on the hand.[9]

While others, like John Roberts of Westminster, paid a much higher price for their crimes; John was indicted for stealing nine loaves from the bakery he worked at and then selling them on at a profit. Found guilty, he was sentenced to transportation.[10]

Many convicts during the 1700s were transported to Australia for relatively petty crimes, like John Skyrme, a baker who trained in Bristol but lived in London, who stole a tweezer case, scissors, a bodkin and a gold ring in 1744; and Francis Otter, also a baker from London, who stole shirts and a gown. Daniel Thoroughgood (aka Dann the baker) was even unluckier with his sentencing, the outcome of which was execution in 1751, for carrying out a bit of highway robbery alongside his baking work. Others like Robert Humphreys, a journeyman baker, and Richard Smith, also a baker, who both stole bread in 1768 and 1771 respectively were flogged for their crimes.[11]

The first fleet of convicts to enter Australian shores in 1788 included just one baker. I wouldn't have wanted his responsibilities. Unsurprisingly, perhaps, for a colony full of convicts, thieving was rife down under, from human teeth, to 'bung-diving' (taking purses) 'speaking to the tattler' (lifting a watch) to 'pricking in the wicker for a dolphin' (stealing loaves from a baker's basket).[12] Wicker being the basket, pricking is a pun on an old word for stealing, 'prigging'. I am unsure what the dolphin refers to. Maybe fishermen were most liking to be carrying out this sort of theft? And that was just in newly populated areas. It was a whole different ball game if you found yourself incarcerated.

The all-male penal settlement of Norfolk Island, located between Australia and New Zealand originally colonised by Polynesians, but uninhabited once the British settled there in 1788, was not somewhere you would have wanted to end up. The reports conducted by Robert

The Old Jail on Norfolk Island, early 1900s.

Pringle Stuart in 1846 describe an intensely miserable place. Prisoners were half starved, with diseases such as gonorrhoea, dysentery and ophthalmia being rife. Rape was inevitable and many men would sell themselves for a hunk of bread. The daily rations of meal per man equated to twenty-four ounces. Twelve of these were issued every morning for hominy (dried maize soaked in lye) the remaining meal was made into bread which the prisoners prepared themselves and then carried a great distance to the bakehouse, which made prisoners vulnerable to theft, blackmail and bartering.[13] The maize itself, used to make bread, was 'in a foul and dirty state',[14] and the resulting bread products were known as 'scrubbing brushes', due to the abrasive scarring and inflammation that it left behind in the prisoner's gut.[15]

It is important to remember that not all colonists were convicts. Many were migrant free-settlers who moved to Australia with the prospect of starting a new life, to seek employment or even to just find a husband. An entry from the diary of George Fletcher Moore, an early western Australia settler, reads: 'Got from the natives a piece of bread made of the root of the flag which they called yand-yett. It tastes like a cake of oatmeal. They peel the root, roast and pound it, and bake it. The root is thick as your finger, and a foot long.'[16]

George is referring to the Typha root, an ancient food first consumed by the Noongar culture, indigenous peoples of Australia. The business of baking in Australia was significantly improved and influenced by Thomas Pye Williamson, the son of Irish immigrant David Campbell Williamson, who moved to Australia in the mid-nineteenth century. By the 1890s, as a young man, Thomas had relocated to Yass, a town in New South Wales and opened his first-class bakery, called the Times Bakery, selling and delivering bread to the community in his reconditioned motor van which he made out of a Model T Ford. In 1900 he wrote *The Colonial Baker*, described by the *Tas Evening Tribune* as 'the most comprehensive and useful book on baking that has ever been published in Australia', declaring that 'no baker should be without a copy'.[17] Very few copies of this book have survived. Newspapers of the time reported that applications for copies were being made daily and only one print run was made.[18]

Here is Williamson's recipe for yeast and it is certainly a powerful sounding one:

Most bakers will be able to make yeast, and make a success of it, from the forgoing remarks. But there are others who will require the recipe for each particular yeast written out exactly as it is to be used. Anyone, by multiplying the quantities given by six, will find that the recipe reads:

No.1 Yeast
6 gallons water
9oz. Hops
6oz. Salt
6lb. Sugar
6lb. Malt
6lb. Flour
18lb. Potatoes
1½ lb. Bran

To four gallons boiling water, add the hops, and boil ten minutes. Cool to 160 deg. Fah. Stain on to the crushed malt and bran. Cover closely for two or three hours. In the meantime, have the potatoes boiled, also have a couple of gallons of water boiling. Strain the potatoes, saving the water that they were boiled in. Mash the potatoes up, and cool them down with a dipper of cold water. Mix in the salt, sugar and flour, and bring the scald up to about 150 deg. Fah., using the potato water, and a sufficient quantity of the water that is boiling, to do so. If there should be too much boiling water for the purpose, replace it with the same amount of cold water, it will help to cool the scald down.

When the malt has mashed sufficiently, rub it up well, then strain, squeeze it well to extract as much as possible; mix everything together and cool to eighty or ninety; stock with four pints old yeast or cover it up and allow it to work through without stock. When the yeast is worked through, stir in 1/2lb. salt in winter, and lb in summer time. This is very rich yeast, and according to theory, should supply all the wants of the trade, but practical experience has proved that it is not advisable to continue on the preceding recipe. For, as we stated before, the yeast requires a change. Why it requires a change is too deep a study for this work. But brewers have recognised the fact long ago, and whenever their yeast becomes weak, they send to another brewery for a stock, or as they term it, 'pitching'. This change can very often be affected by allowing the yeast to work through without stock. But it is not a plan to be recommended, because when the yeast is allowed to work through without stock, it depends on the germs of fermentation that have fallen into it from the atmosphere, or from germs that may have been in the mixing cask to start it, and they are just as likely to be weak ferments as good. Practical experiments have proven that the yeast depends more on the germs that are present in the wood of the mixing tub than what it does on any germs that may fall into it from the atmosphere.[19]

Street-sellers, pedlars and hawkers

Back in Blighty the sale of baked goods continued to thrive in the streets and market places. The media of the eighteenth and nineteenth centuries is crowded with stories relating to street-sellers. Many sellers of

Eighteenth-century Biscuit Seller. (*Wellcome Collection Creative Commons Attribution (CC BY 4.0)300*)

baked goods are reported as having committed suicide, or frequently pop up in convictions for drunken behaviour, assault or other minor crimes. Many are simply recalled for their idiosyncratic natures. Mrs Wood, an oat-bread hawker, could regularly be seen trudging between Huddersfield and Leeds (a good fifteen miles) at a speed of three miles an hour, carrying a two-stone load of bread on her head. Most impressive of all was the fact that she was 87.[20] While Catherine Murrie was a well-known resident of Swansacre in Kinross during the nineteenth century. For some forty years she could be found travelling the district with a basket in either arm selling bread.[21]

Bread Seller. *Wellcome Collection Creative Commons Attribution (CC BY 4.0)300*

Street food today, in many ways mirrors the peddlers and hawkers of old – despite its now obvious gentrification. Although, it was unquestionably the personalities that made Georgian and Victorian traders so distinctive, the type of eccentricity that is rare to find today. Nonetheless, some baked goods traders were definitely more savoury than others (excuse the pun).

William, or sometimes listed as John, Jones was a bread hawker from Nafferton, a picturesque village in Yorkshire. It would seem that he was often under the influence of alcohol and frequently charged with being drunk and disorderly when controlling his horse and cart, or leaving his business unattended in the street, while he drank in the pub. By 1869 he faced a summons amounting to 12*s* 12*d* for committing this same crime a total of fourteen times.[22] Jones's crimes included involvement in an 'extensive robbery' of a variety of goods including gloves, stockings, silk, tweed, table-cloths, gowns and other sundries in 1866.[23] He was also the victim of an assault, in which his bread products were stolen, his cart upended and his horse injured in 1872,[24] but this doesn't appear to have deterred him as he was once again fined for allowing his horse and cart to be left unattended, two years later.[25]

One of the largest producers of steel pens in the country during the Victorian age was self-made industrialist and philanthropist Josiah Mason. Born in Kidderminster, he started life on the streets there hawking cakes. He bought the cakes from a local baker for a shilling in batches of sixteen. He then sold them on individually for a penny. By the age of 15 Mason had made enough of a profit to invest in a donkey and panniers to sell fruit and vegetables alongside his cakes. From there he learned to make shoes, taught himself to read and write, and took a succession of jobs before entering the steel pen business, earning his fortune and becoming a knight of the realm in honour of his charitable work.[26] Josiah Mason is one of those amazing life-stories illustrating how hard work, determination and self-belief can break the cycle of adversity. His narrative is not well-known and although he is immortalised in local statues, I am giving him another mention here, alongside my previous homage to him in my book *More Than a Sauce.*

At the other end of the success scale, Charles, or Charlie, Wood, was more affectionately known as 'Cha Wid' to the locals of Brechin in Scotland. Growing up in this area during the early 1800s and coming from nothing, legend has it that Charlie's heart was savagely broken at an early age by a relationship that turned sour. He turned to scavenging, but carried out this activity with humour and good spirit, being, as one newspaper described him, 'weak in intellect', and apparently eccentric with it. He wore a close-fitting skull cap and clothing which had been repaired so many times that all that was left in places was thread and no actual fabric. He had stockinged feet, also well-patched up, and no shoes. He also wore 'a ghost of an apron', which he lifted up to deposit old fish heads in. He sold manure to farmers in exchange for food and drink and assisted at a local bakehouse for the penny pie baker, Mr Strachan. This was a place that other pie hawkers congregated and they would encourage Charlie to sing 'The Old Wife of Eighty', and other well-known ditties of the time. He died at around 60, and the spirit of his personality is said to have lived on locally for generations.[27]

There was no other place for street characters to parade their wares like London, a city full of quirky, unconventional personalities. Personalities like Tiddy Doll, whose real name was James Ford, known for his eccentric dress sense – attired as he was like a person of rank, which, being tall and handsome, he carried off with style. A charming man, who sang a regular ballad and approached men and women with an introductory address requesting them to visit his premises, opening with 'Mary, Mary, where are you now, Mary?' He was famed for his gingerbread, although several newspaper articles of the nineteenth century recall him as a pieman. Despite the charm and outwardly cheery nature, I found an account of Tiddy Doll in 1746, arrested in Westminster for severely beating up his landlady and threatening to blow up her house.[28]

Tiddy Doll from *The Everyday Book or the Guide to the Year, volume 1300*.

I have read several narratives describing James Ford as Jewish, French and also black. Of course, he may well have been all three. He was

Idle Apprentice's Execution at Tyburn, Hogarth, featuring Tiddy Doll in the foreground.

Hot Spice Ginger
Bread, Smoking Hot
1796.

immortalised in Hogarth's painting of the 'Idle Apprentice's Execution at Tyburn', standing to the right of the painting looking at it head on, his one arm raised holding a cake of gingerbread and calling to the crowd. This and one other drawing I have found of him reveals little of his features. He famously just vanished from his regular trading spot in the Haymarket one day in 1752, sparking grubby rumours of murder, although I have also read that he tragically drowned by falling through the ice on the Thames at a Frost Fair.

A character who appears to have almost entirely been removed from the street-seller archives is Peter Wilkins, listed as a muffin-man, who also served in the American Revolutionary War in an unknown capacity. He committed a crime that was punishable by death, an order issued by General Green. He was hanged over in America for his crimes, but was successfully revived by a surgeon when he fell from the gallows. Described in several articles of the time as 'one of the most sordid, grovelling worms.'[29] It appears that Wilkins amassed a substantial sum of money during his lifetime, some £1,300, or around £100,000 today. Whether this was accrued from his muffin vending, or through other ill-gotten gains, remains undetermined, but he never got to spend it, as it all reverted to his wife in death. He died in London in 1791.

Then there was Harry Dimsdale, also a muffin man pedalling the streets in the 1700s, who acquired a mock knighthood by the local community for his abilities to speak out about local matters. Recorded

Henry Dinsdale aka sir Dimsdale in 1800. *Wellcome Collection, Creative Commons Attribution (CC BY 4.0) 300 – Copy (3))*

as being a dwarf, 'Sir' Harry was quite a character and someone who was cruelly and frequently labelled as 'deformed' and an 'idiot'. A notice of his arrest for being drunk and disorderly is recorded at the old 'watch-house', near St Anne's Church in Soho. When questioned about his behaviour Harry responded:

> May it please ye, my magistrate, I am not drunk; it is *languor*. A parcel of the bloods of the Garden have treated me cruelly, because I would not treat them. This day, sir, I was sent for by Mr Sheridan to make my speech upon the table at the Shakespeare Tavern, in *Common* Garden; he wrote the speech for me, and always gives me half-a-guinea when he sends for me to the tavern. You see I didn't go in my royal robes; I only put'um on when I stand to be member.

He requested an escort from the constable that night, for fear of being attacked by street gangs and was taken to his lodgings, which was a public-house opposite St Giles's Church. By day, as a muffin merchant, Sir Harry rang a little bell which he held up to his ear and cried 'Muffins! muffins! ladies, come buy *me*! pretty, handsome, blooming, smiling maids.'[30] Harry died in 1811, an alcohol-related demise. His image survives on canvas, in several portraits, perhaps an indication of the level of his celebrity status at the time. Typically, muffin men sold flat-bread muffins, leavened with yeast and often unsweetened, which shot to popularity in the 1700s. They probably derive from early griddle cakes. Muffin puddings were also very popular for a time in the nineteenth century. This was a dish where muffins were layered and covered with a cream and egg mixture, brandy, nuts and fruit before being boiled, or more often, baked. Here is Maria Rundell's recipe from 1832.

Henry Dinsdale. (*Wellcome Collection, Creative Commons CC-BY-4.0 Creative Commons 300*)

Muffin Pudding

Cut six stale muffins in the thinnest slices; lay them in a soup plate with half a pint of brandy, with which baste them. Simmer half a pint of cream, with a good piece of genuine cinnamon broken, the grated peel of a lemon and four ounces of sugar ten minutes. Stir till cool; then mix with it by degrees the yolks of eight eggs well beaten. Butter a plain mould of moderate size; lay the crust side of the muffin's outwards; and with alternate layers of dried cherries, put the crumb in. When cold, pour into it the cold custard flavoured with orange flower water. Let the mould stand in a dish of bran till the custard be sunk in then bake it half an hour.[31]

The word muffin either derives from a Saxon word for small cake. *Muffe*, or the old French word *Moufflet*, relating to a quick bread. The contemporary French word muffin, translates as a small round unsweetened cake, as does the contemporary German word. So, it's anyone's guess who gifted Britain the word. The cake version of the muffin, the one we're all now used to seeing in high street coffee-shop chains, has a very different heritage. The first recipes for sweetened baked muffins start appearing in American cookbooks of the early twentieth century, although their ancestor is undoubtedly the much older baked cornbread muffin, generally associated with the southern states. The first UK-published sweet-baked muffin recipe I can find is from 1912, which incidentally appears together with a recipe for brownies, which the writer adds 'are not commonly known'.[32] She was right, as once again brownies were the brainchild of the Americans. Originally baked individual cakes, made gooey by the inclusion of large quantities of molasses and butter, were invented by revered American cook and one-time principal of the Boston Cooking School, Fannie Merritt Farmer. Her first recipe of 1896 was without chocolate, which she added a little later. I'm assuming they were nicknamed brownies as a consequence of all the brown sugar that was added to them. Although it's not a British bake, I have included it here as a cake which has now become almost as popular in the UK as it is across the Atlantic. This is the original brownie recipe in all its simplicity:

Brownies

¼ cup butter. 1 egg well beaten.
1 cup powdered sugar. ½ cup bread flour.
¼ cup Porto Rico molasses. 1 cup pecan meat cut in pieces.

Mix ingredients in order given. Bake in small, shallow fancy cake tins, garnishing top of each cake with one half pecan.[33]

Crumpets were also popular in the 1800s and sometimes get confused with pikelets which, according to Florence White's *Good Things in England* and *A Glossary of North Country Words*, is just the Lancashire-

Brownies. (@ *Emma Kay*)

Yorkshire term for a crumpet, where they were also split in half and buttered.

The role of pieman, or as it was called in medieval times, *pastelar*, is one of the most ancient of baking crafts, next to bread. It was a profession that attracted characters. You needed charm, a good pair of lungs to get noticed, talented hands to craft your wares and a keen business sense, a way to stand out in all the competition, like Peter Stokes, a street-seller also known as 'the Flying Pie man of Holborn Hill'. He was described in great detail by a Mr Harvey, writing in 1863:

> When I was a youngster, the steep roadway from Hatton Garden to Fleet Market was highly attractive to me on account of the 'Flying Pie man,' though he did not vend pies, but a kind of baked plum-pudding, which he offered smoking hot. He was a slim, active, middle-sized man, about forty years old. He always wore a black suit, scrupulously brushed, dress-coat and vest, knee-breeches, stout black silk stockings, and shoes with steel buckles, then rather fashionable. His shirt, remarkably well got up, had a wide frill, surmounted by a spotless white cravat. He never wore either hat or

cap; his hair, cropped very close, was plentifully powdered, and he was decorated with a delicate lawn apron, which hardly reached to his knees. In his right hand he held a small circular tray or board, just large enough to receive an appetite-provoking pudding, about three inches thick. This was divided into twelve slices, which he sold at a penny a slice. A broad blunt spatula, brilliantly bright, which he carried in his left hand, enabled him to dispense his sweets without ever touching them. His countenance was open and agreeable, expressive of intellect and moral excellence.[34]

Peter Stokes was apparently a professional painter of considerable talents. He married young for love, but was unable to sustain his family on the wages of a struggling artist. This is when he turned to trading on the streets of Holborn Hill and from twelve to four o'clock he could be seen shouting, 'Buy, buy, buy!' as he moved along Fetter Lane to Ely Place, onto the once prominent Thavies Inn, or to Field Lane and then Hatton Garden or Fleet Market. Once home after his day of trading, he returned to his lodgings in Rathbone Place where he would once again take to his easel and palette.[35]

In the 1840s the journalist and social reformer Henry Mayhew observed and documented one of the largest and most significant studies of working people in London. From his records we learn that street selling pie men, were usually bakers, unable to obtain employment or their own premises. One pieman that was interviewed by Mayhew, complained about his lack of financial success in the trade. Even when working from six in the evening until well into the early hours of the morning, this particular hawker might receive

The Flying Pie man 1815 Wellcome Collection, Creative Commons Attribution (CC BY 4.0)300

no more than seven shillings in a week. However, he could also earn as much as five shillings in a night, eight shillings on a summer's night and between ten and fourteen shillings pitching at fairs, such as the infamous ones staged at Greenwich, or Hyde Park. The busiest time for pie sales was between 10 pm and 1 am. Mayhew counted some fifty pie sellers in total operating throughout London, with consumers larding down around three-quarters-of-a-million pies annually. Many of these were boys or young men, with women rarely buying pies in the street. Some piemen would also be able to sell their wares in the public houses. There is a lovely account from a pieman in 1837 who, on pleading not guilty to owing a baker money, describes to the jury – while making the court laugh – how business is difficult for him. He found himself restricted to selling pies to drunken customers, the 'muzzy ones', being his biggest clientele.[36]

The average pieman needed about two old pounds, around £120 in today's currency, as capital to start trading, for keeping the pies warm in a metal can fuelled by charcoal, with two tin drawers – one for heating and one for storing the cold pre-made pies, an apron and ingredients including, as listed by Mayhew: flour, meat, apples, eels, fat, sugar, cloves, pepper and salt and eggs for 'washing' the pies to give them that appetising shine during baking.[37]

By the mid-nineteenth century the street piemen were being undercut by the penny pie shops, where you could get more pie for your money.

Commerce, Industry and Empire

As well as producing some of the world's finest shortbread, the Scottish company Walkers continue to manufacture one of the country's most famous baking exports, the Dundee cake. They are not, however, the originators. James Keiller succeeded his mother in 1797, taking over their small confectionery business, that specialised in preserves, jellies and cakes in Seagate. From here the company grew in strength and became adept at specialising in marmalade. It was the leftovers of these products that provided the ingredients for what has become known as the Dundee cake.[38] Certainly, Keiller became associated with the name of Dundee cake in 1839, when its presence in the market was overwhelming, although

I have found slightly earlier references to Dundee cakes, without the Keiller ownership attached. It is a cake likened to seed and pound cake, but it was the addition of the particular qualities of Keiller marmalade that really popularised the Dundee. Cooking with marmalade was not a new practice in the 1800s. It first entered the British language with the Anglo-Norman name of 'charedequynce', a word I have been able to trace back to at least 1407,[39] referring to a spiced quince preserve, which maintained popularity until the late 1500s. Following the use of quince, apricots became the fruit primarily applied to marmalade making in the sixteenth century.[40]

Orange marmalade was a product of the eighteenth century. One of the earliest printed recipes for Dundee cake actually appears in the American manual *The Successful Housekeeper* 1882 and includes lemon rather than orange peel.

Dundee cake

Whip to a cream one and one-half cups of butter and the same amount of sugar; add eight eggs, two at a time, beating five minutes between each addition, one-half cup of cream or milk, one and one half pints of flour, sifted with two teaspoonfuls baking powder, one half of a lemon peel cut in thin slices, one cup of washed, picked, and dried currants, one and one-half cups sultana raisins, one teaspoonful each of extract nutmeg, cloves, and vanilla; mix into a firm batter, pour into a shallow, square cake pan; chop one cup of almonds coarsely and sprinkle over the top; then bake one hour in a moderate oven.

Shortbread is also a prized part of Walkers baking heritage and has been since the late 1800s. As a biscuit, shortbread or short cakes have a history that exceeds this. There are a few theories about how we acquired shortbread. One being that excess bread dough was sweetened and dried in the oven, a process that later included the addition of butter. Hence, a short bread. Short meaning the act of adding fat. However, the shorte paste of early medieval baking is what we still recognise today as short crust pastry. Certainly, in the 1500s, short paste was often made with eggs and butter. Might it be just as likely that the short paste used in pastry making, may have had sugar added to it, thus turning it into a short cake?

Thomas Dawson's *The good Huswifes Handmaide for the Kitchin*, first published in 1594 includes an early printed recipe for shortcakes.

To make short Cakes

> Take wheate flower, of the fayrest ye can get, and
> put it in an earthern pot, and stop it close, and set it
> in an Ouen and bake it, and when it is baken, it will
> be full of clods, and therefore ye must searse it
> through a search: the flower will haue as long
> baking as a pastie of Uenison. When you haue done
> this, take clowted Creame, or els sweet Butter, but
> Creame is better, then take Sugar, Cloues, Mace,
> and Saffron, and the yolke of an Egge for one
> doozen of Cakes one yolke is ynough: then put all
> these foresaid things together into the cream, &
> temper them al together, then put them to your
> flower and so make your Cakes, your paste wil be
> very short, therefore yee must make your Cakes
> very litle: when yee bake your cakes, yee must bake
> them vpon papers, after the drawing of a batch of
> bread.[41]

Despite the endless citations linking Mary Queen of Scots with 'Petticoat tails', I cannot find any legitimate or authentic links with shortbread and its conception in Scotland. Admittedly, during the 1700s it was the predominant country of manufacture, but not solely and certainly not the first to. Here is a recipe which actually has the title of 'short bread', perhaps one of the first to do so. Despite being published in Ireland, it is supposedly written by a Scottish cook and teacher of cookery based in Edinburgh. Interestingly, the recipe contains yeast.

To make the best Short Bread

Take a peck of flour, and keep out about a pound of it; beat and searce a pound of loaf sugar, and cut half a pound of orange-peel, half a pound of citron, and half a pound of blanched almonds; mix them all well together with your flour, and make a hole in the middle of it; rhind three pound of sweet butter with a teaspoonful of salt and pour it into your flour, with half a mutchkin of good barm; work it, but not too much; divide the paste into four quarters, and make up each quarter into an oval; then roll out each quarter by itself into what thickness you please with the flour you kept out, and cut it through the middle, so as to have two fardels out of each quarter; prickle it well on the top, pinch it round with your fingers, and strew carraways on the top. Fire it on grey paper, dusted with flour, in a slow oven – if you want it plain, keep out the sugar and fruits, in place of three pounds of butter, take two pounds, and mix it with half a mutchkin of water, and half a mutchkin of more barm.[42]

If you are of a certain generation like myself and those before me, you will remember the delights of the 'squashed fly' or Garibaldi biscuit. That yummy, both buttery and crispy, fruity sandwiched layer of uniqueness. A packet of which my grandmother would thankfully nearly always have to hand in her kitchen cupboard when I was a child. The Garibaldi was the brainchild of Jonathan Carr – Carlisle-based baker/inventor extraordinaire, and he of the famed water biscuit. At the time of its invention, in 1861, which he created for the London biscuit firm, Peek Freans, the Italian General Giuseppe Garibaldi was a popular political figure in Britain and a new King of Italy had just been crowned. There are numerous stories surrounding the naming of the biscuit, along with its recipe. These range from Garibaldi's grandmother having to hastily put together a sweet snack for visiting soldiers, using grapes drying in the parlour, to horse-blood soaked bread with the addition of wild berries concocted out on the military field by Garibaldi himself, in a desperate attempt to sustain his flagging troops.

Peek Freans launched a campaign throughout the Second World War, with the promise to restore old favourites like the fruit cream, with

THE ILLUSTRATED LONDON NEWS, DEC. 5, 1874.—536

SKETCHES IN A BISCUIT MANUFACTORY.

Peek Frean's in the nineteenth century. (*Wellcome Collection, Creative Commons Attribution (CC BY 4.0) 300*)

its 'crisp biscuit, sweet fruit jelly and vanilla cream', and the custard cream.[43] Consisting of two long, rectangular, chocolate-flavoured biscuits sandwiched together with a chocolate cream filling, the Bourbon biscuit was a British family favourite for decades. Also, the brainchild of Peek Freans, it was originally marketed as the 'Creola'. According to *1857–1957, A hundred years of biscuit making* by Peek, Frean and Company Limited, the biscuit was rechristened 'Bourbon', in the 1930s, after the European royal household.[44] Despite this, I have found newspaper advertisements by Peek Frean & Co. for the Bourbon as early as at least 1894.[45]

The first batch of biscuits to be made by Fox's back in the 1870s were brandy snaps, baked by founder Michael Spedding and swiftly distributed out to shops, stalls and fairgrounds, from his home in Batley, Yorkshire. His son-in-law, Fred Fox, took the business over, eventually renaming the company F.E. Fox and Co. Today Fox's continues to operate out of its four sites: Batley, Kirkham, Uttoxeter and Birmingham. There remains a great deal of ongoing debate about the actual start of the business in Batley, with local historian Malcolm Haigh arguing that Spedding was working in a woollen mill in 1861, almost ten years after Fox's themselves claim that he was earning money from his baking business. Fox's also regard Whitaker Street as the birthplace of the business, even having a plaque erected at this site, while Haigh believes Michael Spedding was living in Spring Gardens when he launched the business. I discovered a newspaper article of 1927 recording Spedding's death and confirming that he commenced his business peddling 'various kinds of eatables' in Batley in 1863, following a long career in the cotton mill at Meltham,[46] West Yorkshire – and had been practising bone-setting in his spare time. Fox's website claim that Spedding baked his first batch of brandy snaps in 1853, as opposed to trading them, which arguably came quite sometime after this date.

Another obituary in the *Yorkshire Evening Post* remembers Spedding in a more detailed way, suggesting a life much richer than the one recorded. Like the *Leeds Mercury*, it also cites the baking business commencing in 1863, followed by a move to Whitaker Street, where he spent more time running his bone-setting business before finally retiring in 1900. In addition, the article makes reference to Michael Spedding's journal, which recorded local events, along with numerous examples of his prose and poetry, including:

> When first I came to Batley,
> Fifty years ago, to dwell,
> There was neither gas nor water,
> Only in the tubs and well.
> The streets were then village lanes,
> And nigh o'er tops in mud.[47]

Spedding visited America in 1866. The journey over was a difficult one, with the ship springing a leak; for some twenty days, both crew and travellers were concerned that the vessel would sink. Spedding's role included regularly pumping out the excess water.

In 1822 another biscuit giant, Joseph Huntley, formed J. Huntley & Son. Huntley's son, Thomas, joined him in the bakery business and by 1841, they had taken on George Palmer as partner, a trained baker and wealthy gentleman, at the very young age of just 23. By this time Joseph senior was elderly, in ill-health and retired. By 1844, Thomas Huntley and George Palmer were successfully trading out of number 72 London Street, Reading, selling biscuits in tins of varied sizes costing 3*s* 6*d* and 2*s*. Ginger and caraway seed wafer-biscuits were for sale at 2*s*, with tins of 'fancy biscuits' retailing at a range of prices. Cracknels/krakenelles, an ancient hard and crispy British biscuit with a heritage extending as far back as the thirteenth century, were on sale in tins costing 4*s* or 2*s* each, available from grocers and in shops across London. Here is a recipe from *The Complete Cook* of 1658.

To make Cracknels

Take halfe a pound of fine flower, dryed and searced, as much fine sugar searced, mingled with a spoonfull of Coriander-seed bruised, halfe a quarter of a pound of butter rubbed in the flower and sugar, then wet it with the yolks of two Eggs, and halfe a spoonfull of white Rose-water, a spoonfull or little more of Cream as will wet it; knead the Past till it be soft and limber to rowle well, then rowle it extreame thin, and cut them round by little plates; lay them up on buttered papers, and when they goe into the Oven, prick them, and wash the Top with the yolk of an Egg beaten, and made thin with Rose-water or faire water; they will give with keeping, therefore before they are eaten, they must be dryed in a warme Oven to make them crisp.[48]

You could also order wedding cakes from them by post.[49] Eight agents were employed to sell Huntley and Palmer biscuits throughout the country, with new factories proposed for London by the middle of the nineteenth century. This little family enterprise had become the biggest biscuit factory in the world, complete with its own railway system. By 1903 Huntley and Palmer were manufacturing in excess of 400 varieties of biscuits, testament to the Victorian popularity for these little baked treats and they had rechristened Reading, 'Biscuit Town'. The company even manufactured a special type of ration biscuit designed for British troops serving in the First World War.

A favourite of mine is their Long Jamaica, created in 1865. This is the original factory recipe:

Long Jamaica Biscuits

The factory recipe ingredients are –
26 lbs White Flour
4 lbs Butter
5 lbs Loaf Sugar
5 pints Milk

For home baking scale this down to –
570 grams Plain Flour
100 grams Butter
110 grams Caster Sugar
¼ pints Milk

Crumble the butter into the flour. Add the other ingredients. Roll out and cut into the shape of your choice. Bake in an oven at Gas 5 (375 Fahrenheit) until golden brown. This makes a very plain, pastry-like biscuit. To give it a bit more of a 'Jamaican' flavour you could substitute Muscovado sugar.[50]

Carr's biscuits was founded by Jonathan Dodgson Carr in 1831. Once the largest baking business in Britain, endorsed by George V, who also gave his seal of approval to M&D Biscuits (Meredith & Drew) which were founded a year before Carr's, boasting the title of largest biscuit manufacturer in Europe. William Meredith and William George Drew parted ways around 1850 following a quarrel. Drew established his own biscuit business. Initially Meredith focused on building up his public house trade, trading biscuits, pound and Banbury cakes. Their sons merged their business interests in the late 1890s and gained their first royal warrant from queen Victoria in 1894. The company continued in strength into the twentieth century with their Betta Biscuit range. This was a form of economy biscuit making them a European success by 1934. At one stage M&D owned some six factories across England, but by the 1940s United biscuits had become the market leader and acquired an ailing Meredith & Drew in 1967.[51] M&D has been confined to the archives and its name erased over time, unlike its many peers of the same era. Jacob's biscuits were initially a modest family biscuit bakery, located in Waterford Ireland in the early 1850s. It was inherited by William Beale Jacob who introduced steam-based machinery and built a new factory in Dublin. By 1862 Jacob's was exporting to North Wales and expanding rapidly, becoming a limited company in 1883, the same year William's son George became Managing Director and began developing the infamous cream cracker, based on a similar product he had discovered on a tour of the United States. An English factory for the firm was opened in Liverpool. George Newson Jacob was a controversial and often unpopular figure. During the major Irish industrial dispute of 1913, which lasted some five years, he responded unwisely to his employees, punishing those who went on strike and enforcing harsher terms and conditions on their return to work. In 1916 the Dublin factory was stormed during the Easter Rising and occupied by rebels, but George still managed to supply soldiers with some 1,200,000 packets of biscuits throughout the First World War and turn a nice profit.[52]

Incidentally, Waterford, the home of Jacob's biscuits and Waterford Crystal, also produces another legendary Irish commodity – the Blaa. Thought to have emerged during the 1600s when the city attracted swathes of French exiles, Huguenot communities allegedly arrived with small batch loaves, perfect for breakfast and light snacks.[53] A theory which has been disputed over the centuries, but eventually led to the Blaa gaining Protected Geographical Indication status in 2013, making the loaf now officially attributable to Waterford. I searched high and low for a period specific Blaa recipe, to no avail. So, the next best option was to seek out a good Irish food writer who knows this bread. Niamh Shields' book *Comfort & Spice* yielded the outcome I desired:

Blaas

Makes 8
¼ ounce active dry yeast
2 heaping teaspoons superfine sugar
3½ cups bread flour, plus more to dust
2 teaspoons sea salt
2 teaspoons unsalted butter

Dissolve the yeast and sugar in one heaping cup lukewarm water. Ensure that the water is warm, not cold or hot. Leave for 10 minutes. It should be nice and frothy, indicating that the yeast is alive and well.

Sift together the flour and salt, to introduce air. Rub in the butter. Add the wet to the dry ingredients and mix until combined. Knead for about 10 minutes, until the dough is smooth and elastic. It will go from rough to a little shiny.

Place in a bowl, cover with cling wrap, and leave in a warm place for 45 minutes. Remove from the bowl and punch it down, pushing the air out the dough. Rest for 15 minutes, to give the gluten time to relax; this will make shaping easier.

Divide the dough into eight pieces. Roll each piece into a ball. Rest for five minutes more, covered.

Dust a baking dish with flour and place in the balls, side by side. Dredge with flour. Leave in a warm place for 50 minutes. Nearly there!

Preheat the oven to 410 degrees Fahrenheit. Dredge the blaas with flour for a final time and bake for 15–20 minutes.[54]

Displaying the Hovis Sign at Darvell's of Chesham. Bakers since the 1700s The Chesham Society.

Bread-making throughout the nineteenth century became large-scale, innovative and commercial. The original home of Hovis is Macclesfield and it was its birth-father, Richard Smith, who ended up developing the means to preserve wheatgerm in bread – the science of which I will spare you. To formerly christen his discovery, Smith launched a nationwide competition in 1890 to name his patented product and voila, Hovis – derived from the Latin homo vitalis, meaning strength in man – arrived. Once the brand had been established, Hovis immediately set about marketing and selling all the merchandise that went into making the final product. Bakers wanting to sell it could buy the Hovis flour, the stamped tins to bake it in and paper bags for customers to store it.

Following the public announcement in the media during the earlier part of the twentieth-century, reporting on the benefits of vitamin B and its presence in wheatgerm, demand increased and Hovis was flying high on its own success. Advertisement cards, boxes and sign boards were now also provided to bakers buying the Hovis brand, making it easily recognisable to consumers on every street where it was sold.[55]

During the 1950s Hovis merged with McDougall, swiftly followed by Rank. It is now a limited company, following several years sitting under the umbrella of Premier Foods.

Unlike Warburtons, which continues to remain a family business today. A company which began like so many others, in the Victorian era. Ellen and Thomas Warburton's grocery store in Bow-Street, Bolton, Lancashire, was in decline by 1876 and to help boost sales Ellen began baking a few loaves and cakes each day. These were so popular that they began selling faster than she could make them. Their nephew, Henry Warburton, was recruited to help deliver the bread products as demand increased. Eventually he would purchase the baking business, which was inherited by his three sons.[56] Thomas and Ellen's daughter, Sarah, died tragically in 1879,[57] which is perhaps why their nephew carried on the baking baton. Today it lists itself as the largest family-owned bakery in the country.

Like so many of the larger more commercial bakeries, Warburtons apply the Chorleywood method of bread-making, where bread is mixed rapidly and mechanically and treatments and raising agents are added, together with preservatives, to both manufacture the products quicker and increase their shelf-life.

Right at the end of the Victorian era, Wales founded what would become another of the UK's largest and most successful family-run bakeries: Brace's Bakery. George Brace was a one-time miner from Monmouthshire who had the notion to set up a bakery business alongside his colliery work. A catastrophic mining disaster persuaded him to give up colliery life and, following a lifetime spent baking, the business was inherited by his son Ernest, and then onto George's grandson, Colin. After the Second World War, Colin ran Brace's Bakery right up until his death at the age of 96.[58] Today it continues to be managed by his sons Jonathan and Mark, and long may it remain a family-run enterprise.

Puddings, of all categories and description, expanded rapidly in the eighteenth and nineteenth century, with batter puddings deriving from the roasting juices of meat, marrow and suet with fruit, eggs and milk combinations of the past continuing to evolve.

Industrialisation, hard labour and early factory, mill and manufacturing meant long working hours for much of the population. People would walk long distances daily to work, wages were poor, hours were long and the working conditions often harsh. Perhaps puddings during this period filled the need required in British diets for carbohydrates and sustenance.

Vermicelli and macaroni baked dishes, sweetened and spiced were also extremely popular in the early part of the 1800s. Both had been on the menu in England the century before and used in pottages and soups, or accompanied with parmesan cheese. One theory for this could be attributed to The Grand Tours of the seventeenth and eighteenth century, a period of foreign travel that enabled young men of sufficient means to experience the delights of Europe, particularly Italy, introducing them to these pastas. Maria Rundell's 1808 edition of *A New System of Domestic Cookery* provides an interesting recipe for macaroni pudding encrusted with pastry:

> Simmer an ounce or two of the pipe-sort, in a pint of milk, and a bit of lemon and cinnamon, till tender; put it into a dish, with milk, two or three eggs but only one white sugar, nutmeg, a spoonful of peach-water, and half a glass of raisin wine. Bake with a paste round the edges.

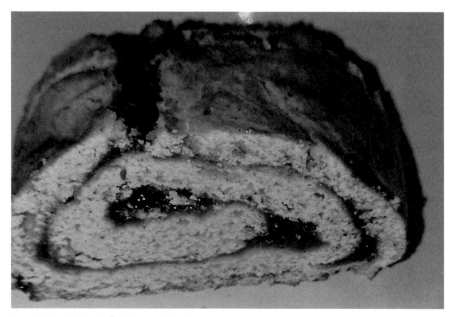

Jam Roly-Poly. (@ *Emma Kay*)

Rundell also recommended the addition of some raspberry jam or marmalade to achieve 'great improvement' to the dish.[59]

It is this enhancement of jam and other conserves to puddings in particular which inspired many of the popular favourites that live on today.

Despite jam-making being a commonplace activity since at least the first century AD, large-scale production didn't occur until the 1800s, with the development of pasteurisation. The earliest reference I can find to one of the country's most treasured of jam puddings, the roly-poly, appears in an 1835 edition of Issac Hurkstone's *The Fatal Interview* when the character 'Mrs.M' declares: 'I have heard such puddings called blankets and sheets, and a hunting pudding; but commonly we call it a rolley polley.'[60]

However, the origins are much earlier. The phrase roly-poly or rowley powley comes from a gambling term used to describe a form of roulette that was extremely popular with the English nobility, but was outlawed in the 1700s.[61] It's possible that the pudding was first served at the type of exclusive gentlemen's clubs that flourished in the eighteenth century, where the game of roly-poly would have been played. If so, it might mean that it is worthy of a much earlier provenance than that of the nineteenth century. The old nursery rhyme, *A Frog He Would a wooing Go* has the line: 'With a rowley, powley, Gammon and spinach. Heigh-ho says Anthony Rowley.' And the rhyme *Georgie Porgie* (a satire of George IV) has 'Rowley Powley, pudding and pie, Kissed the girls and made them cry', could also both potentially have a connection with the jam roly poly pudding.

In 1850, the celebrated Victorian chef Alexis Soyer included a recipe for Rowley Powley, in *The Modern Housewife*:

Rowley Powley

Roll out about two pounds of paste, cover it with any jam or marmalade you like, roll it over and tie it loose in a cloth, well tying each end; boil one hour and serve, or cut it in slices and serve with sauce.[62]

So how did we inherit the suet, baked pudding we recognise today? By the end of the nineteenth century, suet crust jam roly poly recipes appear with more regularity, although they remain boiled. By the early twentieth century, steaming is recommended as the best option and it's not until the 1920s that the notion to bake the roly poly becomes a reality.[63]

The jam roly poly is a homage to the stodgy boiled and hasty puddings of the past, an eighteenth-century reinterpretation that got rolled up and baked in a more modern context. Reading Charlotte Mason's much earlier recipe for raspberry dumplings in her *Lady's Assistant* from 1777, it's not hard to imagine how the roly poly evolved:

Raspberry Dumplings

Make a good puff paste; roll it, spread over its raspberry jam; roll it up, and boil it a good hour; cut it into five slices; pour melted butter in the dish.

It's clear that the roly poly definitely started its life as a pastry, rather than suet pudding. Even more interesting is Mason's recipe, also published in the *Lady's Assistant*, for suet dumplings with currants, which could easily be construed as an early version of that other Victorian classic, Spotted Dick. A dish that has remained steamed.[64]

Bread puddings, which included anything from fruit, to citrus, meat, rice, eggs, milk, cream and so on, superseded the white pots of the previous centuries. By the 1800s the familiar bread and butter pudding of today was christened, the earliest version of which comes courtesy of Eliza Smith, whose 1727 edition of *The Compleat Housewife* recommends bread and butter pudding for fasting days:

A Bread and Butter Pudding for Fasting Days

TAKE a two-penny Loaf and a pound of fresh Butter; spread it in very thin slices, as to eat; cut them off as you spread them, and stone half a pound of Raisins and wash a pound of Currants; then put Puff paste at the bottom of a dish and lay a Row of your Bread and Butter and strew a handful of Currants, and a few Raisins and some little bits of Butter, and so do till your dish is full then boil three pints of Cream, and thicken it when cold with the yolks of ten Eggs, a grated Nutmeg, a little Salt, near half a pound of Sugar, some Orange-flower water and pour this in just as the Pudding is going into the Oven.[65]

The Whole Duty of a Woman, published in 1737 is widely understood to be the first known recipe for Yorkshire pudding, in that it instructs for a batter mix to be placed in a dripping pan, set under a roasting lamb and cooked on the fire.[66] That said, I found a much earlier reference in *The Accomplished Housekeeper and Universal Cook* by T. Williams, dated 1717, which actually christens the pudding as Yorkshire, and I'm quite certain its patronage is probably even earlier than this.

A Yorkshire Pudding

Beat up five eggs in a quart of milk, and mix them with flour till it is of a good pancake batter and very smooth. Put in a little salt and some grated nutmeg and ginger. Butter a dripping or frying pan and put it under a piece of beef mutton or a loin of veal, that is roasting and then put in your batter. When the topside is brown cut it in square pieces turn it and let the under-)side be brown. Put it in a hot dish as clear from fat as you can and send it hot to table.[67]

Yorkshire Puddings. (@ *Emma Kay*)

An article in the *Leeds Intelligencer* of 1765 reflecting on the plight of labouring families in Yorkshire, reported on what little disposable income there was for food. Funds were primarily allocated to bread, 'pudding-flour', milk and beer.[68] It's perhaps not surprising then that every single part of a joint of meat – if they were lucky enough to have one, would have been utilised, with dripping puddings being an essential part of this.

East India Company and minority

Britain's presence in India during its early days of Empire heralded the establishment of the East India Company in 1600, a company whose role was to conduct official trade between Britain and India. Spices for cooking, such as cloves, nutmeg, ginger and cinnamon were in high demand. Early merchant adventurers secured the first working depot in 1619 in Surat, by hijacking the city and defeating the Portuguese in the race for usurpation. There would have been bakers, British and Indian, serving the company both home and abroad. Some 3,000 labourers alone were employed across its London warehouses including eighty-three bakers between 1801 and 1832.[69]

There were numerous lucrative bakehouses in India supplying the company with hardtack, or ship's biscuits. William Farmer was a Company civil servant and as such was allowed to conduct his own trade in addition to Company business, on the proviso that the two did not compete. His post of Assistant to the Marine Storekeeper in Bombay paid him a paltry allowance of £126 annually by the Company, but enabled him to acquire a significant amount of information on matters relating to ships' cargoes. As a consequence, he set up a bakehouse close to the stores supplying hardtack to seamen. Farmer wrote in a letter home in 1774:

> The greatest profit … is supplying the Company's fighting vessels here with Biscuit I do not know what I should have done – in the last year here between you and me I made one thousand pounds of it but do not expect to make this year more than 500 and shall be content with that for among other reductions the Company have lessened their Marine Force here almost a half, the consequence of which you now must be that there will be fewer biscuits cracked.[70]

There was frequent conflict involving legal, cultural and language issues, widespread corruption and shady business practices, but Indian military efficiency was often praised for the ease with which soldiers were able to function in difficult circumstances compared to that of the European armies. Indian bakers would go ahead of the troops, carrying mud, water and iron cradles to form skeleton ovens capable of turning out a thousand loaves at a time over the course of a few hours in mid-conflict.[71]

As foreign commerce increased, Britain established a trading post in Bantam, Java (Indonesia) a geographically strategic port town, which became the location for one of the biggest trading markets in the world. Here you could trade goods for just about anything, from clothing, to drugs, spices, rice and even military weapons. Hundreds of thousands of pounds worth of spices were regularly transported back to the main trading port cities of London, Liverpool and Bristol for domestic consumption. British merchants and an elaborate slaving system run by the East India company shaped them into central participants in the transatlantic slave trade, forcing millions of Africans onto slave ships before transporting them across the Atlantic, mainly to the British colonies in the Caribbean and North and South America. These sordid practices became the centre of Britain's richest source of trade throughout the eighteenth century, eventually making the sugar colonies of the West Indian islands Britain's most valuable assets.

During the 1930s, a project involving 100 interviews with former slaves held in bondage in the Southern districts of the USA revealed the harsh cruelties, daily indignities, exploitation and drudgery they endured. Slaves relied heavily on cornmeal for baking. Julia Brown was a young child when she was torn apart from her family and sold into slavery. She talked about baking 'light bread', made with corn and flour, the yeast was prepared from hops and unless slaves lived with very wealthy southerners, access to stoves and ovens was limited. Everything was cooked on coals from a wood fire.[72] Often corn bread or pone bread was eaten for both breakfast and supper, and diets were high in fat and starch, which would have led to inevitable health issues. Sometimes corn bread was crumbled up in a large trough and covered in buttermilk for a late supper and on some of the larger plantation's pies, cakes and biscuits might be baked.

A number of participants in the project talked about slaves receiving biscuits on a Sunday as well as frequently eating ash or hoe cakes and baked 'taters'. Hoe cakes were so called because they were originally baked on the blade of a primitive garden hoe, which later became a griddle. Traditionally made of cornmeal, hoe cakes were often pancake shaped.

Abbey Fisher was mixed race and born into slavery in the 1830s. After the Civil War and abolitionism, she settled into a new life in San Francisco with her own family, working as a successful caterer. In 1881, Fisher wrote what is now considered to be one of the first original soul-food cookery books, titled, *What Mrs Fisher Knows about Old Southern Cooking*. Including everything from cornbread to Jumberlie. Here are her recipes for Plantation Corn Bread or Hoe Cake and Light bread pie.

Plantation Corn Bread or Hoe Cake

> Half tablespoonful of lard to a pint of meal, one tea-cup of boiling water; stir well and bake on a hot grid-dle. Sift in meal one teaspoonful of soda.

Light Bread Pie

> Take stale bread and grate it. To one and one-half teacupfuls of the grated bread, add two teacupfuls of sweet milk, the juice of one orange, and half of the peel grated. Stir the yolks of four eggs beaten light into it. Take the whites of the four eggs beaten very light and meringue the pies after baking. Put half teacupful of sugar and one tablespoonful of butter to the prepared bread. Have one crust only, and that at the bottom of plate. Bake quickly. [73]

It is confusing to see how slave or soul food continues to shape modern American cuisine today, but failed to influence Britain in any way. Let's not forget the foundations of America were built on British settlers, Britain once colonised and owned thirteen American colonies, yet never embraced any of the rich mix of colonial foods that evolved from there,

Maison Bertaux, London. (@ *Nick Kay*)

not even those consumed by Native Americans, before we usurped them. Britain did, however, inherit a significant love of Indian cuisine and would, some several hundred years later (somewhat ironically) gain a fondness for West Indian cuisine, owing to modern migration and the *Windrush* era of influence.

The slaves who occupied British kitchens in the eighteenth and nineteenth centuries would undoubtedly have been instructed on which foods to cook, depending on the fashion and the type of household they were working in. They would have cooked with ingredients that were more native to Britain and Europe, just as the slaves in the British colonies had to improvise with local ingredients, combined with any existing influences from their own cultures. Nonetheless, there were probably few slaves in Britain working as kitchen staff and even fewer responsible for baking and pastry tasks, with this period so dominated by French, Italian and European influences. Most slaves who made their way to Britain, were brought back by Naval or Military officers, government officials or plantation owners. Some escaped en route to, or from, their masters' houses and would have ended up living in the overcrowded slums of the East End of London, eking out a living from all sorts of lowly trades.

That's not to say that some Africans living in households who respected and educated their slaves, eventually became free men and women, like Olaudah Equiano and Ignatious Sancho.

Although not a slave, Abdul Karim, Queen Victoria's Indian cook, is said to have initially made a chicken daal for the queen, who delighted in the flavours and requested his curries regularly. Eventually a team of chefs were recruited to assist Karim, as he cooked a daily lunch dish for Victoria in the final years of her life. Karim is perhaps one of the few examples of high ranking non-European culinary experts working in Britain during the nineteenth century.

Many migrant and victims of Empire ended up working as bakers at sea for the Navy or other British merchants. The lives of these cooks, was probably not a happy one, with numerous examples ending tragically. In 1857 the press were fixated with the story about Cheung Alum, a Chinese baker under contract to supply bread to the British government in Hong Kong, who was arrested for attempting to murder all the European forces and overseas residents by poisoning their bread. The arsenic mix that Alum used was so strong that it induced immediate vomiting, allowing for a swift arrest.[74] In 1845, four of the crew members of a British ship, *The Driver*, heading for Hong Kong had a disagreement with a Chinese baker, which resulted in him being bound hand and foot, thrown overboard and left to drown. When they arrived at Hong Kong they were arrested and

Austrian Strudel, pastries favoured by Queen Victoria and her grandchildren. (*@ Emma Kay*)

tried for their crimes.[75] A Lascar Baker for the steamship *The Shadow* died in a police cell in the East End of London in 1902, aged just 21; he was found dead as a consequence of alcohol poisoning.[76]

Other migrant bakers finding themselves in London would discover great success, however. According to the media at the time, Queen Victoria was purported to be an admirer of Viennese bread and had it supplied daily from a Polish baker named Petrozywalski, located in London's Regent-Street. Apparently, this baker was able to create curious shapes and figures out of his dough, for the amusement of her majesty's grandchildren.[77] By 1893 Petrozywalski was suppling the queen with some twelve varieties of breakfast rolls daily including milk rolls, pretzels, cinnamon loaves and Viennese twists.[78]

Harris and Judith Grodzinski, established themselves in the East End of London around the 1890s, as Kosher bakers. They went from having a barrow, to premises, and then moved into various other sites over a short period of time, introducing family members into the trade. Over time the Grodzinski baking business has expanded as far as Canada and there are countless references to this family of bakers being involved in small crimes over a period of fifty years or so. These included anything from keeping bad eggs on the premises, to selling bread that was considered stale and for trading outside legal hours on a Sunday.[79] Many migrant bakers came up for frequent criticism during the Victorian and early twentieth centuries, which is possible to attribute to an underlying level of prejudice.

Inventions and Innovation

During the early 1800s a canal linking Carlisle to the Solway Firth was constructed, which heralded Carlisle as the location for one of the largest baking enterprises in the world. Housed in a large red-brick quadrangle courtyard, this consisted of a fifty horsepower steam engine, which ground down some 157,000 stones of flour each year, into roughly 8,000 bags. These were then baked into bread and biscuits on site. The bakery employed around eighty to ninety people and had a reading room, library and schoolroom, together with a heated bath.[80] Premises like these became the powerhouses behind Britain's economic success in the eighteenth and nineteenth century. But it was baking powder that revolutionised the way in which people baked at home. An invention which is commonly attributed to Alfred Bird,

a consequence of his wife's allergies to both yeast and eggs. Bird was the man behind Alfred Bird and Sons Ltd, creators of Bird's Custard who also combined corn-starch with bicarbonate of soda to make a basic leavening agent. There were many others in the race to secure a patent for the perfect mix of chemicals to artificially raise baked products. Dr Whiting and a Mr Sewall both had a go with mixtures containing muriatic acid, while George Borwick & Sons ltd, created a mix of

Alfred Bird & Sons Ltd, Book of Pastry, late nineteenth century.

starch and citrate powder, sold as penny packets. Americans Church and Dwight, best known as Arm and Hammer, produced baking soda in 1846. Cream of tartar was a popular by-product of wine making and it became an important element to leavening.[81] Baking powder releases carbon dioxide when mixed with a liquid, whereas baking soda becomes a leavening agent when mixed with acids like sour cream or yoghurt.

Active dry yeast was developed in the 1930s and 40s, but not commonly used domestically until the 70s. The earliest reference I can find for baking powder in Britain is in 1846, which is an advertisement for an American product – Matthews Baking Powders.[82] Although, Bird is said to have manufactured his at least three years before in 1843.

Potash was one of the earliest forms of leavening, simply taken from the embers of the fireplace. In its commercial context it was better known as Pearlash, basically a refined by-product of burnt plant material.

Originally the contents of the fireplace, once cold, would be placed in a cast-iron kettle and boiled down. This was then scorched to burn out the bits of vegetable matter, usually a yellow-grey colour.[83]

No one really understood the principles of yeast until Louis Pasteur explored it further, discovering its properties as a living organism, one that created carbon dioxide when it reacted with gluten. It is this gas which leavens the bread naturally.

Baking Powder really came into its own during the First World War, when a solution for economising flour became integral to the wartime effort. It was thought to make an excellent substitute for eggs, as well as helping to make loaves larger and more substantial. Borwick's, headed by the drysalter and innovator George Borwick, was one of the leading manufacturers of Baking Powder, recommended by royal bakers and once patronised by both the Army and Navy. Borwick's was the focus of a high-profile criminal investigation during the nineteenth century when an individual, John Smith, was convicted of forging Borwick trade labels, that were printed with all of the company's standard information except the name itself. He then substituted his own powders and secured them in the counterfeit wrappers selling them off as Borwick's, to a range of druggists, grocer's and oilmen. John Smith was found guilty of forgery in 1858. The case went before the Old Bailey and was deferred, before Smith was sentenced on 10 May 1858 to provide sureties for good behaviour. Essentially this meant that he would needed to have found a willing man of property to post a bond, guaranteeing the convict's future good behaviour. A comparatively lenient sentence for the time. It was the Americans who came up with a way of baking a cake that didn't require a chemical leavener, instead they chose to double-up the quantities, creating a fuller cake. The ingredients were measured rather than being weighed. Sometimes called the 'numbers' or 'measure cake', it is perhaps most familiar to us as the 'cupcake'. Essentially the recipe went one cup of butter, two cups of sugar, three cups of flour and four eggs.[84]

Perhaps the greatest development for finding a way of adding leavening-potential to baking with more convenience, was with Henry Jones's invention of self-raising flour in 1845. A Bristol-born baker, he spent years waiting for the admiralty to make a decision about requisitioning his innovative flour, along with a new bread oven designed to be used on board ships. Such was the level of bureaucracy, that after ten years he gave up waiting for a reply and sent details of both of his inventions to every member of parliament to consider and within a month he had the contract with the Navy's Victualling Office.[85] From there on in, ships crews would be treated to fresh-baked bread every Sunday.

In 1741 Aaron Peever invented a new machine for grinding malt, which used less friction and guaranteed a working life-span of at least forty years.[86] In fact, Peever was responsible for a whole cache of new baking related products. Together with his business partner Robert Delziel they made perpetual ovens that came in a variety of sizes ranging from 1ft to 6ft wide, as well as small ovens designed to sit in the side of the kitchen chimney. These came in a choice of materials: either brick or iron plates.[87]

Masters Fahrenheit and Celsius battled it out with their invention for recording levels of hot and cold on a temperature scale during the 1700s, but it would be at least another 150 years before the invention of the oven thermometer, attributed to the American inventor, David G. Cooper, came around in 1886.[88]

By the end of the 1700s, an Anglo–American physicist, Sir Benjamin Thompson – or Count Rumford – as he was better known, was credited with revolutionising the oven, creating a source of heat with a closed range that could be regulated and keep the building warm all at the same time. A process made possible by reflecting the heat back into the room. Rumford narrowed the chimney and angled the bricks around the hearth itself to both alter the amount of up-draught and circulate the air, diverting the flow and pressure of the smoke and heat. By sealing the top of the fire with an iron plate, the sides and front of the hearth itself became warm and a type of enclosed interior oven was formed. One of the first examples of this was built into the kitchens of the Foundling Hospital, London, which would become a benchmark design for future public kitchens.[89]

Gas cooking was made possible as early as 1802, but wouldn't become a domestic reality until several decades later when James Sharp patented his gas stove. People were only just getting used to this technology before the inevitable emergence of the electric oven crashed onto the scene towards the end of the nineteenth century.

There was also a drive to move away from hand-kneaded bread during the latter-half of the nineteenth century, with the introduction of bread-making machines. These were not only labour-saving tools, but they were also considered more hygienic, a way of avoiding the transference of disease and bodily fluids into the bread mix, a now-known component of Pasteur's recognised germ theory. The earliest of these machines that I could find available in Britain was developed in Switzerland around 1822 and appears to have consisted of a crude box, into which the dough is placed, and the handle turned.[90] By 1836 bread-cutting machines were being used in hotels and other venues that called for its mass consumption.

Edwardian Bread Oven and Peal. (@ *Emma Kay*)

In fact, by the latter part of the Victorian period, bakeries could expect to host a wealth of new machinery, like the one that opened in Mann Street, Hastings, in 1888. It boasted a sifting machine for the flour, a kneading machine complete with temperature gauges and water pumps, moveable troughs on castors to enable portable proving, and a cake mixer for producing batters and sponges, capable of beating and mixing up to 200 eggs at once. There was even a currant-cleaning and washing machine, which had the facility to remove stalks and then dry the fruit. All of the machinery was cleverly powered by six gas-engines. At the time it was thought there were at least thirty to forty bakeries to the exact specifications of the Hastings premises and often larger in size, dotted around Britain.[91]

Illustration of Aerated Bread Company (ABC) shop in London.

In the 1860s The Aerated Bread Company Ltd, or the ABC conceived a revolutionary new method of baking, with Dr John Dauglish at the heart of its success. Victorians had begun to get sceptical about fermented bread, the traditional and historical method of baking naturally. They contrived some notion about fermented bread, fermenting a second time in the stomach leading to the acceleration of bad acids. They hit upon the notion that carbon dioxide could replace yeast and Dauglish was the man to put this theory to the test, producing a product that was free from adulterants and could almost entirely be made by machinery. He exploited the 'health benefits' of this new bread and persuaded numerous medical professionals to endorse it, including Guy's Hospital.[92] The entire process of the dough being saturated under pressure with carbon dioxide, divided into portions and then baked, took just ninety minutes.[93]

Dauglish's empire expanded into multiple retail outlets, tea shops and bakeries across the whole of London and into the then British colonies, the first tea shop of which opened in 1864 in the courtyard of London's Fenchurch street Railway Station. But his crusade was to be short-lived, dying as he did from over work and exhaustion at the age of just 42 in 1866 in Malvern, Worcestershire. The ABC chain continued to expand after his death, remaining an independent company until the 1950s. At its peak it owned over 200 tea shops across London. The ABC shops and bakeries have been immortalised throughout literature, from Virginia Woolf's *Night and Day*:

> She would write him a letter and take it at once to his house. She bought paper and pencil at a bookstall, and entered an ABC shop, where, by ordering a cup of coffee, she secured an empty table, and began at once to write.

To T.S. Eliot's *A Cooking Egg*:

> 'Where are the eagles and the trumpets?' His answer:
> Buried beneath some snow–deep Alps.
>
> Over buttered scones and crumpets
> Weeping, weeping multitudes
>
> Droop in a hundred ABC's

And even Agatha Christie, in *The Secret Adversary*:

> First of all, he must have a square meal, he had eaten nothing since midday yesterday. He turned into an ABC shop and ordered eggs and bacon and coffee. While he ate, he read a morning paper propped up in front of him.

Despite aerated bread often being reportedly bland, lacking in flavour and always distributed cold, it became a hit with the middle classes and provided a revolutionary shift away from the long hours and exhausting labour of the traditional baking trade. In 1848, bakers died younger in London than in any other of the main five crafts of that time, with the average death of a male baker being just 49 years, followed by tailors at 49 years and 3 months, shoemakers at 50 years, carpenters, 52 years and 4 months and weavers living the longest to 57 years and 9 months.[94]

If you were cynical, you might think the ABC represented the start of the downward slope for quality bread-making. Mass consumerism, commercialisation and diluted standards. As George Orwell somewhat scathingly observed:

> [as the] sinister strand in English catering, the relentless industrialisation that was overtaking it: the 162 teashops of the Aerated Bread Company, the Lyons Corner Houses which rolled out 10 miles of swiss roll every day and manufactured millions of 'frood' (frozen cooked food) meals, the milk bars that served 'no real food at all … Everything comes out of a carton or a tin, or is hauled out of a refrigerator or squirted out of a tap or squeezed out of a tube'.[95]

Military

In 1758 a young Duke of Marlborough wrote:

> Seventy bread waggons are absolutely necessary even for one delivery of bread to the army. I hope the bread will be of wheat, or half of our men will die of fluxes (the process of blood flowing out from the body, presumably from conflict wounds) on the march; 1½ pound per day is the constant allowance.[96]

Bread, and in particular good, well-manufactured bread, was essential in times of conflict; without it soldiers would perish or lack the strength required to perform their duties. Portable field ovens had been introduced into the French army under Louis XIV in the 1700s. They were simple constructions of iron bars, filled between the rods with stones, with each oven having the capacity to bake 450 rations of bread in one batch, or 2,250 rations across twenty-four hours.[97]

Field ovens were crucial to the military and in the nineteenth century, were forged by digging trenches in the earth or by constructing basic chambers of wood. Kneading troughs were improvised by digging two trenches, parallel to each other of unequal size. The smaller of which was then lined with wooden boards, so that the baker could stand in the larger trench and awkwardly knead in the other.[98]

Towards the latter part of the 1800s it would be the task of an early celebrity chef to alter the course of cooking in conflict. In 1858, following the public hype over Soyer's time spent feeding the troops out in the Crimean War, and the subsequent publication of his memoires, *A Culinary Campaign*, Alexis Soyer was invited to Whitehall to lecture on the subject of military cooking. During his very successful speech to a packed house, Soyer announced his proposals for a 'travelling cooking carriage'. The designs were taken forward and a prototype built, along with Soyers' advisory guidelines for how to cook on the front line. His new 'stove' was adopted by every regiment and just before his death he helped to design a model kitchen for the Coldstream Guards.[99]

One of the first indicators of any looming conflict, was the baking activity that took place in Naval victualling offices. The baking of provisions, thousands of biscuits in particular during the eighteenth century, required advanced planning. These activities were often reported in the press, alerting the public to impending warfare. Ground was also marked out to build temporary ovens to bake ammunition bread, denoting the location of military camps. Nine permanent new ovens were constructed at Rotherhithe in 1740, specifically to supply the king's Navy with biscuits.[100] This provides some indication of the extent of baked provisions required to supply this division of the British Armed Forces. Military biscuits were hard and tasteless, designed for their longevity. A biscuit from the Battle of Trafalgar survives today, testament to its rock-hard qualities. I believe it was auctioned in 2018, having remained in the family of the sailor who returned from sea with it back in the early 1800s. Biscuits of a more domestic kind were hugely popular during this period, including the favoured fruit biscuit:

Scald your fruit, dry it well from the water and rub it through a hair sieve; set it in a pan over a slow fire, and stir it till it is pretty dry; then sift fine sugar through an hair sieve; and having a spoonful of Gum dragon very well steep d and strain d and about a quarter of a pound of fruit, mix it well with two pounds of sugar, beating it with a biscuit beater; then having the Whites of 12 eggs beaten up to a very stiff froth, put it in by little and little at a time, beating it till it is all in, and looks as white as snow, and very thick; drop this on papers, and let them into a very cool oven, and shut it up to make them rise.

The lemon biscuit is made the same way, only instead of fruit put in the juice of three lemons, less will make two pound; it must have juice enough to make it to a paste, and the rinds of two lemons grated, and when it has been beaten enough, you may put in a little Musk or Ambergrease and drop and raise it in the oven as the other.[101]

The scourge of contaminated bread and biscuits on board ship, in the early days of naval sea power, couldn't be attributed solely to weevils. More often than not, the culprit was a reddish-brown beetle, similar to a cockroach but called the 'cadelle beetle'. Its larvae grow up to 20mm in length and these black-headed maggots would worm their way out from the confines of a nice warm biscuit and into the 'barge', the tub used to store them in. It is the larvae, and not the beetle itself that eats the biscuits, so they would be almost invisible to the naked eye and therefore managed with great ease to hide themselves away in bread bags and bakeries. The warm, damp conditions of the ship suited them perfectly. According to a letter from the Admiralty of 1813, one curious method adopted for ridding ships of these undesirables was to place a live lobster in each cask of flour or biscuits for a total of three days. Unsurprisingly, the lobsters were almost always found to be dead, crawling with hungry bugs, by the time the casks were opened.[102]

The Victualling Office (or Victualling Board) was established in 1683, but its powers changed and increased over time. It was the department of the Royal Navy responsible for managing all the victualling or storage and supply yards, of which there were some thirty plus from the 1830s up until the 1960s, located both in Britain and overseas. For many years they experimented with making different breads that might be suitable to be stored and consumed on board ships. These included wheat, molasses and potato, and wheat molasses and barley combinations, the former being likened to gingerbread.[103] Most concoctions proved futile, which is why the Navy settled on biscuits for so many years, particularly as the

Ships Biscuits being stamped with a Georgian Biscuit Docker. (@ *Emma Kay*)

process of making them was so simple. The biscuits themselves were so hard that they required soaking first. If they became damp in storage, which they frequently did, they would deteriorate quickly and become inedible.

Following three successive fires destroying bakehouses at Dover, Plymouth and then Rotherhithe, a new substantial bakehouse at an estimated cost of £4,000 was built at Deptford, sometime after 1747, to handle all of the Navy's baking in the London area.[104]

Deptford in South East London was one of the biggest victualling yards making biscuits. They ground their own flour and meal in two separate mills until 1797, when they realised production would be cheaper using a private mill. Pay records for the Deptford site reveal that there were twelve teams of bakers, working across twelve ovens. If these ovens were operated at full capacity throughout the year, they were capable of producing enough ships' biscuits to feed 12,310 men annually.[105] During The 1700s the British Navy lost numerous bakeries, in part due to the vulnerable nature of the business, in addition to the fact that the work got so hot the bakers tended to drink too much beer and made careless mistakes. Vice Admiral Sir Issac Coffin built an oven for the British Navy in the early nineteenth century specifically for baking biscuits. It was called the 'perpetual oven'. So named because it could continue baking for any length of time, with a conveyor belt running the whole length, constantly pumping out bread and biscuits. Personnel at Deptford did not view it as a viable labour-saving device that would decrease wages and so refused to build an experimental version to trial.[106] Coffin's oven became a promising invention that was sadly never implemented.

Victualling stores in the nineteenth century were problematic to manage. Letters with requests for goods would arrive late, communication would be chaotic and unpredictable, depending on when and where the conflict was taking place. It also took a number of weeks or months to ship goods directly from one port to the next. In 1809 for example, an order was placed with urgency to send 1,500,000 lbs of bread to Portugal. This request was then altered to half bread and half flour and the goods were shipped from the victualling store at Portsmouth. Four months later a further 1,000 barrels of flour were sent to Portugal from Plymouth. A letter was received some two months after this instructing no flour or bread to be sent to Portugal from either Portsmouth or Plymouth, as Lisbon was over-stocked. Both shipments should instead be sent to Gibraltar. So, in the end, Portugal would have been drowning in a dearth of provisions, while Gibraltar would have to wait another few months.[107]

Adulteration

The Bread Reform League was formed in 1880 by May Yates, following a visit she made to Sicily. Yates observed that the labouring classes there were thriving on brown bread, inspiring her to lobby against inferior white bread production in Britain. It was thought that by retaining as much of the germ of the grain itself in baking, a loaf would contain higher levels of nitrogen, positive fats and gluten, leading to reduced incidents of malnutrition. Baked goods have been adulterated for centuries. One baker's assistant from Northampton in 1758 revealed that his master dissolved a pound of alum with a gallon of urine and mixed it with eight bushels of flour before baking and selling it to the public. This is one of the foulest combinations I think I have read, and there are more than a few, believe me.[108] In this same year a bill was passed in the House of Commons 'to punish persons who shall adulterate meal, flour, or bread...',[109] a bill that extended to include Scotland in 1763. It wasn't just Britain that suffered from this abhorrent crime. While you could be expected to be thrown in jail and have your name publicly bandied about in the press, in Istanbul, formerly Constantinople, it was not uncommon for bakers who adulterated their products to be served the most horrific punishments in the eighteenth century, including the chopping off their hands and public lynching.

It wasn't until the nineteenth century, with the publication of the German chemist Fredrich Accum's *A Treatise on Adulterations of Food and Culinary Poisons* that a real change in the law began to emerge. His controversial paper of 1820 exposed numerous high-profile businesses who were adulterating not only bread, but beer, cheese and other mainstream products manufactured for the food market. As a consequence of targeting many of society's big players, Accum became a wanted man and was covertly framed for a crime he did not commit, leaving him with no choice but to flee the country in a great hurry. Nonetheless, the seed had been sown and the *Lancet* boldly followed on from where Accum was forced to capitulate, by publishing the names and addresses of repeat offenders in the corrupt business of adulteration some thirty years later. By 1860 Britain had introduced its first administrative Food and Drink Act that would lead to much greater country-wide regulation and increased legislation in this area.[110]

Yet the Victorian era remains the worst period in history for recorded cases of adulterated bread. In 1853 the *Staffordshire Advertiser* published a guide to eke out contaminants, first printed in the *Economist* and based on the following observations:

Pure bread is of a clean colour and mellow texture; the crust is brown, the crumb soft when moderately new, the smell is fresh, pleasant and wholesome and the taste sweet. On the contrary, the crumb of adulterated bread is harsh, and the crust pale; the smell is raw and disagreeable and the taste has nothing of that sweetness; neither has the crumb at any time the due consistence, for it is made up of ingredients which will not mix with the yeast and the water in the manner that flour does. The paleness of the crust is one great test, and it depends upon this plain cause: flour when burnt becomes brown; but the ingredients added to bread by those who adulterate it, remain white in the fire. Whiting, lime, alum and ashes of bones are alike in this respect; they will continue white when burnt; and therefore, the more there is of them in the bread the paler will be the crust.

I remain somewhat dubious of the pure and sweet tasting bread described here, but often the colour would be a giveaway as to its contents. A dazzling white appearance was thought to be appealing to consumers demanding the archetypal perfect loaf, which was one of the reasons for incorporating toxic additives, along with the desire to reduce manufacturing costs.

Be it with ground bones, lime, gypsum or plaster of Paris, flour has been adulterated for centuries to mimic colour and texture, increase weight and density.

Finally, in 1846 the assize of bread was repealed. Essentially, this allowed bread to be made with wheat, barley, rye, oats, buckwheat Indian corn, peas, rice or any other grain, or potatoes. salt, water, eggs, barm, butter, yeast, sugar and seeds. The addition of any other ingredients came with a fine of £5 (equivalent to around £400 today). This fine also applied to any type of adulteration either found in baked goods or on baking premises. Justices of the Peace were given powers, on receipt of a warrant to enter either bakehouses, mills or shops and search for any suspect ingredients. Bakers could also sell bread of any shape, weight or size and priced according to weight and were encouraged to keep their own scales and weights on the counters, to allow consumers to check the weight against the price, if required.[111]

The role of bakeries and training

So what would it have been like working in a bakery of this era? During the trial of a rather grisly murder involving a bakehouse oven in 1898, one of the testimonies contained a lengthy description of the typical working practices of a baker's assistant:

> his duty in the bakehouse would chiefly be at night—he begins
> work about 7 o'clock to make the dough, which takes about forty-

five minutes—he would use the larger trough for it—after that he goes, up to bed again—he used to have his food in the bakehouse— he gets it himself when he likes—I call him about 11.30 for his night duties—he then cuts the same dough back again which takes about half-an-hour, and puts away the ferment for the buns, that takes about five minutes—then he has got nothing to do till about 1 o'clock—he would stay in the bake house and at 1 o'clock he would make the next dough, which takes about half-an-hour—after that he starts the oven—the fire is on one side—he heats the oven till about 3.45, when the dough would be put into the oven—I go to bed about 11.30 after I have called the *chap*, and get up about three—the baker calls me—I go down and help him to get the dough ready for the oven—the baking continues till about 11 o'clock next morning, my assistant stays there till then, at 11 o'clock all the baking is over for the day—I have had several assistants…

The owner of this particular bakehouse was William Ross. He also described the clothing of his assistants as – '…a soft cap, a shirt, and a pair of trousers, and a blue-striped canvas belt round his waist with two buckles on it'.[112]

Many commercial enterprises also had bakeries attached. A 'cake house' was another name applied to a confectioner's from the seventeenth to the nineteenth century. As well as sweets, confection and candied fruits, they also sold small baked products. It wasn't a term that seemed to be used with any frequency and is often associated with the selling of cheese-cakes, which were a very popular bake during this period. Cakes could also represent anything from soap to explosives, so it makes archive research a little confusing. There was a notorious cake house in Hyde Park, sometimes called the mince-pie house in the seventeenth century. It was popular with young couples who would court there and refresh themselves with a drink and snack. It was immortalised in William Draper's poem 'The Morning Walk':

> some pretty collation
> Of cheesecakes, and custards, and pigeon-pie puff,
> With bottle-ale, cider, and such sort of stuff[113]

Cake House, Hyde Park
from *Old and New London*.

The Old Chelsea Bun House, located in Jews Row near the former Pleasure Gardens of Ranelagh, has also maintained a legacy, patronised by several of the King Georges and home to the Chelsea Bun. Sadly it was demolished around 1839, but was captured by several artists of the day. Chelsea in the seventeenth century was nothing more than a quiet country village, with a population of around 1,000. A century later it had become one of the most fashionable suburbs of the city of London, with an infamous coffee house called Don Saltero's, and public gardens encompassing thirteen acres of lime and chestnut tree avenues.[114] Allegedly, there were frequent queues outside the shop, which caused public disturbances and numerous breeches of the peace, particularly around Easter when they also sold some of the best Hot Cross Buns in

Chelsea Bun House,
1839, Frederick Napoleon
Shepherd.

Inside Old Chelsea Bun House, 1838.

London, reportedly selling in excess of 240,000 buns on Good Friday, 1829.[115]

The premises themselves also housed a wealth of antiquities and curiosities of museum status, making it even more of a star attraction to wealthy visitors. George III and Queen Charlotte presented the Chelsea Bun house proprietor, Mrs Hand, with a silver half-gallon mug, together with five guineas as a token of their appreciation.[116]

During the mid-nineteenth century, bakeries began to be established inside workhouses, opposed to having the bread delivered or collected from an external source. It was thought that this would cut costs, and generate training and employment opportunities inside the workhouse itself, in addition to raising the quality of bread and sustaining the poor. The city of Bath's workhouse bakery in 1869 appears to prove this point, with its annual statement documenting the production of 130,634 loaves, of which 68,546 were consumed by the inmates and 62,089 by 'out-door' paupers. The bakery cost £2,683 9s and 2d to run, saving at least £130, and producing bread that was 'considerably better than that previously supplied by the contractors'.[117] Reports from Waterford, Ireland, were not so positive, leading with the statement that 'the bread was very inferior… [a] consequence of being badly handled'.[118] Workhouse bakery reports generally throughout the latter part of the nineteenth century appear to be mixed, but on the whole more positive than negative. Some schools, like those in East London, also turned to local workhouses for the supply of their bread, who offered competitive prices. Some schools, such as Uppingham Public School, even had the resources to build their own bakehouse. While the distinguished boys' boarding school, Harrow, went one step further and established their own baking enterprise which was supported financially by the schoolmasters acting as the shareholders.[119] By 1930, Harrow School Bakery Company was producing around 250 4lb loaves a day.[120]

Prisons had also established their own bakeries by the nineteenth century. Brixton Prison housed female convicts, with their bakery described as:

> a pleasant and large light building adjoining the kitchen, [where] more females in light blue gowns [were] at work on the large dresser with an immense heap of dough that lay before them like a huge drab coloured feather bed, and with the master baker in his flannel jacket standing beside the oven watching the work. Some of the female prisoners were working the dough that yielded to their pressure like an air cushion, and some were cutting off pieces and weighing them in the scales before them, and then tossing them over to others who moulded them into the form of dumplings or small loaves. At the end of the bakery was the large prison kitchen, where stood kind of beer trays such as the London pot boys use for the conveyance of the mid-day and nocturnal porter, to the houses in the neighbourhood. These trays at Brixton however served for the conveyance of the dinner cans to the several parts of the prison, while the huge bright spouted tin beer cans that stood beside them, were used for the dispensation of the cocoa that was now steaming in the adjoining coppers and being served out by more prisoners, ready against the breakfast hour at half past seven.[121]

The traditional way to access a career in baking was as a journeyman. A journeyman was someone who had completed their apprenticeship in various trades but who hadn't yet been promoted to master. They were paid by the day and worked relentlessly. Countless stories exist of journeyman bakers; one of the best, summarised first-hand accounts appear in Henry Mayhew's *London Labour and the London Poor*.

…so much night work and the heat of the oven, with the close air, and sleeping on sacks at nights (for you can't leave the place) so that altogether it's a slave's life … a journeyman baker's life drives him to drink, almost whether he will or not.[122]

The above is quoted from a journeyman baker who disliked his job so much that he took to selling stale bread on the streets, his clientele were mainly the very poor, but he made about a guinea a day, roughly £85 pounds in today's worth.

Urban bakehouses were often located underground, possibly to reduce the risk of fires, and were more akin to dungeons, with their poor drainage, lack of ventilation, sweltering hot conditions and ghastly fumes. Most journeyman bakers slept in a room adjacent to the oven, also underground. It was a miserable existence, which is why so many died at such an early age.

One of the most detailed and well-researched accounts of journeyman bakers was compiled by John Lilwall in 1859, in an attempt to incite further legislative measures in this field. He revealed that for most, their working day began at 11.00 pm, and continued until 4.00 pm the following day. After the kneading, proving and baking, they then had to make their deliveries. This often involved carrying in excess of 100 lbs of weight on their backs, or wielding hand-carts through the streets. On average, many journeyman bakers worked in excess of 112 hours a week, having to snatch meals whenever possible without leaving the ovens and getting just a few hours' sleep, if that, each night. For this they received between twelve to eighteen shillings a week, around £45 today.[123] Is it any wonder that Henry Mayhew's interviewee chose a different course? It would be hard to sustain a marriage and family in this line of work, so many had no choice but to remain single. In fact, any form of social life was almost out of the question, with many journeymen rarely even being able to attend church on a Sunday. If the exhaustion, long hours of laborious work and loneliness didn't get to you, then the asthma and rheumatism would finish you off.

Eventually parliament did listen to the plight of the Journeyman baker and in 1863, The Bakehouse Regulation Act introduced formal inspections of all bakehouses, new policies on work conditions and sanitation. The

Act also cracked down on the exploitation of young people under the age of 18 labouring long hours in bakeries.

By the end of this period in history, there was only one school devoted to the technical and practical education of bakers and confectioners – the National School of Bakery and Confectionery, located at Borough Polytechnic, on the South Bank, which was established in 1894. Over the course of the next 100 years or so it would be impossible to calculate the number of training centres and courses that sprung up all over the country with a remit for baking.

As Britain literally marched into the twentieth century, bread would become more significant, life dependant and contentious than ever.

Chapter 4

War, Progress and Mass-consumption

T ea and cake, the epitome of Edwardian culture, transformed London into a giant tearoom of Lyons and ABC venues on every street corner, enterprises that eventually expanded across the provinces and throughout wider Britain. The prosperous new department stores also offered afternoon tea in decadent surroundings, with the chance to follow this up with a trip to the in-store bakery, to purchase the very finest of cakes and luxury patisseries. Selfridges bakery department sold specialist items like Idolice rolls of strawberry and lemon for 2*s* 9*d*, almond genoa cake for 3*s* 9*d*, and Japona Gateaux, which consisted of almond meringue and butter cream layers, for the same price.[1] Idolice rolls have disappeared from the bakery shelves now and it is hard to find any substantial references to them, aside from the fact that they were considered to be a 'new delicacy for afternoon teas' in 1909. It also appears that the variety of flavours including chocolate, coffee, pineapple, raspberry and so on, came from a powder of the same name.[2] Every afternoon at 4pm Selfridges would also sell off its bread at a reduced price, with queues outside the door.[3] In 1905, Harrods bakeries undertook a refurbishment which was so significant, including the very latest equipment, that they advertised for members of the public to apply for a personal inspection and tour of the new premises.[4]

Henry Gordon Selfridge was a great supporter of the suffragette movement and secured regular advertising space in the campaign pamphlet of the 1900s, *The Suffragette*. One such advertisement read:

Selfridge's have taken this space in the 'Suffragette', out of compliment to many of their customers who have expressed a wish that this House should be represented among the advertisers in this paper. Selfridge & Co. Ltd. Oxford Street, W.[5]

In the age of suffrage and the formation of the WSPU in 1908, suffragette cakes were all the rage. The purple, green and white colours adopted by the party were coincidentally the same as those of the Wimbledon Lawn Tennis Championships, and as such the two have often come together collaboratively in the district of Wimbledon. A reception at the Wimbledon Cottage Hospital in 1908 was adorned in decorations of purple, green and white with a 'suffragette cake' as the central feature, while a local Wimbledon confectioner was known to display a doll in his window, dressed in bespoke gowns of the same colours.[6] Suffragette cakes were visible at numerous baking competitions and exhibitions, like the one at Holborn Town Hall, in which a local newspaper commented on the symbolic harp, worn by many Irish suffragettes which was displayed on a cake, with the body of the harp serving as a banana and the strings made of currants.[7]

During the First World War female bakers enlisted en masse, a responsibility previously attributed to men. They were also given the task of driving bread delivery vans, while the National Bakery School established its first classes for women in 1916.[8] Initially women were only considered for fancy bread and confectionery work. It was assumed they were too delicate to undertake the 'heavier side of bakery', which essentially meant working overnight in the bakehouses. A law was passed in 1917 that would negate this, with the proviso that bread could not be sold until it became twelve hours old. Women factory workers in the Great War predominantly worked in the munition factories, but they also played a significant role in creating staple rations for soldiers by manufacturing biscuits, a role which continued into the Second World War. In 1945 the Carr's biscuit factory based in Carlisle employed 4,300 people, half of which were women.[9]

In 1915, an inspection of women workers at an anonymous biscuit factory found they had sore and swollen fingers, a consequence of the heat of the biscuit and roughness of the tins that were used to cream and stick together a cream sandwich biscuit. The task required two women, one to place the cream on the bottom layer, the other to stick the top layer onto the cream. Over time the skin on their fingers split and broke, causing swelling and bleeding. For this they received 7*s* 8*d* a week, roughly £23 in today's money, working from 7am until 6pm.[10]

Perhaps the most significant historical event involving women biscuit-factory workers occurred in 1911, when thousands withdrew their labour from Jacob's Biscuits in Ireland to pursue a pay claim. James Larkin, who founded the Irish Transport and General Workers' Union (ITGWU) commented that conditions for the biscuit workers at the time were 'sending them from this earth twenty years before their time'.[11]

Women also worked in other baking related professions throughout both wars, including Brunner, Mond & Co in Northwich, a company that manufactured sodium bicarbonate, and in flour mills like that of Rank & Sons in Birkenhead.

Perhaps one of the most renowned female activists of her day was Emily Davison, who protested at the Epsom Derby in 1913 by throwing herself in front of King George V's horse. King George V would be the monarch to steer Britain through the First World War and beyond. His coronation in 1911 was a grand affair and the cake even grander. Representatives from the Universal Cookery and Food Association, better known as the Craft Guild of Chefs, whose original founders included Escoffier and Cesar Ritz in the 1880s, collaborated on the creation which demonstrated highly skilled sugar workmanship. The cake stood 3ft high and was three months in the making. It contained 6 lbs of egg, based on a macaroon mix, and was one of the first royal cakes to break the mould of using the old traditional plum-cake mixture. The cake had two tiers divided into five plinths, each creating a scene depicting the five continents of Empire. There were sections from the National Anthem inscribed throughout, coats of arms and heraldry. The central 20in-high figures depicting

THE SISTERS SEARLE.
of Chertsey, employees of the Coxe's Lock Milling Co., Addlestone.

World War One Female Millers, Chertsey, Surrey Herald. (*Courtesy of Chertsey Museum*)

the king and queen wearing their coronation robes and seated on thrones were one of the main features, including an intricate fully rigged ship, all constructed of icing.[12]

The population at the start of the twentieth-century was around a third of what it is today, and Britain was still a largely rural country where many people continued to work the land. Domestic service remained the leading occupation and life expectancy was relatively low. As the century progressed, great social and economic changes emerged as a consequence of the burgeoning industrialisation and modernisation of the preceding centuries. One such advancement was the luxury cruise market, engineered to make long transatlantic crossings more comfortable and pleasurable. Not so for the passengers of RMS *Titanic.* This fatal liner had the most advanced electrics ever to be installed on a ship, powered by four enormous steam-driven generators. While passengers enjoyed the daily 6,000 meals on offer, the staff worked around the clock in its vast catering divisions, spanning seven decks and including three bakeries.[13]

One of the most characterised survivors of the *Titanic*'s cataclysmic voyage is Charles Joughin, the ship's 33-year-old head baker. Portrayed by actor George Rose in the 1958 film *A Night to Remember,* famously hanging from the ship's rails, swigging from a flask of whiskey. He is also seen running along the deck alongside Rose and Jack, played by Kate Winslett and Leonardo Di Caprio in the iconic 1997 movie, while Joughin also featured in episodes of both the US and British versions of the television series *Drunk History* in 2016.

The British Wreck Commissioner's Inquiry contains the testimony of Joughin, recounting that last horrific night in detail. In his own words Joughin stated that he was asleep in his bunk, located in the middle of the ship on the left-hand (port) side when it hit the iceberg. When asked if he was ordered to gather any provisions, Joughin noted that tack biscuits were already stored on board the lifeboats as standard, but they also received orders to grab what they could. He rallied the thirteen bakers he was managing at the time, who grabbed four loaves each, weighing around 40 lb in total. They were then sent to their stations on the lifeboats, followed by Joughin who went to his assigned lifeboat, number 10. He recalled how the men made a line and passed the ladies and children down. Some women refused to get in the lifeboat, resolute in their decision to stay on board where they thought it safer. Joughin clarified that all third-class passengers had easy access from the lower decks to the upper deck via an emergency door and a staircase, which was opened early and was in constant use. This rather contradicts many of the stories about third-class passengers not having any access to the decks above. Joughin and some of the other male passengers forcibly picked up women and children from the promenade deck, who were refusing to get in the lifeboats and threw them in. When his own lifeboat, the one he had been allocated command of in advance, was full, he did not get in and simply watched as it was lowered into the sea. Joughin then returned to his quarters and lubricated himself with alcohol before returning to the upper decks and discovering that all the lifeboats had been launched. He threw deck chairs in an attempt to help those stranded, before returning below decks for a drink of water. There was a loud crack, followed by a rush of people overhead running down the decks and clambering to get onto the poop, or the highest deck. Joughin followed but stayed behind the crowd. *Titanic* then shifted violently over to the left and he watched as 'many of hundreds of people in front of him were tossed overboard'. He clung to a rail and within minutes the ship had moved again. Joughin found himself in the sea, where he stayed for a number of hours treading water but with a lifebelt on. As daylight broke, he attempted to climb a lifeboat already laden down with survivors. Pushed off, he continued to stay with the boat before spotting one of his colleagues, a ship's cook, who gave him his hand, enabling Joughin to hold onto the side of the boat. Not long after, another passing lifeboat approached with plenty of space, so Joughin swam to it and was taken in. The Cunard liner, *Carpathia* was sent to retrieve survivors, Joughin being one of those eventually picked up later that day.[14] Over 1,500 people died that night, the same night that first-class passengers would have indulged in a menu including Waldorf Pudding, had the ship never hit that iceberg.[15] The making of this pudding may even have been supervised by Charles Joughin himself. Here is a recipe for Waldorf Pudding which doesn't appear to have been that well-known at the time. Many variations exist, of which the majority were concocted after the last menu was published and have a relationship to the eponymous salad. Apparently, there is no known connection between the pudding and the famous Waldorf Astoria Hotel in New York,

Veranda Cafe and Palm Court on the *Titanic*. (*Library of Congress*)

or London's Waldorf Hilton Hotel. However, Waldorf Astoria Pudding, also a type of bread pudding, was popular in the United States in the very early 1900s.

The following recipe was published prior to the *Titanic*'s voyage, so to me, represents perhaps a more authentic version of what might have been served up, although there is another 1903 recipe published in a Presbyterian church collection, that also contains apples, together with an even earlier variant from 1899, cited below. The 1899 Waldorf Pudding is a much richer recipe, which might make it a more likely candidate for an appearance on a first-class dinner menu, but the bottom line is that we are unlikely to ever know for sure.

Waldorf Pudding (1911)

Break up half a pound of stale lady-fingers and cook to a smooth paste with a quart of cream. Add half a cupful of sugar, three tablespoons of butter, a wineglassful of sherry, and a sprinkling of grated nutmeg. Cool, add the well-beaten yolks of four eggs and three tablespoons of almonds blanched and pounded to a paste with lemon-juice. Turn into a baking dish, sprinkle with sugar, and bake in a quick oven.[16]

Waldorf Pudding (1899)

Peel and slice sufficient apples to fill a baking dish; butter the dish thickly and put in the apples in layers, alternating them with stale cake crumbs and a little melted butter, using two tablespoons of the latter to a pint of apples; let the last layer be crumbs. Cover, and put in a hot oven until the apples are soft; then beat together two eggs and two tablespoons of sugar, add one cup of cream or rich milk; add this, return to the oven until the pudding is a rich brown. Serve with cream.[17]

The cabin biscuits featured on the evening menu for third-class passengers would have resembled more of a cracker and were a simple bake consisting of flour shortening (probably lard) water and salt. They were thought to prevent seasickness, something passengers below decks would have had considerable experience of. Cabin biscuits were available at both dinner and supper, along with Swedish bread at breakfast. Here is Sarah Tyson Rorer's recipe, which is a very common example of the early colonial 'rye and Indian' version from the United States and most likely similar to what *Titanic*'s third-class travellers would have eaten.

Swedish Bread

Scald one pint of Indian meal with one pint of boiling water. Cover and cool slowly. Add a quart of warm water, a salt spoon of salt, one cake of compressed yeast; dissolved in a quarter cup of warm water, Now stir in rye meal until you have a dough. Knead well, using graham flour (coarsely ground whole wheat flour) on the board. Break off a bit, about a pint; roll it out into a thin sheet, the size of a dinner plate. Place it on a cloth cover for one hour and bake in a moderately quick oven (300 degrees Fahrenheit) for forty minutes.[18]

Like the Waldorf, it was extremely popular to name cakes and puddings in the early twentieth century. A traditional cake was baked during the First World War specifically for soldiers in the trenches, Christened (unsurprisingly) *Soldier's Cake*. These would be posted to loved ones serving on the front line. They were typically eggless cakes with vinegar or milk added to help react with baking soda and aid more of a rise/increased texture. The dried fruit mixture would also have given the cake its much needed longevity. Always a bonus during wartime.

A good Soldiers' Cake

1½ lb. Flour. ½ lb of cooking butter or dripping. ½ lb brown. ½ lb currants, ½ lb raisins stoned half teaspoonful of ginger, ½ ounce of candied peel, two teaspoons of carbonate of soda and little nutmeg. Rub the butter well in the flour. add all the dry ingredients, mix all well together, dissolve the soda in half a pint of milk (warmed). Mix all well together and bake two hours and a half.[19]

Many of the bigger towns and cities pulled together during the Great War to provide the necessities of conflict; baking being one of those chief necessities. Sheffield's Personal Comforts Depot, established in 1914, supplemented the local hospitals struggling with the dying and wounded with food and aided the wives and children of military personnel fighting overseas. Items like pork pies and cakes were channelled through the depot at a rate of thousands a week.[20] The Personal Comforts Depot made a public appeal in 1915 for people to come forward with homemade cakes to help sustain the additional 400 wounded soldiers that arrived in the city over a period of just six days.[21]

Two years later these comforting treats were under threat when orders were issued by the Minister of Food Control, Lord Devonport, to regulate cakes and pastries. Declaring that:

… no person shall after April 21 make or attempt to make for sale, or after 24 April sell or offer to sell or have in his possession for sale:

(a) Any crumpet, muffin, tea cake, or fancy bread, or any light or fancy pastry, or any other article.

(b) Any cake, bun, scone, or biscuit which does not conform to the requirements of the two following provisions of this Order.

In the making of any cake, bun, scone, or biscuit, no edible substance shall be added to the exterior of the cake mixture or dough after it has been mixed, or to the article during the process after baking.

CAKE – No cake shall contain more than 15 per cent of sugar or more than 30 percent wheaten flour.

BUN – No bun shall contain more than 10 per cent of sugar or more than 50 per cent wheaten flour.

BISCUIT – No biscuit shall contain more than 15 per cent of sugar.

These restrictions were increased just weeks later when the baking of pikelets, crumpets, dropped scones, Eccles cakes, sausage rolls and the filling of any type of sponge cake were all prohibited.[22]

Bread itself wasn't rationed during the First World War, but the fresh bread ban introduced in 1917, making it illegal to sell bread less than twelve hours after baking, enabled more women to participate in breadmaking, as it was formerly considered inappropriate to let women carry out night duties. The twelve-hour law made night baking obsolete. 'War bread' as it was known, was mixed with barley, rye, oats, soya and potato flour giving it a darker colour and heavier consistency.

The 'Aldershot oven' method of baking used previously in times of military conflict was a primitive one and proved difficult for British soldiers out in the Balkans in a location where rising Serbian nationalists and the Austro-Hungarian government came to blows, prompting the assassination of Archduke Franz-Ferdinand and the onset of the First World War. The weather was wet and stormy, washing away the earth and grass built up around the front, back and sides of the oven. The 1910 publication, *The Manual of Military Cooking*, provides an excellent description of this oven which consisted of:

Two sections, two ends, one bottom, four bars, nine tins, one peel and weighing 874lbs. Roughly one pound of wood was needed to bake each pound of bread.[23]

The mouth of the oven needed to face the prevailing wind to heat it quickly. Once an appropriate site was found it needed to be cleared and sods of earth cut up. The four bars were then placed down, the back one overlapping the front. The back of the oven was then placed in position while the bottom plate was fitted and the front portion fixed. Sods were then built up around it, covering the front, back and sides, while a trench was cut for the baker to work in, about 18in deep and 6ft long. The clay and soil taken from building the trench was then used to bind the whole oven structure together, forming a sloping roof to drain off the rain. The oven required lighting each morning and the embers drawn out with a rake. The dough tins needed to be placed in the oven about thirty minutes after the fire was drawn, to prevent it cooking too quickly or burning, and a makeshift door put in place. Essentially, the Aldershot principal could be improvised out of different materials, including corrugated iron, barrels, biscuit tins, beaten out into an arch shape. The Aldershot oven was named after the army's largest camp and training centre, including the Army School of Cookery established in Aldershot in 1885, which became indispensable during the Great War. With the Aldershot ovens

Military Baking 1915, from *Kitcheners Army and Territorial Forces the Full Story of Great Achievement.*

in the Balkans proving inadequate, the troops had to wait for the delivery of Perkins ovens, a long cylindrical and portable steam oven, designed by A.M. Perkins and Son, which soon began to replace the Aldershot method altogether.

Transporting fresh food and baked goods directly to the front line could take several days and as a consequence, field bakeries and butcheries were established on railway lines, capable of turning over 22,500 rations of fresh bread or fresh meat. The bread was baked, cooled and packed in what were known as 'offal sacks', cheap, jute bags used in the butchery trade. Each of these sacks could hold fifty 2 lb loaves, the equivalent of rations to feed 100 men. Ten sacks would feed a whole battalion. Following comparative exercises, it was proved that this process was too costly and wasteful. Instead, bread began to be made in Aldershot in bulk and delivered directly to the troops. Soldiers also needed to carry emergency rations which included a 1 lb tin of preserved meat, 1 lb tin of biscuits, sugar, salt and tea.

The allocated daily rations for soldiers in 1917 included:

Meat, fresh or frozen . . . . 1 lb.
Bacon . . . . 4 oz.
Bread . . . . 1 lb. or 10 oz. biscuit.
Butter . . . . 2 oz. (3 times a week).
Jam . . . . 3 oz.
Tea . . . . $^5/_8$ oz.
Sugar . . . . 3 oz.
Condensed milk . . . . 1 oz.
Cheese . . . . 2 oz.
Oatmeal . . . . 2 oz. (3 times a week).
Potatoes . . . . 2 oz.
Fresh vegetables . . . . 8 oz. (or 2 oz. dried vegetables)
Tobacco or cigarettes . . . . 2 oz. (once a week).
Matches . . . . 1 box (3 times a fortnight).

With salt, pepper and mustard, rum was also permitted at the discretion of the GOC Army Service Corps.[24]

The Army Service Corps, consisting of that vast body of workers including cooks, carpenters, blacksmiths, drivers, saddlers, grocers, domestic staff and so on, also provided travelling bakery waggons where bakers could knead and prepare the bread. These came with dough-troughs and all the baking implements required.[25] As well as knowing how to bake, field bakers needed to be adept at constructing the steam and sometimes electric ovens that would service the troops in camp, in addition to improvising things like makeshift beer barrels converted into ovens in the field. This was achieved by placing the barrel upright in a trench and knocking out one end. The interior was then filled with fuel and the top and sides covered with clay. Now comes the clever bit – when the fire was lit, the woodwork of the barrel burned away, leaving the clay which was held together by the barrel's iron bands, thus forming the shell of a usable oven.[26]

Bread, of course wasn't the only baked product made in the field. Meat was an essential element of a soldier's diet, like this original recipe designed to feed 100 men in 1917.

> Baked meat and potatoes – wash, peel and rewash the potatoes, cutting the large ones into halves lengthways. Bone, roll and skewer the meat, cover with slices of fat if lean joint. Place the potatoes into a baking dish, clean and cut up the onions, put in centre of the potatoes, add ½ oz. Pepper, 3ozs.salt, then pour over a little stock or water. Place dish in oven, turn joint at half-time, add stock when necessary. Time 15 minutes for each pound of meat.[27]

The government's Wheat Commission was responsible for buying grain, allocating it to millers and corn merchants, and ensuring bread supplies were maintained to avoid rationing, but by 1917, Germany's attempts to sink ships carrying provisions became so successful that the government were forced into introducing a voluntary scheme of rationing and British citizens were advised to restrict their weekly consumption to 4 lb of bread, cakes and puddings.

These were desperate times and the 'ploughing up' campaign of 1917 persuaded farmers to grow more arable in an attempt to increase the country's production of wheat, oats and potatoes. The Women's Land Army would be key to this initiative.

The Ministry of Food urged people to substitute flour for potatoes in their bread-making and the newspapers during this time are strewn with advertisements for potato bread, alongside articles praising its merits as a wholesome and tasty alternative. Potato bread was by no means a new approach to baking in Britain. During the 1700s it was seen as a means of feeding the poor and labouring classes cheaply. Just as it was promoted in the twentieth century as a surrogate for wheat, it was also widely reported on during the eighteenth century, with potatoes recommended to be mixed along with flour to both bolster and reduce the price of an average loaf, as this detailed article from *Derby Mercury* in 1789 exemplifies:

RECEIPT for making POTATO BREAD.

Communicated to the Committee of the Bath Agriculture Society, with an improved Sample of the Bread. THE Potatoes should be clean washed, and pared, and every eye mould be cut out; they should then be boiled in as much water as will barely suffice to cover them, and should remain over a slow fire till reduced to a pulp; after which they should be put into a knead-ing trough, together with the water they were boiled in, which should always be of the softest: kind; they must be well bruised after they are in the trough till no lumps remain, and the flour may be then mixed with them together with the barm or yeast; and this should be done while the potatoes are about blood warm: This will make the bread light, and the water in which they were boiled will be fully sufficient to incorporate the mixture; but care mull be taken to reserve a proper quantity of flour to make the bread into separate loaves, previous to its being put into the oven, and after it is well kneaded; and the harder and drier the dough is, the better the bread will be. The oven in which the bread is to.be baked should be made very hot, and the mouth thereof should be stopped some time before the loaves are introduced, and scarcely eatable. In the making this bread, the following proportions should be observed:—To every four pounds of potatoes, add one pound, and a half of the second sort of wheaten flour from found corn, and the like quantity of fine barley flour. This, with the water the potatoes-were boiled in, (and the barm or yeast added) will make about eight pounds of wholesome bread. Suppose the wheat flour to be 2d. per lb. which is 9s. 4d. per bushel, and the barley flour one 1d. per lb. which is 4s. 8d. per bushel of 56lb. and the potatoes four pounds for 3d. — a high price; I say, admitting these prices, the bread may be afforded at one penny per lb. including barm and fuel. Barley is an excellent ingredient, and its cheapness is another recommendation; nor can it be discovered by the nicest palate. I have used this bread in my family several winters, and am confident it need only be tried to be approved. I hope the humane and affluent will be induced to make it in the winter, for the comfort of their poor neighbours, and you have my leave to make it public in any manner you think proper; and believe me to be, Gentlemen, Your very obliged humble servant, Holt, near Bradford, Wilts. JOS. HAZARD.[28]

Unless you wanted to live on potato bread for any length of time, the most intrinsic element of baking is the growing of wheat, barley or corn to mill for flour. A difficult task during times of conflict.

We tend to associate the 'Land Girls' with the Second World War, but the Board of Agriculture created the Women's Land Army (WLA) as early as 1917, although many women had unofficially been working in the fields to meet the shortfall of male workers for some time. After receiving training at one of the many centres set up across the country, women ploughed fields, harvested crops and milked cows among other tasks. This account from one of the training centres established at St Augustine's College Canterbury provides a glimpse into what was expected of a Land Army Girl during the Great War:

At 5.30 every morning the reveille rings down the long oak corridor, and echoes through the cloisters, warning the occupant of each little cell that it is time to be up and doing. As the clock in the clock tower strikes 6 the 'army' crosses the quadrangle to the raftered kitchen and each member of it drinks an early cup of tea and eats a 'wartime' sandwich. At 6.15 all set out with their ration baskets to their various farms for a strenuous day's work … The girls are now even allowed to cart manure, which for a long time was a stumbling block. Men and women work together in the hayfields and harvest fields, in the stables and cowsheds, on the maure dumps and turnip fields. Laughter, song and strenuous work can go together, and the former often helps one to forget that the latter is 'hard'. By 6 pm. They have returned – a hot and dusty or soaking wet company according to the type of weather provided. Hot baths and a change of clothing work a miracle, and the 6.30 supper bell finds a jovial party seated on the benches which run along the sides of the long, narrow oak tables. Their adventures during the day appear to have been innumerable and are related with much spirit and laughter. At 7 pm a move is made to the kitchen to pack up rations for the following day, and application is made for the weekly 'late leave pass', which is granted for one evening a week, and which permits the holder to stay out until 9 p.m. On other nights all must be present at the 8 p.m. roll call – on the terrace in fine weather, in the cloisters if it is wet. Compline follows in the chapel, bed at 9 o'clock, and 'lights out' at 9.30.[29]

In contrast, the reality of life for a Land Army girl once in post was often rather different, as this article published in the *Landswoman* in 1918 suggests:

As days shorten and winter deepens, women on the land, especially if they have been accustomed to towns or have been trained in agricultural classes, feel the loneliness of their lives. They have little chance for rest or recreation. They pine for some congenial soul with whom to compare notes … Let me mention two of the obstacles they had at first to face. One is the reluctance of farmers to employ them, the other is the aloofness of the villagers … All honour to the pioneers who have, to a great extent, conquered both difficulties. They have set the standard and by so doing have smoothed the way for those increasing numbers of women who will, we hope, follow in their steps.[30]

As a consequence of German blockades and failing harvests, there was something like an estimated three weeks' supply of food left in the country before this essential band of the women's services was established. It was stressful, backbreaking and not nearly as glamorous as the WRNS, also formed in 1917. Working in the Women's Land Army meant long hours and very low pay. These women have, in my opinion, never been given the proper recognition they deserve. Without them Britain would have suffered a much harsher, hungrier war and their legacy would go on to significantly alter the role of women in society.

Land Army women also heralded the introduction of calcium to flour in 1941, as a consequence of high-levels of rickets detected on signing up. The ramifications of this socially were evident in the press, with a backlash against the use of additives in bread. From demonstrations to angry letters published in newspapers, many people believed that the government were slowly poisoning consumers, or had concerns that calcium raised blood pressure levels significantly. The Minister of Food at the time, Colonel Llewellin made a formal statement in 1944. 'I am advised on the best authority that the addition of the small amount of calcium now added to bread is beneficial for the continued good health of the nation'.[31] And again in 1945, with the public continuing to remonstrate over the benefits of calcium, Llewellin remained resolute,

Wholemeal
Bread.
(@ *Emma Kay*)

declaring: 'I am advised that substantial advantages have been obtained from the addition of calcium and I am not prepared to make available an alternative national loaf without it.[32] Around the time that calcium was added to flour, the British government established an organisation to 'assist in organising wartime production and distribution of bread', the Federation of Bakers, an organisation that became responsible for introducing the 'National loaf', a predominantly wholemeal-based bake containing a mixture of vitamins and calcium and a compulsory bread designed to combat both the shortage of white flour, while tackling issues related to nutrition. Bakers were paid a subsidy to ensure every loaf sold remained at a consistent price. They also found the mix difficult to work with, with early loaves often under-cooked and turning mouldy after just two days. As a consequence, the National Association of Master Bakers collaborated with the Ministry of Food to roll out a series of national bread-baking competitions designed to help bakers create the perfect loaves made to the specifications of the Federation recipe. This rather unpalatable and unpopular product was finally abandoned in 1956. It didn't take the Rank, Hovis McDougall group long to popularise their new Mother's Pride, perfectly white fluffy loaf, with tantalising advertisements for the bread, 'we know you really want', filling the newspapers just a few weeks after the National loaf was retired.[33]

Over the last few decades, consumers have become used to buying bread that is mass produced, containing numerous additives, the likes of which the wartime generation would never have tolerated. But there is a growing backlash against synthesized bread products today, and a move towards authentic additive free, natural methods of traditional bakery. Undoubtedly it was the two world wars that altered the nature of breadmaking in Britain with plant or factory baking, designed to produce large quantities of bread at lower costs and the advent of advanced road networks, transportation and improvements in machinery. No food was as affected by legislation as much as bread was during and immediately after the Second World War.

In February 1941 a cap was placed on the price of all sales of bread, specialist breads and rolls. A price that was not allowed to exceed that of December 1940. With the cost of a 2 lb loaf totalling 4½*d*.[34] In theory this worked quite effectively, until it became apparent in 1942 that some parts of the UK, less populated areas in particular, were being charged considerably more than others for their average loaf. As much as an extra farthing. Local councillors rallied to subsidise bakers in these regions to enable people to purchase bread at the standard price, but all resolutions were defeated.[35] Basically, if you lived more rurally during the war, you paid the price.

In 1942 the Minister of Food announced to the House of Lords that there would be no white loaves available on the shop shelves, only brown. A restriction that would continue until 1956.[36] During this same year it also became unlawful to put sugar on top of cakes.[37]

There were endless advertisements and public notices addressing the issue of using the most of your bread, from how best to store it, to how to make it go further. Bread and butter pudding became a staple dish for using up stale bread. Like this one published in the *Belfast News-Letter* of 1940.

Required — Stale bread cut thin slices, margarine, 1 egg. to 1 pint milk, 1 oz. currants or sultanas, 1 oz. sugar, a few drops of vanilla essence, or a little grated lemon rind, and a grating of nutmeg. Spread the slices of bread with margarine, and cut Into fingers. Put a layer of the bread in the bottom of a greased pie-dish, and sprinkle with half the currants and sugar; then another layer of bread, and the rest .of the currants and sugar. Cover With bread, with the margarine side up. Beat the egg thoroughly, stir in half pint of the milk, add a few drops of vanilla and strain the whole over the bread. Leave to soak for to 1 hour, according to the staleness of the bread. Add more milk if necessary. There should be sufficient liquid almost to cover the bread, and the staler the bread the more milk will be necessary. Grate a little nutmeg over the top, and bake in a moderate oven for about 30 minutes, until risen and nicely browned. Dredge with sugar, and serve at once. Stale cookies or cake may be used up in this way.

For much of the Second World War, Lord Woolton retained the position of Minister of Food. It was a monstrous task for any government minister. One fraught with public dissatisfaction, criticism and unpopularity.

Overseeing rationing at a time of great shortage and hardship, Woolton's reputation in history is a mixed one. His relationship with Churchill was strained, but he implemented vast UK wide campaigns, establishing advice centres, mobile cookery demonstrations and a constant stream of recipe and advisory food and drink propaganda. He even provided children with free school meals during one of the harshest times of the conflict. The public berated him for the high cost of food products and his position as food minister came into jeopardy on more than one occasion.

Lord Woolton is perhaps best known in culinary terms for his 'Woolton Pie'. A timely piece of good PR which appeared in the spring of 1941, launched at the Savoy Hotel, London, following a spate of bad press and public lack of confidence in his abilities. The pie itself began to be served in restaurants, canteens and hotels throughout the country, born out of a need to promote the benefits of vegetables at a time when meat was scarce. Woolton Pie was created by the then head chef of the Savoy, Francis Latry, and consisted of diced and cooked potatoes, cauliflower, swedes and carrots, spring onions, vegetable extract and a tablespoon of oatmeal. It was then covered with the obligatory wholemeal or potato pastry, baked and served hot with gravy. It is said that when offered a slice, Churchill pushed his plate away and requested some beef. Still, the pie became quite renowned in the 1940s and into the proceeding decades, a symbol of British austerity and courage.[38]

Here is the original recipe, first published in *The Times* newspaper, 26 April 1941:

Take 1 lb each diced potatoes, cauliflower, swedes and carrots, three or four spring onions – if possible one teaspoonful of oatmeal. Cook altogether for 10 minutes with just enough water to cover. Sir occasionally to prevent the mixture from sticking. Allow to cool; put into a pie dish, sprinkle with chopped parsley, and cover with a crust of potato or wheat-meal pastry. Bake in a moderate oven until the pastry is nicely browned and serve hot with a brown gravy. The ingredients can be varied according to the vegetables in season.[39]

Baking became difficult, with the stringent rationing of items such as butter and sugar during the Second World War. Generally, the allocated amount of sugar per adult for a week was around 12oz (340g) but this decreased to as low as 8oz, or 225g, at one stage of the war. The weekly allowance for butter was approximately 4oz, a weight which reduced to 2oz per week, or around 56g. Households could also choose a butter plus margarine combination ration. This averaged out at about 6oz (170g) in total per week, per adult. A 'points' system was also introduced in 1941. Each person was allocated sixteen points a month, which later increased to 20. A variety of foods, such as biscuits, worked on a points scheme, valued according to availability. Eggs, (both fresh and powdered) an ingredient so crucial to baking were not included within any of these schemes. You had to register for these separately and they were not guaranteed.[41]

During the Second World War, bread and potatoes remained unrationed. A surprise and unwelcome bread rationing proposal was, however, launched by the Ministry of Food in July 1946, a scheme heavily opposed by bakers. As a consequence of drastic world food shortages, all bread manufacturers and traders were required to submit a detailed return showing how many units they had purchased, number of sales made and stock remaining every eight weeks.[40] Severe penalties were threatened if the scheme was not upheld. These included a fine of £500 or a year's imprisonment, with a maximum fine of up to £5,000 for repeat offenders. This post-war rationing of bread stayed in place for a further two years.

Perhaps one of the UK's biggest community-inspired movements associated with baking began to flourish in Wales in the early twentieth century. Emerging from the Women's Institute formed in Canada, almost a decade before, Madge Watt was appointed Canadian Ambassador and sent to Britain to spread the word and inspire interest in establishing a similar format. In 1915 she delivered a talk in Bangor, Wales, and was asked to speak again to the village of Llanfairpwllgwyngyll (the shortened version of the infamously quoted Welsh village name ending in gogogoch) on the isle of Anglesey, by some of the interested members of the audience. The meeting was so successful, it was agreed there and then that a Women's Institute would be set up in the village. The subsequent 'formation meeting', was chaired by Watt and Jane Stapleton-Cotton was elected as Founding President.[42]

By the end of the First World War in 1918, there were some 700 Women's Institutes, a figure that doubled just a year later. By the Second World War they were a well-established part of British rural society, with institutions set up in over 5,000 villages. They helped significantly with the war effort, in particular with supporting evacuees, helping them settle into rural areas and organising activities like tea parties.

The Ministry of Food distributed sugar to WI Preservation Centres which had been established to make jam and canned goods. Making jam was of course one of the main activities most associated with the WI during Second World War, a task they completed on an epic scale from surplus fruit and vegetables growing wild, on allotments and in private gardens. Members of the WI also sold surplus fruit and vegetables from market stalls in rural locations across the country, from as early as 1919, to assist vulnerable out of town communities when food supplies were scarce.

'Make do and mend' was the order of the day during Second World War and many women were already skilled in this art from the previous war. They had to make cakes from vegetable peelings, bread from mashed potatoes, biscuits from oatmeal. Butter or margarine had to be mixed with boiling water to increase the volume, while flour was sometimes substituted with cornflour. Eggs were often powdered, while almost obsolete sugar was replaced with honey, syrup or sometimes dried fruit. The absence of sugar would have produced a tighter dough and smaller volume of cake. It wouldn't have been possible to simply replace sugar in a standard recipe with honey or syrup, as the consistency would have been completely different. New recipes had to be explored and invented. It was also recommended to overcook cakes being sent to the Front Line, so that they didn't deteriorate as quickly. Newspapers and magazines published ideas for women in the home to experiment with, such as these for Honey Cake, Date Cake and gingerbread which appeared in the *Ormskirk Advertiser* on 22 February, 1940.

Honey Cake

Ingredients: 4 oz. dripping. lb. wholemeal flour. ½ lb honey, teaspoon bicarbonate of soda, 1 egg, little milk, 1 small teaspoon ground ginger.

Method: Beat the dripping with the honey. Stir in the flour with the ginger and the beaten egg. Beat well. Fold in the bi-carbonate of soda mixed in a little milk. Put into a hot oven, lower the gas and bake in a moderate oven for 2 hours.

Date Cake

Ingredients: 4 oz. flour. 4 oz. ground rice, 3 oz. margarine or dripping. ½ lb. chopped dates, 1 teaspoon bi-carbonate soda, 1 egg.

Method: Mix the flour and ground rice, rub the fat well, add the chopped dates. Whip the egg and stir into the dry ingredients with the carbonate soda dissolved in little milk. Add more milk if necessary but keep the dough fairly stiff. Put into a well-greased baking tin, and bake in moderate gas oven for 1 to 1½ hours.

Gingerbread: (No sugar, no eggs)

Ingredients: 1 lb. self-raising flour. 5 oz. margarine, 3 oz treacle and 3 oz. golden syrup (if treacle unobtainable use 6 oz. golden syrup). 4 oz. sultanas, 4 oz. chopped crystallised ginger. 1 teaspoonful bi-carbonate of soda, ¾ pint of milk. Method: Rub the margarine into the flour thoroughly. Add the powdered ginger. Warm the milk and syrup until they blend. Stir in the bi-carbonate of soda and when the mixture foams pour into the flour. Mix to a soft dough and fold in the fruit. Thoroughly grease (or line with greaseproof paper) a flat baking tin or gingerbread tin. Pour in the mixture, smooth the top and brush with milk. Cook in a slow oven for about two hours.[43]

You could forget real cream too. A 'mock', or 'emergency' cream was often fashioned from a mixture of margarine, dried milk and vanilla

Marshall's of Pewsey, Bread Van, 1940s courtesy of Richard Marshall.

essence. Baking powder adverts, particularly those issued by the Royal Baking Powder company, were everywhere at this time, highlighting the powder's benefits to baking, by saving on eggs and preventing waste as a consequence of faulty raising. The Ministry of Food issued a constant stream of leaflets, advisory short films and advertisements promoting and teaching all aspects of working within the rationing system and advising on how to make things last longer using the right recipes. The Board of Education was also integral to this drive and published numerous pamphlets during the 1940s, including *Good Fare in War-Time*, 1941, from which the following recipe for patriotic Pudding is taken:

Patriotic pudding

Ingredients:
4 table-spoons Flour
4 table-spoons grated raw Potato or Fine Oatmeal
1 table-spoon Fat
½ table-spoon Jam, Treacle or Milk and Water to mix Syrup and 1 grated Carrot

½ tea-spoon Bicarbonate of Soda
Pinch of Salt
2 tea-spoons grated Orange or Lemon Rind (if available)
Milk and Water to mix

Method:
Rub the fat into the flour, add the rest of the dry ingredients and mix well. Add the jam and carrot, heated in four table-spoons of milk and mix to a soft mixture adding more milk or water if necessary. Turn into a well-greased bowl, cover and steam for 1 hour.

OR: Place jam and carrot in the bottom of a well-greased bowl make the mixture as above, mixing the dry ingredients with the milk only.[44]

It was very popular to have 'wartime cake' competitions at summer/garden fetes or special events. These might just be cakes entered into a competition, or actual practical demonstrations to show women how to get the most of their meagre rations.

There was even a special wartime dog biscuit, issued sometime around 1940. These were specifically manufactured with 'damaged flour'. The Canine Defence League issued a statement to reassure dog owners and to remind them that there were plenty of alternatives including horseflesh, offals, stale bread and cheap rice boiled with bones. Yummy.[45]

Among one of the great bastions of wartime cooking was Marguerite Patten. Working for the Ministry of Food she became well known for broadcasting and demonstrating on how to best cook with rations and instructing on the principles of basic cookery. A few years ago, I was lucky enough to acquire a collection of cookware and miscellaneous culinary paraphernalia mostly belonging to Brenda Russell, whose daughter, Carolyn Findell, donated to my private kitchenalia collection. Included in these items is a wonderful collection of recipes and training notes written during classes delivered by Marguerite Patten herself in London and attended by Brenda from January 1948 – October 1948.

Among Brenda's numerous jottings, Marguerite provided advice on classic pastry-making mistakes. If the pastry ends up too hard or 'cakey', then the cook has clearly added too much water; if tough, either the oven was too slow or the pastry too roughly handled. If the pastry ends up crumbly, then not enough water was added. She also recommended to her students that a dry bowl is essential for mixing the ingredients for pastry, with the fat (preferably grated) to be added first. Next comes the flour that should be mixed into the fat using 'forefinger and thumb', lifting the mixture high to add air.

After the Second World War most of Britain's flour was imported from Canada. It was during this period that domestic millers and bakers began to both protect and promote themselves in a growing competitive market, clawing their way out of the ruins of war. The

Margurite Patten 1948 Recipe For pastry from Brenda Russell's training notes. (@ *Emma Kay*)

Flour Advisory Bureau, established in 1956, which continues to thrive under the umbrella of 'nabim', The National Association of British and Irish Millers, founded in 1917, has a remit to promote the use of flour and bread products nationwide.

Today the UK grows the majority of its own wheat for flour production. Flour milling is as important to the nation now as it was hundreds of years ago, the difference being that water and windmills have evolved into highly technical automated systems. Some fifty-one mills, operated by thirty-two companies exist in the UK, of which the majority are members of nabim, there has been a resurgence in both the revival of old working mills as well as opening mills up as visitor attractions in recent years. Near to where I live, Shipton Mill stands as a working reminder of a structure that has been in place since at least the eleventh century. Lovingly restored some thirty years ago, it continues to produce the finest stoneground flour, which is stocked in shops throughout the

1930s flour bin and sifter. (@ *Nick Kay*)

Cotswolds and beyond and used by numerous local bakers, including one time TV and media favourites, The Fabulous Baker Brothers, AKA Tom and Henry Herbert, who run a small family chain of bakeries called Hobbs House.

Eling Tide Mill in Hampshire offers a vast array of activities with a Visitor Centre, Discovery and Activity Rooms. Rebuilt in the eighteenth century, it is one of just two known remaining Tide Mills in the UK. The other, Woodbridge, is located in Suffolk. A Tide Mill is a very specific structure driven by the rise and fall of the tides, an engineering feat thought to have been invented by the Romans.

Today, large-scale modern commercial milling is carried out on roller mills, consisting of two cylindrical steel rollers that break down, separate and sift the wheat. Some would argue that this method damages the grain considerably and dilutes its quality. The history of grinding is lengthy, with so many inventions, patents and types of mills developed throughout history, that I become quite dizzy with it all. I do know that if I could physically grind wheat myself in some way, using traditional methods, that this would always be my preferred way of accessing flour to use in baking.

Migrants and the Market-place

Possibly the most significant, and some might argue, damaging impact on post-war baking in Britain occurred with the introduction of the Chorleywood method in 1961. Developed by the British Baking Industries Research Association, in – you've got it, Chorleywood, Hertfordshire. They essentially pumped the dough with so many additives that the proofing time was drastically reduced, longevity of shelf-life increased and a softer loaf at a fraction of the cost was created. The Chorleywood process is a technically complex one, which is a book in itself. In fact, there are a number of small publications that specifically focus on this revolutionary development. For the purposes of remaining succinct, the upshot of this method worked on the principal first discovered by researchers Swanson and Working in the 1920s, who found that by mixing small amounts of dough for longer periods or at higher speeds, the outcome was a lighter bread.[46] It took many years to perfect this mechanically developed dough, which uses lower protein-based wheats, which are easier to grow in the UK, negating the need to import flour, among other benefits such as generating high-volume bread production in a short amount of time. Some of the disadvantages of this process include a loss of nutritional value, the creation of a bread with a much

Traditional Cypriot Baking.
(@ *Emma Kay*)

higher water, yeast and gluten content, dangerous fatty compounds and a concoction of additives and preservatives, including salt, linked to detrimental health issues. This industrial bread represents much of what Britain consumes each year, but remains increasingly controversial.

The revolution in post-war innovation and mass-production intrinsically altered the way we bake. The food mixer, electric whisk, electric ovens, electric everything. It was now possible for every British housewife to become a Cordon Bleu chef and patissier. Magazines for women were big business, publishing recipes and tips on a weekly basis. The television showed you how to cook, with TV chefs from Philip Harben, to the glamorous Fanny Craddock in the early days of broadcast, leading to a boom in this field, with the likes of Delia Smith and Keith Floyd, who initiated a cultish passion for cooking and baking that continues to grip national interest today with the Great British Bake Off leading the way.

Britain needed rebuilding after the war and The *Empire Windrush* has become synonymous with post-war migration, a time when citizens of the Caribbean responded en masse to British recruitment advertisements offering the chance of a new life. The long road to trading independently as

Rinkoff's Russian Bakery, London, founded 1911. (@ *Nick Kay*)

a migrant in Britain specialising in baked goods was not a new one. German and Jewish bakers, as well as Russian and Eastern European artisans were well established in London way before the *Windrush* era. The London Jewish Bakers' Union existed from 1905 to 1970; established to support the thriving Jewish Labour movement in the East of London at the end of the nineteenth century. The union protected and legitimised Jewish bakers who could guarantee kosher and well run, safe bakeries with decent working conditions. As with many bakeries during the Victorian era, stories circulated about poor working conditions and unsafe working environments. The *Grantham Journal* of Saturday 9 September, 1893 reported on Jewish bakers in London who alleged that they commenced work at five or six o'clock in the evening, continuing until around noon or 1pm the next day. For this they were paid an average weekly wage of 10*s*, a salary with the purchasing power of around £45.00 today. Conditions were described as 'frightfully insanitary', with many having to work on the Sabbath, behind closed shutters. Nonetheless, those early struggling founding Jewish bakers have left a legacy that continues to thrive today. The famous Beigel Bake of Brick Lane, London, which I have been to only twice, the last time probably in the 1990s, but which I still think of as a bakery for traditional hedonists,

Beigel Shop, established 1855, London. (@ *Nick Kay*)

where you don't mess with the tough counter-ladies seeking sustenance on your way back from the city's late night pubs and clubs. Founded in 1974 by the Cohen brothers (no, not the movie duo) it still provides a wonderful selection of traditional beigels (opposed to the Americanised Bagel) throughout the night. A few stops down the same road you can find the Beigel Shop, which boasts the title of the original and oldest beigel bakery in London, established in 1855. I bought a significant batch on a recent visit and they were really rather good.

Wonderful Patisserie, Chinatown, London. (@ *Nick Kay*)

Colonial returnees had been enjoying Indian food in London since the Victorian period and by the 1990s there were some 8,000 Indian restaurants operating in Britain.[47] The Chinese communities in the Limehouse district of London during the 1800s, expanded to Manchester after the Second World War, when a large wave of migrants descended from Hong Kong. Moon cakes could be found in all the Chinese grocers' shops in Britain from as early as the 1920s, while specialist Chinese bakeries have built a presence in the country since at least the 1970s, if not earlier.

Lotus seed Mooncakes

½ cup (125ml) Golden syrup
2 cups (300g) flour, sifted
1 teaspoon baking powder
½ cup (125 ml) oil
1 teaspoon alkaline water or bicarbonate of soda solution

1½ cups (450g) sweet lotus seed paste
10 salted preserved egg yolks(optional)
1 mooncake mould
1 egg yolk, beaten, for brushing

Sweet lotus seed paste

2½ cups (150g) skinned dried lotus seeds, soaked in water for 1 hour
½ cup (150ml) oil
¾ cup (150g) sugar
1 teaspoon maltose syrup

Make the lotus seed paste by boiling the lotus seeds in a pot of water over medium heat until soft, about 1 hour, then draining and grinding them to a smooth paste in a blender. Heat 2½ tablespoons of the oil in a non-stick wok or saucepan over high heat. Add 2 tablespoons of the sugar and stir until the mixture caramelises, 2 to 3 minutes. Reduce the heat to medium, add the lotus seed paste and mix well. Stir in the remaining sugar and mix until the sugar is dissolved. Gradually add the remaining oil and stir until the mixture is thick and pulls away from the sides of the pan, 20 to 30 minutes. Finally stir in the maltose syrup and remove from the heat. Cool the paste overnight before using. This makes about 1½ cups (450g) of sweet lotus paste.

To make the mooncake dough, combine the flour and baking soda in a mixing bowl. Make a well in the centre and gradually stir in the golden syrup, oil and alkaline water or bicarbonate of soda solution) mixing well with a wooden spoon. Flour your hands and knead the mixture into a soft dough. Cover with a cloth and set aside for 3 to 4 hours.

Once the dough and sweet lotus paste are ready, divide the sweet lotus seed paste into 10 equal portions, and then roll each portion into a ball between your palms. If using preserved egg yolks, press each paste ball with your thumb to make a depression, then insert a yolk and gather the edges of the paste around the yolk to enclose it.

On a floured surface divide the dough into 10 equal portions and roll each portion into a ball in a similar fashion. Repeat until all 10 mooncakes have been formed.

Bake the cakes in a preheated oven 400 degrees f (200 deg c) for about 15 minutes. Remove and brush the top of the cakes with the beaten egg. Return the cakes to bake for 6 to 8 more minutes or until golden brown.

To allow the pastry to mellow and taste better, leave the cakes to cool uncovered in a well-ventilated place for 1 to 2 days before eating.[48]

First and then second generation West Indian bakers also slowly began making their own culinary impression on the streets of post-war Britain. Sunrise Bakery, which was up until very recently (before it went to court for breaching hygiene regulations) still trading and providing the largest distribution of Caribbean baked products in the country from its premises in the West Midlands. Sunrise began trading in the mid-1960s, formed by Herman Drummond and his partner William Lamont. The business was based on Drummond's abilities to recreate his family recipes for hard dough, or 'hardo', bulla cake and spiced fruit buns for the UK market. They delivered the products to both domestic and commercial properties, expanding out from Birmingham, into Wolverhampton, Dudley, Walsall, Sandwell and other areas in the West Midlands where Caribbean and African communities were growing. Demand soon spread across the country and contracts were agreed with major supermarkets.[49] Similarly, Alvinos Caribbean Bakery in Manchester has sold its special patties and

Victorian Mooncake
Mould. (@ *Nick Kay*)

dumplings since the 1950s; the Old Trafford Bakery in Manchester, with its coco and banana bread and ginger cake, all lovingly baked since 1960, along with numerous other mid-twentieth-century Caribbean bakeries in London, one of the oldest still trading being Cornfield Bakers in Thornton Heath. All remain survivors of the *Windrush* era of culinary transfer to Britain.

Beef Patties

2 lbs ground turkey or beef
8 sprigs fresh thyme
2 oz scallion or about 10–13 stalks
2 scotch bonnet peppers, seeded
2 loaf French bread
6 cups water
2 tablespoons Jamaican seasoning
2 teaspoon garlic powder
2 teaspoon onion powder
2 teaspoon ground allspice
2 tablespoon beef base
2 tablespoons browning
2 teaspoon accent AKA MSG (optional)
2 small onions
2 oz gelatine
2 teaspoon salt

Grind scallions/onions and peppers in mincing ill

Add to the ground beef/turkey with all the other seasonings

Cook without adding any water or fat until the meat has lost its broth and only a certain amount of oil remains.

While meat is being cooked, pour sufficient boiled water over bread in a saucepan. Cover and soak for a few minutes.

Pass bread/little water through mincing mill until it is a semi-thick paste. Add to cooked meat, along with water. Continue to cook until meat mixture is thickened similar to the texture of warm oatmeal, about 10–15 minutes.

Remove from heat. Cool for filling pastry circles.

If patties need more seasoning, blend spices as listed and add until desired taste is achieved.[50]

Locally based UK bakers began to evolve and develop pioneering brands during the twentieth century, many of which retain a presence today.

Despite having its origins in the early Georgian era, William Crawford and Sons didn't become national distributors until the early 1900s, with large-scale factories operating out of Liverpool and Edinburgh. Their biscuits were popular with the troops in the First World War, with many fundraising towns like Stockport adding up to 1 lb of Crawford biscuits to food parcels sent to soldiers on the front line in far flung locations such as Greece, Mesopotamia, India and Malta.[51]

You would be forgiven for thinking that the vegan-sausage-roll-bragging, convenient high street pasty and doughnut outlet Greggs, is an example of a modern-day baking enterprise. It is, in fact, a company that started in the 1930s, against the backdrop of the Second World War by John Gregg, who built his empire up from selling eggs and yeast around Newcastle upon Tyne off the back of his bike.[52] The sausage roll is a much earlier incarnation, with the phrase coming into popular use around the turn of the nineteenth century, when they were nothing more than seasoned minced pork, rolled into sausage or cake

Turkish Bakery, Yunuslar Karadeniz, Bodrum. Turkish pastries influencing British pastry making. (@ *Emma Kay*)

shapes and fried. They were satirised for their characteristic greasiness in an 1844 edition of *Punch*.[53] The Italian *cannelon* – a stuffed sweet or savoury cone of pastry – was popular in Britain in the 1800s and at some stage, by my reckoning, the sausage meat began being wrapped in pastry like the *cannelon*, or any of the other continental pastry parcels of inspiration that would have existed at this time. Initially, a suet-based pastry was used to encase the sausage meat, which by at least the 1870s, had advanced to puff pastry. In hindsight, sausage rolls are probably an amalgam of many popular sausage-meat and sausage-based novelty dishes such as 'angels on horseback', originally oysters wrapped in bacon, pinned together with a wooden toothpick and served on toast with lemon. It was quite typical to insert two cloves at one end of the roll to make 'ears'. Perhaps this was an early pig in a blanket?[54] There is a well-known old Polish or Slavic dish comprising of minced meat, mixed with rice and herbs, then wrapped in cabbage leaves. In fact, there are versions of wrapped up meat encased in small sausage shapes all over the world, from the Danish 'sausage in a blanket', to the Chinese sausage wrapped in pastry, 'Lap Cheong Bao'. Any one of these may have inspired the sausage roll as we know it, which has been a staple savoury snack of choice in Britain for 150 years – be it meat or meat free – and one so basic in its composition, as this recipe from 1871 demonstrates. It is no wonder it remains a firm favourite.

Sausage Rolls

Have ready some nice sausage meat, which can always be obtained from the pork butchers. If you wish to make it, get some nice pork chops, cut the meat from the bones, or take two-thirds of lean free from gristle, and one-third fat, chop the meat very fine, and season it well with pepper, salt and spices, add a small quantity of sage, or basil, use a little water in chopping the meat, or else a little soaked bread.

Roll out some paste into square pieces, lay a roll of meat in the centre, lengthways; fold them so as to form long puffs, and wash them with egg before they are baked.[55]

Supermarket favourite, Jus-Rol pastry products also harken back to an earlier time of 1954, when Scottish baker Tom Forsyth had the notion to sell ready rolled pastry to his customers for convenience. His advertisements at the time boasted the product 'Gives More for Your Money'.[56] Similarly Mr Kipling – incidentally, never a real person, but you all knew, that right? Although it was said that the name was chosen by Rank Hovis MacDougall for its association with the writer and poet Rudyard Kipling, as a figure considered to be wholesome and trustworthy with an old-fashioned appeal. In today's social climate he is a little more controversial. The company capitalised on the fact that by the mid-1960s, women were spending more money on cakes than any other branded products at their local grocery stores. Six thousand women were surveyed by Ranks Hovis MacDougall, who used them as guinea pigs to sample twenty different varieties of their cakes in 1967.[57] Subsidiary company Manor Bakeries Ltd took responsibility for Mr Kipling cakes and ran a large-scale recruitment campaign for salesmen and merchandisers in 1967 in order to start distributing the new brand.[58] From this point, Mr Kipling became well received and remains a firm favourite across the nation.

The Ginster family roots are not Cornish, but West Midland based, with a legacy of working in agricultural produce. By the late 1960s the family had migrated to the West Country and were rapidly distributing their baked savoury products far and wide. Ginsters are now the biggest selling pasty-maker in the UK, but their origins lie in a deserted egg-packing warehouse in Callington, East Cornwall. From here they installed a few food mixers, some large ovens, a vegetable dicer and a conveyor belt; using a heavily protected recipe, said to hail from an old ships' cook method, began churning out their little baked parcels of joy at a rate of around two dozen a day. Back then they were mostly hand-made with staff 'peeling potatoes, crimping, baking, cleaning down and loading the delivery van'. A year after production began in 1970, Ginsters maintained a workforce of thirty, manufacturing some 48,000 pasties each day. Convenience foods were on the rise and it wasn't long before the company were supplying to major grocery stores across the country. They couldn't meet demand fast enough and expanded into sausage rolls and meat pies, gaining an annual profit of £200,000 by 1977, with a turnover of £1 million pounds. That same year, flying high on their successes, Geoffrey Ginster sold the company to the Samworth family, British food manufacturers who also make the country's beloved Melton Mowbray pork pies.[59] A descendant of the old traditional raised medieval hot water crust pies, pork pies became synonymous with the town of Melton Mowbray in Leicestershire sometime in the Victorian period. The only original firm left in the town today is Dickinson and Morris, based in Ye Olde Pork Pie Shoppe which was completely refurbished and reopened by the Samworth family in the 1990s following a devastating fire. Stephen Hallam, a master baker, was approached to revive both the business and the pie back to its former glory. In November 1992 the shop reopened with Hallam at the helm, together with a staff of eighteen. By 1997 it was selling over 4,000 pies a week. Ye Olde Pork Pie shop is now an official tourist attraction, with Stephen Hallam still at the heart of it.[60]

The first record I can find of W.D. Irwin trading in Portadown, Co. Armagh, is in 1905 as a grocer and provisions merchant.[61] By 1927 they appear to be running a successful baking business advertising Christmas cakes and fruit loaves 'made from the purest ingredients at our home bakery'.[62] Six years later, W.D. and his wife Ruth are acknowledged in a newspaper article praising their distinction in the grocery trade, alongside the bakery business which is quoted as being 'second to none in efficiency, quality and value'. The article goes on to list the popular baked products which are reaching 'the tables daily in hundreds of homes throughout the district', including 'plain and fancy bread, cakes and pastry'.[63] By the 1940s the business was branching out overseas, with contracts in the United States and Canada, and in 1947 the couple spent three months touring American and Canadian bakeries, visiting the most innovative of modern plants, who had adopted the latest in baking equipment.

Essentially the trip was an exchange of ideas and cultures, a chance for Canadian and American people to promote their nations to would-be Irish immigrants, and to impress the Irwin's enough to encourage them to spread the word on their return to Portadown.

A fashionable revolution in breadmaking came about in Ireland during the 1960s. Termed the 'Nutty Krust'; so called because it was baked on the oven floor to create a unique crusty flavour, this bread could be found across many bakeries in Ireland during the early 1960s, although Irwin's have always taken the credit for it. I'm sure they are the architects of this still hugely popular product, but I also think there is another much richer narrative to be found within W.D. and Ruth's baking history, that of extraordinary, forward-thinking pioneers who went looking for inspiration overseas and created skilled bakes that were often worthy of considerable press interest. Irwin's continues today and thankfully still remains in the hands of the family. The bakery premises relocated and expanded out to the Carne district of Portadown in the mid-1990s and is now Northern Ireland's largest independent bakery. Brian Irwin is quoted as saying that 'we aim to stay aware of customer tastes and needs and are very interested in establishing our products as firm favourites'.[64]

Another family baking institution, which came into its own during the twentieth century is Bradfords of Glasgow. Founded by Hugh Bradford and his sons in 1924 it has moved around the city more than a number nine bus, attempting to retain a shop front for almost 100 years, the bakery finally regenerated itself into an online business in 2013, but not before establishing an associated business – Miss Cranston's Tearooms. Catherine Cranston was herself an integral part of Glasgow's baking past, creating a chain of tea shops adorned with the designs of talented designers and architects including Charles Rennie Mackintosh, H&D Barclay and George Walton. Her father George was a baker and pastry-maker who became a successful hotelier, although it was his cousin Robert who financed Catherine's early tea shop empire.[65] Cranston's tearooms became a distinctive feature of the city. They provided smoking rooms, chess and billiard rooms and separate reading areas. Each table was adorned with a centrepiece – a three-tiered cake-stand predominantly filled with light tea-breads.[66] Here is a recipe for Devonshire Tea Breads, which would have been similar to those served in Miss Cranston's Tearooms

½ oz. yeast
½ teaspoon castor sugar
11/2 gills tepid milk
14oz. flour
Pinch salt

2 ½ medium apples
2 oz. margarine
Mixed spice to taste

Beat yeast and sugar to a cream in a heated basin. Stir in milk. Sift flour and salt into a basin. Mix into flour and cover. Stand in a warm place to rise for one to one and a half hours. Turn onto a lightly floured pastry board. Knead well for five minutes. Peel, core and mince apples. Melt margarine and stir both into dough with spice to taste. Place in a well-greased cake tin. Cover and stand in a warm place to rise for 20 to 30 minutes. Uncover and bake in a fairly hot oven, 375 deg. F., for three-quarters to one hour.[67]

With her first opening in 1874, Catherine, or Kate as she was better known, was one of the pioneers of the teashop trend, which grew out of the popularity of the temperance movement and their struggle to replace the wide consumption of alcohol across the UK during the nineteenth century. Cakes and pastries were a natural accompaniment to tea and I discovered an interesting recipe for a cake named after the society itself. Whether this was served up in any of Kate Cranston's tea rooms or not remains contentious, particularly as this is a recipe that was published in the United States.

Temperance cakes

Take two pounds of wheat flour, three fourths of a pound of fresh lard or butter, one pound of powdered white sugar, one nutmeg grated. After the flour and butter have been incorporated lay the sugar in, and pour upon it a small teaspoonful of boiling water. Have well beaten six eggs, and with a spoon incorporate them all well together, till it can be moulded with the hands: roll it thin, cut with a tumbler, and bake in a few minutes, in a quick oven, without turning.[68]

An alternative tea-bread that may have been served in Miss Cranston's establishments is the deliciously traditional Welsh Bara Brith. One of the major leading twentieth-century established bakeries in Wales, Village

Bakery, would perhaps have manufactured this tea-bread at some stage in its broad history spanning several generations of families and countless craft bakery awards. The small village of Minera in Wrexham is home to this bakery, whose credits include ownership of the UK's largest and most automated gluten-free bakery, Juvela. It is considered to be one of the fastest growing companies in Wales today.

Rival firm Garth Bakery, nearly forty years old, produce another historical Welsh cake, Teisen Lap, which was a well-known favourite in the coal mining villages of South Wales. The name stems from the word llap, meaning moist or wet. It was a cake originally baked in a Dutch oven in front of the fire. The following recipe is taken from Annette Yates's wonderful book of *Welsh Traditional Recipes*:

250g plain flour
1½ tsp baking powder
Pinch of salt
½ tsp grated nutmeg
125g butter, cut into small cubes
125g caster sugar
125g currants or sultanas
2 eggs lightly beaten
150ml milk or buttermilk

Preheat the oven to 190 degrees c/375 degrees F/ Gas 5. Butter a shallow 20–23cm/8–9in round baking tin.

Sift the flour, baking powder, salt and nutmeg into a large mixing bowl and stir in the sugar. Add the butter and, with your fingertips, rub it into the flour until the mixture resembles fine crumbs. Alternatively, do this in a food processor. Stir in the currants. Stir in the eggs with enough milk to give a mixture with a soft consistency that easily drops off the spoon.

Transfer the mixture to the prepared cake tin and level the surface.

Bake in the hot oven for 30–40 minutes, or until the cake has risen, is golden brown and cooked through. To check, a small skewer inserted in the centre should come out clean.

Leave in the tin for 5 minutes then turn out and cool on a wire rack.[69]

Patisserie Valerie, is a teashop come bakery chain that you might be mistaken for thinking of as a modern addition to our high streets. In fact, it was first opened in Frith Street in London's Soho in 1926 by Belgian born Madame Valerie. In 1900, she came to London on a mission to introduce fine continental patisserie to the English. Madame Valerie and her pastries were an instant success and are now synonymous with the brand and her clientele. Ryvita too, which I tend to associate with the 1970s for some reason, is also a brand with much earlier beginnings, started in Birmingham in 1925 and now partnered with an even older brand, Jordans, who have been around since the 1800s. Pork Farms, grew out of a pie shop of the same name purchased in the 1940s by pork pie specialist Ken Parr, who went on to develop their unique dark brown crispy pastry cases. The main post-war bakeries were Allied Bakeries, J. Lyons and Co, Lever Brothers and Rank Hovis McDougall, who absorbed many of the smaller baking companies like Allinson and Kingsmill. The white loaf became the principal bread of choice after the abolition of the National Wheat Meal Bread in 1956 and brown bread consumption

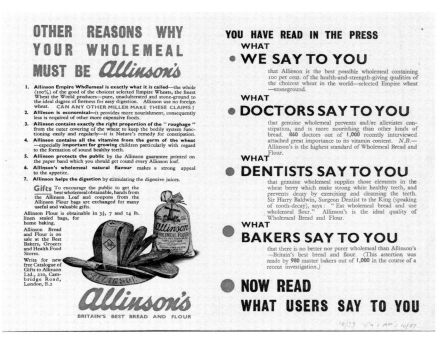

Allinson's Leaflet 1932 Wellcome Collection, Creative Commons Attribution. ((*CC BY 4.0*)*300*)

was almost at zero, while Sunblest sliced bread soon became a household staple.[70]

Post-war baking in Britain was all about convenience. The truck stop pasty and sausage roll, the stodgy white bread and sugar-loaded cupboard treats like Tunnock's caramel wafers, snowballs and teacakes, products that were all developed in the 1950s.

From the mouth of Bakers

In 2008 Andrew Whitley, in partnership with the charity Sustain, founded The Real Bread Campaign. Their overall mission was and continues to be about improving the quality of bread for the benefit of everyone. A whole host of awards have also been designed in the last few years to help raise the profile of craft bakers and champion their work, such as the Great Taste awards, Tiptree World Bread Awards and the Baking Industry Awards. Baking in Britain today is a vast rich mix of independent commercial enterprises, traditional and experimental craftsmen, culturally diverse and corporate mass production.

I visited and interviewed a number of businesses while researching this book to gauge a sense of what was important to them, in terms of

Shop Front, Marshall's Bakery, Pewsey, 1930s. (*Courtesy of Richard Marshall*)

the process of baking and its relevance both personally and for the wider community.

Of the bakers I was in contact with, two were retired and the geographical locations of these business spanned the North of England, Scotland, the South West, the Midlands and London. Only four had any formal college training, three at graduate level. Most bakers were self-taught, took informal courses, or learnt the trade from their parents and grandparents. Naturally there was a significant difference between bakers today and from the past, with the latter serving an ongoing, regular market with a variety of baked goods sold in

Alison McTaggart, Bread on a Bike. (*Courtesy of Alison McTaggart*)

the high street from sausage rolls and pies to cakes and biscuits. Many of today's independent bakers operate from their own homes, making variations of one or two products – mostly bread, cakes or pastries. They operate on a word of mouth basis or use the most popular tool for baking promotion – Instagram, the social media for glossy food-porn shots. It is interesting to note that if you go back far enough in history, working from the home was always how bakers traded. The trade has gone full circle. From street cart to private dwelling, to high street store, to supermarket and back to retailing from your own home or selling at Farmer's Markets. In fact, this is how I visualise most retail businesses evolving in the future. The demise of the high street will force people into trading from their homes or outdoor market places. 'Progress' is simply tipping the balance back into the past. Some bakers like Alison McTaggart from Cambridge's Bread on a Bike, and Elisabeth Mahoney's One Mile Bakery enterprise, which has become a national franchise, have gone a step further delivering their baked goods on two wheels.

Many of the bakers I interviewed felt strongly about the poor quality of supermarket, mass-produced bread. Caroline Walsh of the wonderful Archipelago Bakery in Edinburgh, who has been baking professionally for some thirteen years proclaimed:

Archipelago Bakery, Edinburgh. (*Courtesy of Caroline Walsh*)

I became so jaded with crap supermarket bread and all the rubbish that is in it – full of E numbers, sugar, excess salt, palm oil and a whole number of other things that should not be in there. It felt like the world was turning against bread and yet it is one of life's simple pleasures. But only if it's made properly. I really wanted to change people's perception of bread and wanted to use organic flour.

Incidentally, a large proportion of the bakers I spoke to used organic flour in their products and when questioned on their biggest economic challenges, the majority stated either the cost of flour, or more commonly the rapid increase in the price of dairy products gave them the greatest sleepless nights. Running costs, deliveries and general overheads all appeared in equal measure, as did the long hours and physical labour required to run a small baking business. Aside from the consistent approach to mainly utilising the sourdough method of bread and pastry making, there was also a powerful recurring contempt for the word 'artisan'. This of course, refers to a more craftsman like approach to breadmaking, but since being adopted by many large-scale commercial bakeries has somewhat sullied its original definition.

Artisan Bakery, Bourton on the Water. (@ *Emma Kay*)

Edward Clark of the deliciously tempting and visually impressive Norfolk based Pastonacre goes as far as to say: 'I find it a rather poncey adjective, all too often applied wrongly.' Is it time to dispense with this rather over-used and superficially applied word I wonder?

I think it's safe to say that I approached almost every single major commercial bakery in the UK to contribute to this book in some way. This was no mean feat. Without fail, every one of them declined (some more politely than others). I thought this rather odd, but received a much warmer reception from the chaps that oversee most of them:

Edward Clark, Pastonacre. (*Courtesy of Edward Clark*)

The Federation of Bakers. Despite being an advocate for good bread, made in the most natural way possible, it was logical that I speak to those industries involved in its mass production.

Sadly, Geoff Permain's family bakery was a casualty of this consumerist supermarket-driven boom in the 1970s. W. Permain and Sons Ltd of Southampton was an independent family bakery with four or five shops and a large wholesale customer base. It had traded since the nineteenth

Permain's delivery cart. (*Courtesy of Geoff Permain*)

century, spanning several generations, fighting off competition from the dozen or so other bakers in the immediate locality, but it could not compete with the big players and when the supermarkets moved into Freemantle, the Permains' had to move out. Geoff, the last baker in the family, decided 'if you can't beat them, join them'! And ended up applying his skills to the in-house bakeries for some of the country's leading supermarket chains. Tony Greenwood was also a contributor to the burgeoning post-war baking boom of the 1960s through to the 80s. His father sold G. Greenwood Baker and Confectioner, also based in Southampton, after the war and the following transcript details how Tony went on to use his skills in baking in the changing social and economic landscape of the mid- and latter part of the twentieth century:

> When I was a student, I worked at Mothers Pride in Eastleigh near Southampton, just sweeping the floors but I enjoyed seeing the production process for the sliced bread and the 'morning goods' which were mainly bread rolls, I think. I was lucky to get that job – the company had just taken over and closed another bakery in Eastleigh and so had to absorb as many workers as they could from the one

that had closed. I think it was owned by Rank Hovis McDougal. The machines were mainly Baker Perkins, which I assume was a Perkins Engineering brand. After I finished my degree, I worked at Manor Bakeries for probably about nine months doing all the jobs on the Fondant Fancy plant. It was their policy to train everybody at everything. My main job was watching the fondant section of the process to make sure the tanks didn't run out, the consistency was right, the colour was right, the weight of the cakes was right. There was some mixing of men and women but generally it was women who packed the cakes by hand and mainly men who made them. Women who had been promoted were more likely to be seen doing every job though. Most of the women packers spoke either Hindi or Guajarati (Tony later corrected this to Urdu) but most of the men were white British. One in particular was very keen to use the opportunity to learn an Indian language. While I was there, the first fully automatic production line was installed. It made an individual portion sized tart which was a pastry case containing jam, possibly fruit, and a

G. Greenwood Baker and Confectioner, Southampton in the 1900s. (*Courtesy of Tony Greenwood*)

synthetic cream topping. Even the packing was mechanised. I think they might have called the packing machine a Franklin Transfer but I could very well be making that up! I made the fondant sometimes which was a horrible hot noisy job with temperamental machines but just as I was leaving that was automated. They were also about to start including some automation in the ingredient mixing process.

What I love so much about Tony's description here is the fact that it mentions some of the big contemporary companies that came into their own during the twentieth century, along with the nod to technological advancement and the acknowledgement of the changing face of Britain's diverse multi-ethnic workforce at this time.

With only one exception (they didn't actually answer the question) every baker I interviewed stated that they remember baking at home as children with either their parents or grandparents and they all felt passionately about the importance of educating children to bake, to understand what they are eating and how to eat well. Something that today's school system with its diluted subject curriculums might benefit from.

Where all the bakers did differ was in their choice of favoured baking equipment. I really enjoy asking bakers and cooks generally which item in the kitchen is invaluable to them. As a baker of fine brownies, Heidi Wall, who runs Boutique Brownies from her home in Essex, felt that the spatula was the champion of culinary support. For Alison McTaggart from Bread on a Bike, a pair of scales rated as one of the highest, although she had to admit that a good dough knife, scraper and scorer were also essential. Others mentioned their KitchenAids, ovens and the need to have a good working room with the right temperature, but for me,

Heidi Wall, Boutique Brownies. (*Courtesy of Heidi Wall*)

Vitor Santos of the inspiring Celtic Bakers of London, provided an obvious, perhaps, but certainly the most taken for granted of answers, simply, his hands.

I spent a wonderful morning chatting to Richard Marshall at Marshall's bakery in Pewsey. Richard is the last of his generation to run the bakery after his grandfather and father. He emphasised the difficulties of adapting to modern dietary needs, highlighting the expenses involved with adapting a bakery to be safely gluten or nut free, and the constant issues relating to contamination, which I must admit I had never really considered in much depth. Sesame seeds, it seems, are the

Vitor Santos, Celtic Bakers, London. (*Courtesy of Vitor Santos*)

bane of his life, to the extent to which he has banned them from the premises. Apparently, they spread everywhere, their presence a constant

Interior of Marshall's Bakery, Pewsey. (*Courtesy of Richard Marshall*)

source of annoyance infesting the smallest of nooks and crannies! Richard gave me a tour of his premises, showing me the proofing cabinets, large-scale commercial ovens and huge dough mixers. All a far cry from the beehive brick ovens, wooden kneading boards and troughs of the past. In many larger bakeries today you are likely to find evidence of the 'Koenig' technology invented by Helmut Koenig, whose baking engineering skills of the 1960s and 70s led to the invention of numerous labour-saving baking aids offering regulated temperature and humidity levels, energy efficient ovens with multi-decks and rotating rollers to shape and size bread products and perfect the process of uniformed

Interior Marshalls Bakery, work station. (*Courtesy of Richard Marshall*)

baking. Incidentally, the Village Bakery in Minera, Wales, was the first UK craft bakery to invest in Koenig roll baking plant equipment in 1980.

So, what of the big guns, the large corporate, consumer-driven factories? As mentioned previously, none of them felt obliged to divulge

Marshall's Bread Ovens, Marshall's Bakery, Pewsey. (*Courtesy of Richard Marshall*)

their secrets. However, the Federation of Bakers, established during the Second World War who now 'represent[s] the interests of the UK's largest baking companies', who manufacture sliced and wrapped bread, bakery snacks and other bread products. These include Allied Bakeries, Jackson's Bakeries, DeliFrance, Kerry, Warburtons, Irwins, Roberts and so on. The Federation admitted that there were very different patterns of bread consumption in the South compared to the North and that socio-economic factors also featured within this, but that they didn't have the data to share. They cited 'Below cost selling, competition/market saturation, health perceptions' as the main factors affecting larger-scale bakeries.

Judging by the success of the independent bakers I spoke to and the sheer number of thriving home bakers and small-scale bakeries applying traditional techniques such as sourdough, using high-end, natural ingredients, there is a definite growing market and demand for quality bread, other than that supplied by the larger manufacturers.

Is this a serious concern for the future of Federation bakeries? And what is the overall future for baking? Will technology soon make it possible to generate the perfect sourdough in minutes? Will the world even continue to grow wheat, or breed cows for dairy? We live in such uncertain times, it's impossible to know how the impact of climate change will alter everyday patterns, or how future economies will be able to manage and sustain the lifestyles so many of us depend on. Will the 'staff of life', which has sustained Britain's communities for thousands

Federation of Bakers, courtesy of Federation of Bakers.

of years become a very different kind of staff, one made from alternative resources? Perhaps the cassava bread so readily dismissed in those early days of Empire will dominate the shelves. Maybe we will all be making our own bread.

Over the centuries Britain has learnt to manage the land, adapt and reshape it for purpose. Will this again prove to be the solution? While writing this book, it has occurred to me just how much society has manipulated baking to suit the palette, the climate, the situation, the social and economic environment. People have always found a way to get the best out of baking and I think this is probably where its destiny lies.

Notes

Introduction

1. Buchan, W, *Domestic Medicine: A Treatise on the prevention and cure of Diseases* (U.P. James, 1838).
2. *Magazine of Domestic Economy and Family Review* 1838–1842 (W.S. Orr & Co., London, 1838).
3. Francatelli, C.E., *The Modern Cook,* (Bentley, London, 1846) 395.
4. British Newspaper Archive, *Dundee Courier* (Saturday 14 November 1885).
5. *Ladies Home Journal Volume 29*, (Philadelphia, 1912) 35.
6. Markham, G., *The English Housewife* (Hannah Saw bridge, London, 1615)
7. Tschirky, O., *The Cook Book of Oscar Tschirky* (The Saalfeld Publishing Co., Chicago, 1896) 695
8. Jacob, E., *Physicall and chyrurgicall receipts. Cookery and preserves* (1654–1685). Wellcome Trust Archive, Ref: MS3009.
9. British Newspaper Archive, *Yorkshire Evening Post* (Friday 4 July 1930).
10. *Baking Mad*, 'Classic Wholemeal Loaf by Allinson's', online at https://www. bakingmad.com/recipe/classic-wholemeal-loaf-by-allinson (accessed, 03/10/2019).

Chapter One

1. Sarah Knapton. 'World's oldest bread shows hunter-gatherers were baking 4,000 years before birth of farming', *The Daily Telegraph* 16 July, 2018 https://www.telegraph.co.uk/science/2018/07/16/worlds-oldest-bread-shows-hunter-gathers-baking-4000-years-birth/.
2. Gisslen, W, *Professional Baking*, fifth edition, (John Wiley & sons: New Jersey and Canada, 2008) 4.
3. Spalinger, A.J., *War in Ancient Egypt: The New Kingdom* (Blackwell Publishing, USA, 2008) 151.
4. Ezzamel, M., *Accounting and Order,* (Routledge, New York, 2012).5
5. Amr Hussein, M., *The Pharaoh's Kitchen: Recipes from Ancient Egypt's Ednduring food Traditions.* (American University in Cairo Press, Cairo and NY, 2010) 25–30.6
6. Gisslen, W., *Professional Baking*, fifth edition, (John Wiley& sons: New Jersey and Canada,2008) 4. 7
7. 'Upton St Leonards', in *Ancient and Historical Monuments in the County of Gloucester Iron Age and Romano-British Monuments in the Gloucestershire Cotswolds* (London, 1976) 123. *British History Online* http://www.british-history.ac.uk/rchme/ancient-glos/p123a (accessed 2 March 2019).
8. Cubberley, A.L. Lloyd, J.J., Roberts, P.C., 'Testa and Clibani: the Baking Covers of Classical Italy', *Papers of The British School at Rome,* vol. 56 (1988) 989

9. Elliot, P., *Food and Farming in Prehistoric Britain*, (Fonthill Media, 2017).10
10. White, J., *A Treatise on the Art of Baking*, (Anderson and Bryce, Edinburgh, 1828) 175.11
11. Dommers Vehling, J., (ed.) *Apicius, Cookery and Dining in Imperial Rome, A Bibliography*, *Critical Review and Translation of the Ancient Book known as Apicius de re Coquinaria* ,(Dover Publications, New York,1977) 12
12. 'Roman Baking', Benton, J.T., (2016) (accessed 12 March 2019).
13. 'Bakers and the Baking Trade in the Roman Empire' Morgan, H, (2015) http://www.academia.edu/13319823/Bakers_and_the_Baking_Trade_in_the_Roman_Empire_Social_and_Political_Responses_from_the_Principate_to_Late_Antiquity_(accessed 12 March 2019) 14
14. Dommers Vehling, J., (ed.) *Apicius, Cookery and Dining in Imperial Rome, A Bibliography*, *Critical Review and Translation of the Ancient Book known as Apicius de re Coquinaria*,(Dover Publications, New York,1977) 97.15
15. *Notices and Anecdotes Illustrative of the Incidents, Charcters and Scenery Described in the Novels and Romances of Sir Walter Scott* (Baudry's European Library, Paris, 1833) 350.
16. Faas, P., *Around the Roman Table: Food and Feasting in Ancient Rome*, (University of Chicago, 2005) 6.
17. Bennett, H.S., *A Study of Peasant Conditions 1150–1400*, in Coulton, G.G (ed.) *Medieval Life and Thought*, (Cambridge University Press, London,1938).
18. Gouldman, F., *A Copius Dictionary in Three Parts*, (John Hayes, London 1674).
19. 'Ancient Roman Recipes', Raimer, C, (2000) https://www.pbs.org/wgbh/nova/article/roman-recipes/ (accessed 4 April 2019).
20. Hagan, A., *A Handbook of Anglo Saxon Food*,. (Anglo Saxon Books,1992) 9.
21. Ibid. 11–12.
22. Gautier, A *Cooking and Cuisine in late Anglo-Saxon England*, in Anglo-Saxon England Vol. 41 ,(2013) 373–406
23. Ibid.
24. Gimpel, J., (1977) *The Medieval Machine: The Industrial Revolution of the Middle Ages*, (Penguin, London,1977).
25. Banham,D, Faith, R, *Anglo-Saxon Farms and Farming* (Oxford University Press, Oxford, 2014) 219.
26. Ibid. 22
27. Ibid. 29
28. Cockayne, T.O., *Leechdoms, Wortcunning and Starcraft of Early England*, Vol. 3. 1866, (Longmans, Green, Reader and Dyer,1866) 135.
29. Hagan, A., *A Handbook of Anglo Saxon Food* (Anglo Saxon Books,1992) 59.
30. Ibid. 58.
31. Dewing, H.B. (ed.) *The Wars of Justinian'*, *Procopius*, (Hackett Publishing Co. Inc Indianapolis/Cambridge 2014) 173.
32. Mac Veigh, J, *International Cuisine*, (Cengage Learning,2006,U.S.A) 146.
33. Major, A, P., *The Book of Seaweed*, (Gordon & Cremonesi, 1977).
34. 'Vickery TV', Laverbread bread, https://vickery.tv/phil-vickerys-recipes/this-morning/item/laverbread-bread (accessed 13 september, 2019).

35. The British Newspaper Archive, *Yorkshire Evening Post* (Wednesday 10 February 1915).
36. Smith, E., *The Compleat Housewife: Or Accomplished Gentlewoman's Companion* (J. Pembertton, London) 97.
37. Andrews, C, *The Country Cooking of Ireland*, (Chronicle Books, California, 2012) 120
38. Whelan, F., Petrizzo, F., Spenser, O., (ed.) *The Book of the Civilised Man: An English Translation of the Urbanus magnus of Daniel of Beccles* (Routledge, London, 2019) 137.
39. Ibid.
40. Whelan, F., *The Making of Manners and Morals in Twelfth-Century England: The Book of the Civilised Man*,(Routledge, London and New York, 2017) 164.
41. Riley, H.H., (ed.) *Memorials of London and London Life in the 13th, 14th and 15th Centuries*, (Longmans, Green, London, 1868) 118–123.
42. Taken from John Strype's *A Survey of the City of London* (accessed 2 April 2019) https://www.dhi.ac.uk/strype/TransformServlet?page=book2_022&display=normal&highlight=+Bakers
43. Maitland, W., *The Court-Baron Pub* (Selden Society, 1891) 73.
44. Taken from John Strype's *A Survey of the Cities of London and Westminster* (accessed 02 April 2019) https://www.dhi.ac.uk/strype/
45. 'Folios xci – xcix: Sept 1378 -', in *Calendar of Letter-Books of the City of London: H, 1375–1399*, (ed.) Reginald R Sharpe (London, 1907) pp. 97–111. *British History Online* http://www.british-history.ac.uk/london-letter-books/volh/pp97-111 (accessed 21 September 2019).
46. J.S. Barrow, J.D. Herson, A.H. Lawes, P.J. Riden and M.V.J. Seaborne, 'Economic infrastructure and institutions: Craft guilds', in *A History of the County of Chester: Volume 5 Part 2, the City of Chester: Culture, Buildings, Institutions*, (ed.) A.T. Thacker and C.P. Lewis (London, 2005) pp. 114–124. *British History Online* http://www.british-history.ac.uk/vch/ches/vol5/pt2/pp114-124 (accessed 21 September 2019).
47. Pilkington, M.C., *Bristol*, (University of Toronto Press, Canada,1997) 30.
48. Chansky, D., White, Ann, (ed.) *Food and Theatre on the World Stage*, (Routledge, New York, 2016).
49. Gonzalez-Wippler, M., *The Complete Book of Spells, Ceremonies and Magic* (Llewellyn Publications, Minnesota, 1978) 262.
50. Jolly, K., *Witchcraft and Magic in Europe. Vol 3: The Middle Ages*, (Athlone Press, 2002) 18.
51. Kieckhefer, R., *Magic in the Middle Ages*, (Cambridge University Press, 2014) 89.
52. Worth, V., *Crone's Book of Magical Words*, (Llewellyn Publications, Minnesota, 2004) 58.
53. Ibid. 51.
54. Kay, E., *Dining with the Victorians*, (Amberley, Gloucestershire, 2015).
55. Matossian, M., *Poisons of the Past: Molds, Epidemics and History* (Yale University Press, 1989) 113.
56. Winsham, W., *England's Witchcraft Trials*, (Pen and Sword, Yorkshire, 2018).

57. *Notes and Queries,* (Oxford University Press, 1878) 490.

58. Slater, H. *A Book of pagan Rituals,* 1978 (Weiser Books, Boston USA, 1978) 23–24

59. Redstone, Lilian J., 'The history of All Hallows Church: To c.1548', in *Survey of London: Volume 12, the Parish of All Hallows Barking, Part I: the Church of All Hallows* (London, 1929) pp. 1–20. *British History Online* http://www.british-history.ac.uk/survey-london/vol12/pt1/pp1-20 (accessed 13 September 2019).

60. Bailey, N., *The New Universal Etymological English Dictionary,* (W. Cavell, London, 1775).

61. The British Newspaper Archive, *Illustrated London News* (Saturday 15 August 1846).

62. *Table Talk .Volume 24 number* 12. (London, 1909) 477

63. *The Gentleman's Magazine, Volume 64,* (E. Cave. London, 1794) 1153.

64. May, R., *Accomplisht Cook,* (Obadiah Blagrove, London, 1685).

65. The British Newspaper Archive, *Airdrie & Coatbridge Advertiser,* (Saturday 28 December, 1907).

66. Russell, J., *The Boke of Nurture, c.1460–70,* (J. Childs and Son, London, 1867) 33.

67. Jeake, S., *Arithmetick surveyed and reviewed: in four books, etc.* (1696).

68. 'Prebendaries: Moreton Parva', in *Fasti Ecclesiae Anglicanae 1066–1300: Volume 8, Hereford,* (ed.) J S Barrow (London, 2002) pp. 50–51. *British History Online* http://www.british-history.ac.uk/fasti-ecclesiae/1066-1300/vol8/pp50-51 (accessed 14 September 2019).

69. 'Close Rolls, Edward II: July 1317', in *Calendar of Close Rolls, Edward II: Volume 2, 1313–1318,* (ed.) H C Maxwell Lyte (London, 1893) pp. 556–560. *British History Online.* http://www.british-history.ac.uk/cal-close-rolls/edw2/vol2/pp556-560 (accessed 14 September 2019).

70. 'London tradesmen and their creditors: (G. Unwin)', in *Finance and Trade Under Edward III the London Lay Subsidy of 1332,* (ed.) George Unwin (Manchester, 1918) pp. 19–34. *British History Online* http://www.british-history.ac.uk/manchester-uni/london-lay-subsidy/1332/pp19-34 (accessed 14 September 2019).

71. I also discovered that Henry V forbade the baking of simnel loaves during Lentin 1417. 'Memorials: 1417', in *Memorials of London and London Life in the 13th, 14th and 15th Centuries,* (ed.) H. T. Riley (London, 1868) pp. 644–660. *British History Online* http://www.british-history.ac.uk/no-series/memorials-london-life/pp644-660 (accessed 14 September 2019).

72. Knight, R., *A discourse on the worship of Priapus and its connection with the mystic theology of the anciets,* (London,1865)158

73. Hindley, C., *A History of the cries of London,* (Reeves and Turner, London, 1881) 217

74. Harrison, S., *The House-keeper's pocket-book; And complete Family cook,* (R. Ware, 1739) 134.

75. The British Newspaper Archive, *Bellshill Speaker* (Friday 24 March 1939).

76. 'House of Lords Journal Volume 7: 2 April 1645', in *Journal of the House of Lords: Volume 7, 1644* (London, 1767–1830) pp. 299–301. *British History Online* http://www.british-history.ac.uk/lords-jrnl/vol7/pp299-301 (accessed 28 February 2019).

77. Langland,W, *Piers Plowman: A New Translation of the B-text,* (Oxford University Press, Oxford) 1992.

78. Coote, L.A., (ed.)*The Canterbury Tales*, Geoffrey Chaucer, (Wordsworth Poetry Library, Hertfordshire, 2002) 203, 603.

79. Watkins, A.E., (ed.) *Ælfric's Colloquy*, http://www.kentarchaeology.ac/authors/016.pdf (accessed 15 September, 2019).

80. Monk, M., Sheehan, J., (ed.) *Early Medieval Munster: Archaeology, History and Society*, (Cork University Press, 1999) 81.

81. Russell, J., *The Boke of Nurture*, c.*1460–70*, (J. Childs and Son, London,1867) 1468.

82. *The Forme of Cury, 1390, by the Master-Cooks of King Richard II*, available online. Samuel Pegge(ed.) 2013. http://www.gutenberg.org/cache/epub/8102/pg8102-images.html accessed 21 September 2019.

83. Austin, T., (ed.) *Two fifteenth-century cookery-books*: Harleian MS. 279 (ab. 1430) & Harl. MS. 4016 (ab. 1450) with extracts from Ashmole MS. 1439, Laud MS. 553, & Douce MS. 55 (Oxford University Press, London, New York, Toronto,1996) 47.

84. Wilson, C.A., *Food and Drink in Britain* (Cookery Book Club,London,1973) 56.

85. Morris, R., (ed.) *Liber Cure Cocorum*, (Philological Society, Berline,1862) 95

86. Hensperger, B., *The Bread Lover's Bread Machine Cookbook* (Harvard Common Press, USA) 56.

87. Austin, T (ed.) *Two fifteenth-century cookery-books*: Harleian MS. 279 (ab. 1430) & Harl. MS. 4016 (ab. 1450) with extracts from Ashmole MS. 1439, Laud MS. 553, & Douce MS. 55 (Oxford University Press, London, New York, Toronto,1996).

88. Wilson, C.A., *Food and Drink in Britain* (Cookery Book Club,London,1973) 201

89. Morris, R., (ed.) *Liber Cure Cocorum*, (Philological Society, Berline,1862) 16.

90. Glasse, H., *The Art of Cookery made plain and easy*. (A. Millar, London, 1763) 152.

91. Russell, J., *The Boke of Nurture*, c.*1460–70*, (J. Childs and Son, London, 1867).

92. Warner, R., *Antiquitates Culinarie. Or Curious Tracts Relating to the Culinary Affairs of the Old English* (Blamire, London,1791) 27.

93. Dawson, T., *The Good Huswifes Handmaide for the Kitchin*, (Richard Jones,London, 1594).

94. Austin, T., (ed.) *Two fifteenth-century cookery-books*: Harleian MS. 279 (ab. 1430) & Harl. MS. 4016 (ab. 1450) with extracts from Ashmole MS. 1439, Laud MS. 553, & Douce MS. 55 (Oxford University Press, London, New York, Toronto,1996) 47

Chapter Two

1. Lamb, A.L., Evans, J.E., Buckley, R., 'Multi-isotope analysis demonstrates significant lifestyle changes in King Richard III', *Journal of Archaeological Science*, Vol 50, (2014) 559–565.

2. Napier, A., (ed.) *A Noble boke off cookry ffor a prynce houssolde or eny other estately houssolde: reprinted verbatim from a rare ms. in the Holkham collection* (Elliot Stock, London, 1882).

3. Brander, G., (ed.) *Forme of Curye, 1390*, (1780) 29 https://archive.org/stream/theformeofcury08102gut/7cury10.txt (accessed on 12 September, 2019).

4. Austin, T., (ed.) *Two fifteenth-century cookery-books*: Harleian MS. 279 (ab. 1430) & Harl. MS. 4016 (ab. 1450) with extracts from Ashmole MS. 1439, Laud MS. 553, & Douce MS. 55 (Oxford University Press, London, New York, Toronto,1996)

5. *Letters and Papers, Foreign and Domestic, Henry VIII, Volume 4, 1524–1530*. (Her Majesty's Stationery Office, London, 1875).

6. Gairdner, J., Brodie, R.H., (ed.) *Letter from Marillac to Francis I, 1541 Letters and papers, Foreign and Domestic, Henry VIII, Volume 16, 1540–1541*, (Her Majesties Stationery Office, London, 1898).

7. Lewis, S., (ed.) *A Topographical Dictionary of England*, (Samuel Lewis, 1848) 520–523.

8. *Calendar of the Manuscripts of the Dean and Chapter of Wells: Volume 2*, (HM Staionery Office, London, 1914) 97–98.

9. Riley, T.H., *Memorials of London and London Life in the 13th, 14th and 15th centuries*, (Longmans, Green, London, 1868) 428–438.

10. Cole, M.H., *The Portable Queen: Elizabeth I and the Politics of Ceremony* (University of Massachusetts Press, 1999, USA) 42.

11. Dawson, T., *The Good Huswifes Handmaide for the Kitchin*, (Richard Jones, London, 1594).

12. Evelyn, J., *Acetaria: A Discourse of Sallets*, (Women's Auxilary, Brooklyn USA, 1937).

13. Myers, D., (ed.) *The commonplace book of Countess Katherine Seymour Hertford (1567)'A briefe discourse of the m[…] and order of the d[epar]ting of the Ladye Katherine by one hole night wherin she dyet in the morning.'* (University of Pennsylvania, 2007).

14. Kaufman, H., *Black Tudors: The Untold Story* (Oneworld Publications, 2017)

15. Gregg, P., *King Charles I*, (University of California Press, 1984, USA) 22.

16. White, P., *King: Charles I, Traitor, Murdere, Martyr Leanda de Lisle*, (Random House, 2018).

17. Jenks, J., *The Complete cook: Teaching the Art of cookery in all its Branches* (J. Potts and J. Williams. Dublin, 1769) 239.

18. Markham, G., *The English Huswife, extracted from the original work published in 1653*, (Grosvenor Library, London, 1908) 37

19. Carlton, C., *Going to the wars: The Experience of the British Civil Wars 1638–1651* (Routledge, London and New York, 2003) 95.

20. Ibid. 96.

21. Ibid. 164

22. Askew, R., *The House of everyone:the consumption of material culture in castles during the English Civil War, vol 1.* 44.

23. Mest, M.R., (ed.) *The English Housewife*, (McGill-Queens University Press, Canada,1986) 162.

24. Mayerne, Sir Theodore, *Archimagirus Anglo-Gallicus; or, excellent and approved receipts and experiments in cookery. Together with the best way of preserving. As also, rare formes of sugar works; according to the French mode and English manner* (Bedell & T.Collins, London, 1658).

25. Ibid. 76

26. Holme, R., *The Third Chapter of the Book of the Academy of Armory and Blazon, Chap. VII Academy of Armory*, (Chester,1688) 315–16 .

27. Smith, R., *Court Cookery, or the Compleat English Cook*, (T.Wooton, London, 1725) 165.

28. Eaton, M., *The Cook and Housekeeper's Complete and Universal Dictionary* (J and R Childs, 1822) 286.

29. British Newspaper Archives, *Northern Whig* (Wednesday 19 April 1939).
30. Carraro, L.F., 'Susanna Centilivre', (The Literary Encyclopedia, 2001).
31. Bucholz, R.O., *The Augustan Court: Queen Anne and the Decline of Court Culture* (Stanford university Press, California, 1993) 308
32. Crossley, A., Chane, E., Colvin, C., Cooper, J., Day, C.J., Hassall, T.G., (ed.) *Early Modern Oxford*, in *A History of the County of Oxford: Volume 4, the City of Oxford.*
33. Lewis, C.P., Thacker, A.T., *Early modern Chester 1550–1762: Economy and society, 1550–1642* in *A History of the County of Chester: Volume 5 Part 1, the City of Chester: General History and Topography.* Originally published by (Victoria County History, London, 2003) 102–109.
34. Page, W., A History of the County of Northampton: Volume 3. (Victoria County History, London, 1930) 1–26.
35. Styles, P., (ed.) 'The borough of Stratford-upon-Avon: Historical account', in *A History of the County of Warwick: Volume 3, Barlichway Hundred*, (London, 1945) pp. 234–244. *British History Online* http://www.british-history.ac.uk/vch/warks/vol3/pp234-244 (accessed 27 February 2019).
36. McKinley, R.A, (ed.) 'The City of Leicester: Political and administrative history, 1509–1660', in *A History of the County of Leicester: Volume 4, the City of Leicester*, (London, 1958) 55–75. *British History Online* http://www.british-history.ac.uk/vch/leics/vol4/pp55-75 (accessed 27 February 2019).
37. Malden, H.E., (ed.) *A History of the County of Surrey: Volume 3* (London, 1911) 560–570. *British History Online* http://www.british-history.ac.uk/vch/surrey/vol3/pp560-570 Caccessed 27 February 2019).
38. Farrer, W., Brownbill, J., 'Townships: Manchester (part 2 of 2)', in *A History of the County of Lancaster: Volume 4*, (ed.) William Farrer and J. Brownbill (London, 1911) 230–251. *British History Online* http://www.british-history.ac.uk/vch/lancs/vol4/pp230-251 (accessed 27 February 2019).
39. Crittall, E., (ed.) 'Salisbury: Trade companies since 1612', in *A History of the County of Wiltshire: Volume 6* (London, 1962) 136–138. *British History Online* http://www.british-history.ac.uk/vch/wilts/vol6/pp136-138 (accessed 28 February 2019).
40. Lockyer, R., *Tudor and Stuart Britain: 1485–1714* (Routledge, 2004).
41. Cox, D.C., Edwards, J.R., Hill, R.C., Kettle,A.J., Perren, R., Rowley, T., Stamper, P.A., 'Domesday Book: 1540–1750', in *A History of the County of Shropshire: Volume 4, Agriculture*, (ed.) G.C., Baugh and C.R. Elrington (London, 1989) 119–168. *British History Online* http://www.british-history.ac.uk/vch/salop/vol4/119-168 (accessed 27 February 2019).
42. Dugdale, J., The New British Traveller, (J. Robins and Company, 1819, London) 375
43. Page, C., *The Guitar in Stuart England: A Social and musical history.*(Cambridge University Press, 2017) 122.
44. Shakespeare, W., *Troilus and Cressida*, (Cambridge University Press, 2005) 95.
45. Markham, G., *Country Contentments, or The English Huswife*, 1623 R. Jackson, London, 1623) 231.
46. Shakespeare, W., Uyl, A., (ed.) *Titus Andronicus The Tragedy of Titus Andronicus* (Devoted publishing, Canada, 2016)

47. Darley, G., *John Evelyn: Living for Ingenuity*, (Yale University Press, New Haven and London, 2006).

48. Houghton, J., John Evelyn, *Panificium*, 1666, in *A Collection Of Letters For the Improvement Of Husbandry And Trade* (Woodman and Lyon, London, 1728).

49. Digby Knight, K., *The Closet of Sir Kenelm Digby Knight Opened*, (London, 1669) 215.

50. Francois Massialot, *The Court and Country Cook* (A&J Churchill, M. Gillyflower, London, 1702) 103.

51. Pepys, S., *The Diary of Samuel Pepys*, (B&R Samizdat Express, 2018).

52. Machyn, H., *The Diary of Henry Machyn*, (Camden Society, Longmans, London, 1838).

53. Gouffe, J., *The Book of Preserves* (S. Low, Son and Marston, London, 1871) 230–31.

54. Defoe, D., *A Journal of the Plague Year*, (1722) 209.

55. Ibid. 3.

56. Ibid. 169.

57. Creighton, C., *A History of Epidemics in Britain, Volume 1* (C.J. Clay and Sons. Cambridge University Press, 1891) 539.

58. McCavour, T., *Killed by Fire* (Friesen Press, Canada, 2017) 112.

59. Forsyth, H., *Butcher, Baker, Candlestick Maker: Surviving the Great Fire of London* (I.B. Tauris, London and New York, 2016) 77.

60. Ibid. 24.

61. Kidder, E., Receipts of pastry and cookery: for the use of his scholars, Edward Kidder (London, 1720).

62. British Newspaper Archives, *Daily Mirror* (Friday 24 July 1964).

63. British Newspaper Archives *Daily Mirror* (Monday 13 July 1964).

64. White, F, *Good Things in England* (J. Cape, London, 1936) 320.

65. *English and Foreign Mining Glossary*, (London 1860) 16.

66. Macdonell, A., (ed.) *The Closet of Sir Kenelm Digby Knight Opened* (Philip Lee Warner, London, 1910) 159.

67. Cobb, H.S., 'Petty Custom Account 1480–1: Imports, Oct – Dec 1480 (nos 1–55)', in *The Overseas Trade of London: Exchequer Customs Accounts, 1480–1*, (ed.) H.S. Cobb (London, 1990) 1–19. *British History Online* http://www.british-history. ac.uk/london-record-soc/vol27/19 (accessed 17 September 2019).

68. Wellcome Library, Ref: MS4047, Recipe Book Manuscripts.

69. Dawson, T., *The Good Huswifes Jewell* (Edward White, London,1596).

70. Frere, C., (ed.) *A Propre New Booke of Cokery*, 1545 (W. Heffer &Sons, London, 1913).

71. W.M., *The Compleat Cook* (Nath Brook, London,1658).

72. British Newspaper Archives, *West London Observer* (Friday 29 May 1931).

73. Plat, H., *Delightes for Ladies* (London, 1609).

74. British Newspaper Archives, *Ipswich Journal* (Saturday 4 December 1756).

75. Sharpe, R., (ed.) 'Folios xli – l: 1315', in *Calendar of Letter-Books of the City of London: E., 1314–1337* (London, 1903) 53–66. *British History Online* http://www. british-history.ac.uk/london-letter-books/vole/53-66 (accessed 19 September 2019).

76. Lewis, S., (ed.)'Orby – Ormskirk', in *A Topographical Dictionary of England*, (London, 1848) 479–483. *British History Online* http://www.british-history.ac.uk/topographical-dict/england/479-483 (accessed 19 September 2019).

77. British Newspaper Archives, *Chester Courant* (Tuesday 17 March 1801).

78. Panayi, P., (ed.) *Germans in Britain since 1500*, (Hambleton Press, London and Rio Grande, 1996) 39.

79. Calendar of Letter-Books of the City of London: B, 1275–1312. (Her Majesty's Stationery Office, London, 1900).

80. Kaufmann, M., *Black Tudors the Untold Story*. (Oneworld Publications, 2017).

81. British Newspaper Archives, *Nelson Leader* (Friday 9 November 1934).

82. Amussen, S.D., *Caribbean Exchanges: Slavery and the Transformation of English Society, 1640–1700* (University of North Carolina Press, USA,2009) 73.

83. Braidwood, S.J., *Black Poor and White Philanthropists: London's Blacks and the Foundation of the Sierra Leone Settlement 1786–1791*(Liverpool University Press, 1994) 63.

84. Page, W., (ed.) *Letters of Denization and Acts of Naturalization for Aliens in England, 1509–1603.* (Huguenot Society of London, London,1893) 20.

85. Rabbi Susser, B., *The Jews of South-West England* (2003) Jewish Communities and records. Online at https://www.jewishgen.org/jcr-uk/susser/thesis/thesisacknowledgements.htm (accessed 27 February, 2018).

86. Amr Hussein, M., *The Pharaoh's Kitchen: Recipes from Ancient Egypt's Enduring Food Traditions.* (American University in Cairo Press, Cairo and NY, 2010) 36.

87. Baldwin, H., *The Plays and Poems of William Shakspeare* (1790) 520.

88. Taylor, J., *The great eater, of Kent, or Part of the admirable teeth and stomacks exploits of Nicholas Wood, of Harrisom in the county of Kent His excessiue manner of eating without manners, in strange and true manner described, by Iohn Taylor.* (1610) 13.

89. Jennings, J., *Observations on some of the dialects in the West of England* (Baldwick, Craddock and Joy, London,1825) 38.

90. Patten. M., *Century of British Cooking* (Grub Street Cookery, London, 2015) 100.

91. *The Original Journals of Captains Meriwether Lewis and William Clark. The Journals Proper, vol 5 (1804–6)* 127 http://content.wisconsinhistory.org/cdm/search/collection/aj/searchterm/baking/field/all/mode/all/conn/and/order/extra5/ad/asc/cosuppress/0 (accessed 12 April 2019).

92. *Observations by Master George Percy, 1607* (Wisconsin Historical Society, 2003) 18.

93. Martha Ballard's Diary Online http://dohistory.org/diary/(accessed 13 March 2019).

Chapter Three

1. Petersen, C., Jenkins, A., *Bread and the British Economy, 1770–1870* (Routledge, London,1995) 110.

2. Bailey, N., *The Dictionarium Domesticum of 1736*, (C. Hitch and C. Davis, London).

3. British Newspaper Archives, *Nottinghamshire Guardian*, (Thursday 25 Jan 1855).

4. British Newspaper Archives, *Western Times* (Saturday 29 August 1846).

5. British Newspaper Archives *Bradford Daily Telegraph* (Monday 2 January 1899).

6. British Newspaper Archives *Belfast News Letter* (Monday 21 November 1904).

7. British Newspaper Archives, *Liverpool Echo* (Thursday 22 May 1890).
8. The Old Bailey, ref: t16850429-56.
9. The Old Bailey, ref: tl6910114-28.
10. The Old Bailey, ref: t17220228-66
11. *Digital Panopticon, Tracing London Convicts in Britain & Australia 1780–1925* https://www.digitalpanopticon.org/search?from=40&e0.type.t.t=root&e0._ all.s.s=baker&e0.surname.s.s=&e0.given.s.s= (accessed 30 March 2019).
12. Hughes, R., *The Fatal Shore*, 2003 (Vintage Books, London,2003).
13. *Norfolk Island, 1846 the accounts of Robert Pringle* (Stuart and Thomas Beagley Naylor, Sullivan's Cove, 1979) 38.
14. Ibid. 36.
15. Hughes, R., *The Fatal Shore*, 2003 (Vintage Books, London, 2003) 537.
16. Fletcher Moore, G, *Diary of ten years eventful life of an early settler in western Australia; and also A descriptive vocabulary of the language of the aborigines*, (M. Walbrook., London,1884) 220.
17. National Library of Australia, *Yass Evening Tribune*, (Thursday 10 May, 1900).
18. National Library of Australia, *Australian Town and Country Journal* (Saturday, 1 Dec 1900).
19. Williamson, T. P., *The Colonial Baker*, (A.G. Brander and Son, Yass, 1900) 48.
20. British Newspaper Archives, *Leeds Mercury*, (Thursday 21 October 1858).
21. British Newspaper Library, *Kinross-shire Advertiser* (Saturday 21 October 1882).
22. British Newspaper Archive, *Hull and Eastern Counties Herald* (Thursday 27 May 1869).
23. British Newspaper Archive, *York Herald* (Saturday 25 August, 1866).
24. British Newspaper Archive, *York Herald* (Saturday 28 Dec 1872).
25. British Newspaper Archive, *Hull Packet* (Friday 6 March 1874).
26. British Newspaper Archive, Aberdeen Press and Journal (Saturday 23 July 1881).
27. British Newspaper Archive, *Brechin Advertiser* (Tuesday 24 December 1872).
28. British Newspaper Archive, *Sussex Advertiser* (Sunday 23 March 1746).
29. British Newspaper Archive, *Bath Chronicle and Weekly Gazette* (Thursday 8 Dec 1791).
30. Roud, S., London Lore: The Legends and Traditions of the World's Most Vibrant City (Random House, London,2008) 379.
31. Rundell, M., *A New System of Domestic Cookery* John Murray, London, 1832) 218
32. The British Newspaper Archive *Horefield and Bishopston Record and Montpelier & District Free Press* (Saturday 20 January 1912)
33. Farmer, F.M., *Boston Cooking-School Cook Book* Little Brown and Company, Boston, 1896) 424.
34. Thornbury, W., 'Holborn: To Chancery Lane', in *Old and New London: Volume 2* (London, 1878) 526–542. *British History Online* http://www.british-history.ac.uk/old-new-london/vol2/526-542 (accessed 1 October 2019).
35. Ibid.
36. The British Newspaper Archive *Bucks Herald* (13 May 1837).
37. Mayhew, H., *London Labour and the London Poor, Volume 1* (Cosimo Inc, New York, 2009) 194–6.

38. Brown, C., *Classic Scots Cookery*, (Neil Wilson Publishing, Scotland, 2011).
39. Mackman, J., Stevens, M.,'CP40/585: Easter term 1407', in *Court of Common Pleas: the National Archives, Cp40 1399–1500* (London, 2010) *British History Online* http://www.british-history.ac.uk/no-series/common-pleas/1399-1500/easter-term-1407 (accessed 24 September 2019).
40. Cox, N., Dannehl, K, 'Apaveris – Apulia oil', in *Dictionary of Traded Goods and Commodities 1550–1820* (Wolverhampton, 2007) *British History Online* http://www.british-history.ac.uk/no-series/traded-goods-dictionary/1550-1820/apaveris-apulia-oil (accessed 24 September 2019).
41. Dawson, T., *The Good Huswifes Hamndmaide for the Kitchin*. (London 1594).
42. Mrs Frazer, *The Practice of Cookery, Pastry, Pickling, Preserving &c*, (Dublin, 1791).
43. The British Newspaper Archive, *Newcastle Evening Chronicle*, (Thursday 3 August 1944).
44. Peak Frean & Co, *1857–1957, A hundred years of biscuit making by Peek, Frean and Company Limited*, (Peek Frean and co. 1957) 10
45. The British Newspaper Archive, *The Graphic*, (Saturday 6 January, 1894).
46. The British Newspaper Archive, *The Leeds Mercury*, (28 September 1923).
47. The British Newspaper Archive *Yorkshire Evening Post* (Tues 27 September 1927).
48. W.M., *The Complete Cook* (London,1658).
49. The British Newspaper Archive *Reading Mercury* (Saturday 3 February 1844).
50. *The Huntley & Palmers Collection*. Reading Biscuit town online at http://www.huntleyandpalmers.org.uk/ixbin/hixclient.exe?a=query&p=huntley&f=generic_theme.htm&_IXFIRST_=1&_IXMAXHITS_=1&t=rm-rm-biscuits_content1&%3dtheme_record_id=rm-rm-biscuits_content12&s=FHzVByQxOiH (accessed 20 May, 2019).
51. Farrell, T., *Strange But True: Meredith Drew*, (2015) online at http://letslookagain.com/2015/11/strange-but-true-meredith-drew/accessed on 8 Aug 2019.
52. Biagini, E., Mulhall, D, *The Shaping of Modern Ireland: A Centenary Assessment* (Irish Academic Press, Ireland, 2016).
53. Mulvihill, M., *Ingenious Ireland: A County-by-County Exploration of the mysteries and Marvels of the ingenious Irish* (Town House, Dublin,2003) 439.
54. Shields, N., *Comfort and Spice: Recipes for Modern Living* (Rowman & Littlefield, USA, 2012) 88.
55. The Agrarian History of England and Wales, Vol VII, (ed.) Edward John T. Collins Joan Thirsk, (Cambridge University Press, Cambridge, New York, Melbourne, 2000) 1089.
56. Mottershead, B., Woods, L., *Food Technology* (Heinemann, Oxford,2003)
57. The British Newspaper Archive, *Sheffield Independent* (Tuesday 13 May, 1879).
58. Walford, J., *Chairman of Brace's Bakery dies aged 96* (Wales online, 15 February, 2018, https://www.walesonline.co.uk/business/business-news/chairman-braces-bakery-dies-aged-14291879 accessed, 24 September 2019.
59. Rundell, M.E., *A New System of Domestic Cookery* (John Murray, London and Edinburgh,1808) 147.
60. Hawes, D., *Who's who in Dickens*. (Routledge, London, 2006).

61. The British Newspaper Archives, *London Evening Standard* (Saturday 26 August 1865).

62. Soyer, A., *The Modern Housewife or Menagere* (Simpkin and Marshall, London, 1850) 356.

63. Hammerton, J.A., *Harmsworth's Household encyclopaedia: G–MED*. (Harmsworth Encyclopaedia, 1920) 2284

64. Mason, C., *The Lady's Assistant*, Charlotte Mason (J. Walter, London, 1777) 348.

65. Smith, E., *The Compleat Housewife*, (J. Pemberton, London, 1729).

66. *The Whole Duty of a Woman* (T. Reed. London,1737) 468.

67. Williams, T., *The Accomplished Housekeeper and Universal Cook* J. Scratcherd, London, 1717) 119.

68. The British Newspaper Archives *Leeds Intelligencer* (Tuesday 8 Jan 1765).

69. Makepeace, M., *The East India Company's London Workers: Management of the Warehouse Labourers*(Boydell & Brewer, Suffolk,2010) 53.

70. Finn, M., Smith, K., (ed.) *East India Company at Home, 1757–1857* (UCL Press 2018, London) 374.

71. *Naval and Military Gazette and Weekly Chronicle of the united service* (Wednesday 25 September, 1878

72. Yetman, N.R., (ed.) *Voices from Slavery* (Dover publications, USA, 2012) 49.

73. Fisher, H.K., (ed.) *What Mrs Fisher Knows about Old Southern Cooking* (Bedford USA:Applewood Books, 1995).

74. The British Newspaper Archive, *Morning Post* (Wednesday 15 April 1857).

75. The British Newspaper Archive, *London Evening Standard* (Monday 6 Oct 1845).

76. The British Newspaper Archive, *Bournemouth Daily Echo* (Thursday 10 April 1902).

77. The British Newspaper Archive, *Western Times* (Monday 24 March 1890).

78. The British Newspaper Archive, *Dundee Evening Telegraph* (Saturday 10 June 1893).

79. The British Newspaper Archive, *Western Times* (Monday 29 Oct 1917).

80. *A Topographical Dictionary of England*. (S. Lewis, London, 1848) 511–520.

81. Civitello, L., *Baking Powder Wars: The Cutthroat Food fight that Revolutionised cooking* (University of Illinois Press, USA, 2017).

82. British Newspaper Archive, *Bristol Mercury* (Saturday 18 April 1846).

83. Civitello, L., *Baking Powder Wars: The Cutthroat Food fight that Revolutionised cooking* (University of Illinois Press, USA, 2017).

84. Ibid.

85. Hanson, N., *The Custom of the Sea* (Corgi,2009)60.

86. British Newspaper Archive, *Newcastle Courant* (Saturday 13 June 1741).

87. British Newspaper Archive, *Newcastle Courant*, (Saturday 22 Oct 1743).

88. Giguere, J., *Plymouth Revisited* (Arcadia Publishing, S. Carolina., 2011) 67.

89. Kay, E., *Dining with the Georgians*, (Amberley Publishing, Stroud, 2014).

90. British Newspaper Archive, *Evening Mail* (Monday 23 Sep 1822).

91. British Newspaper Archive, *Hastings and St Leonards Observer* (Saturday 24 November 1888).

92. Naidoo, J., Wills, J., (ed.) *Health Studies: An Introduction* (Macmillan International Higher Education, London, 2015) 71.

93. Edwards, W.P., *The Science of Bakery Products* (Royal Society of Chemistry, Cambridge, 2007) 179.

94. Petersen, C., Jenkins, A., (ed.) *Bread and the British economy, 1770–1870* (Routledge Oxford and New York ,2017) 78.
95. George Orwell as quoted in: Popham, P., 'The Great Escape,' *The Independent* (Friday, 22 September 1995). (accessed 5 August 2019).
96. De Fonlanque, E.B., Treatsie on the Administration and Organization of the British Army (Longman, Brown, Green, Longmans, 1858) 354.
97. Ibid.
98. Craighill, W.P., *The Army Officer's Pocket Companion: Principally designed for staff officers.* (D. Van Nostrand, New York, 1862) 242–243.
99. Ruth Cowen, *Relish: The Extraordinary Life of Alexis Soyer, Victorian Celebrity Chef*, phoenix, 2010.
100. The British Newspaper Archives, *Derby Mercury* (Thursday 22 May 1740).
101. Bailey, N., *The Dictionarium Domesticum of 1736*, (C. Hitch and C. Davis, London).
102. Macdonald, J., *Feeding Nelson's Navy: The True Story of Food at Sea in the Georgian Era.* (Frontline Books, Yorkshire, 2014).
103. Lewis, M., *Social History of the Navy* (London,1961).
104. Baugh, D.A., 'British Naval Administration in the Age of Walpole', *The Historical Journal* Vol. 9, No. 3 (1966) 435
105. Macdonald, J., *The British Navy's Victualling Board, 1793–1815* (Boydell and Brewer, Suffolk, 2010) 61.
106. Ibid. 100.
107. Ibid. 21.
108. British newspaper Archives, *Leeds Intelligencer* (Tuesday 21 Feb 1758).
109. British Newspaper Archives, *Caledonian Mercury* (Tuesday 9 May 1758).
110. Kay, E., *Dining with the Victorians* (Amberley publishing, Stroud, 2018) 12–13.
111. British Newspaper Archives, *Westmeath Independent* (Saturday 10 October 1846).
112. The Old Bailey, Ref: t18981212-85, The case of Johann Schneider and Richard Mandelkow 12 December, 1898.
113. Draper, W., *The Morning Walk, or City Encompassed* (1751, London).
114. Walford, E., 'Chelsea', in *Old and New London: Volume 5* (London, 1878) 50–70. *British History Online* http://www.british-history.ac.uk/old-new-london/vol5/50-70 (accessed 12 March 2019).
115. 'Social history: Social and cultural activites', in *A History of the County of Middlesex: Volume 12, Chelsea*, (ed.) Patricia E.C. Croot (London, 2004) 166–176. *British History Online* http://www.british-history.ac.uk/vch/middx/vol12/ 166–176 (accessed 12 March 2019).
116. Walford, E/. 'Chelsea', in *Old and New London: Volume 5* (London, 1878) 50–70. *British History Online* http://www.british-history.ac.uk/old-new-london/vol5/50-70 (accessed 12 March 2019).
117. British Newspaper Archives, *Bath Chronicle and Weekly Gazette* (Thursday 2 December 1869).
118. British Newspaper Archives, *Waterford Mail* (Saturday 23 April 1853).
119. British Newspaper Archives, *Hendon and Finchley Times* (Friday 23 June 1893).
120. British Newspaper Archives, *Hartlepool Northern Daily Mail*, (Thursday 13 Feb 1930).

121. Mayhew, H., *The Criminal Prisons of London and Scenes of Prison Life*, (Griffin, Bohn and Company, London, 1862) 183.
122. Mayhew, H., *London Labour and the London Poor. Vol 1* (New York, 2009) ,179.
123. Lilwall, J., *Bondage in the bakehouse; or, the case of the journeyman Baker* (Kent & Co, London,1859).

Chapter Four
  1. British Newspaper Archive, *Globe* (Wednesday 11 February 1920).
  2. *Journal of Taste*, volume 16 (1909).
  3. British Newspaper Archive *Daily Mirror* (Saturday 1 September 1917).
  4. British Newspaper Archive *London Evening Standard* (Saturday 1 March 1905).
  5. British Newspaper Archive *The Suffragette* (Friday 27 March 1914)
  6. British Newspaper Archive *Votes for Women* (Thursday 31 December 1908).
  7. British Newspaper Archive, *London Daily News* (Thursday 12 November 1908).
  8. British Newspaper Archive, *War Savings Campaign* (Thursday 17 Feb 1916).
  9. Davies, H., *The Biscuit Girls* (Random House, 2014).
 10. *Women workers; papers read at the conference held in London Oct 4 to 7, 1915*, (National Union of Women Workers (Great Britain) Westminster, London).
 11. Jones, M., *These obstreperous lassies: a history of the IWWU* (Gill and Macmillan, Ireland, 1988) 3.
 12. British Newspaper Archives, *Darlington & Stockton Times, Ripon & Richmond Chronicle* (Saturday 24 June 1911).
 13. 'Powering a Giant', *National Geographic*, 02 August 2015, (accessed on 7 August 2019) https://www.nationalgeographic.com.au/engineering/powering-a-giant. aspx
 14. 'Testimony of Charles Joughin' *Titanic Inquiry Project, British Wreck Commissioner's Inquiry* (accessed on 7 August 2019). https://www.titanicinquiry.org/BOTInq/ BOTInq06Joughin03.php
 15. Hinke, V., *The Last Night on the Titanic: Unsinkable Drinking, Dining and Style* (Simon & Schuster, USA, 2019).
 16. Green, O., *Everyday Deserts* (G.P. Putnam and Sons, New York, 1911).
 17. *Vermont Cookery as practiced in 1899 by the women of the first Congregational Church of Bellows Falls, Vermont 1899* (Argus and Patriot Press, U.S.A) 120.
 18. Rorer, S.T., *Bread and bread-making: how to make many varieties easily and with the best results* (Arnold and Company, Philadelphia, 1899).
 19. British Newspaper Archive, *Derbyshire Courier* (Tuesday 14 November, 1916).
 20. Warr, P., *Sheffield in the Great War* (Pen and Sword, 2015, Yorkshire).
 21. British Newspaper Archive, *Sheffield Independent* (Wednesday 2 June 1915).
 22. Hartley, J., *Bully Beef & Biscuits: Food in the Great War* (Pen and Sword, 2015 Yorkshire).
 23. *The Manual of Military Cooking* (HMSO, Mackie, London 1910) 64–66.
 24. Beadon, R.H., Col., *A History of Transport and Supply in the British Army, Vol. 2* (Cambridge).
 25. Wolseley, G.J. Sir, *The soldier's pocket-book for field service* (Macmillan and Co, London and New York, 1871) 38.

26. Wallace, E., *Kitchener's Army* (George Newnes Ltd, London. 1915) 139–140.
27. Holman, H., *The Trench Cookbook 1917* (Amberley Publishing, Stroud).
28. British Newspaper Archive, *Derby Mercury* (Thursday 19 Nov 1789).
29. British Newspaper Archive, *The Sphere* (Saturday 13 Oct 1917).
30. British Newspaper Archive, *Landswoman* (Tuesday 1 Jan 1918).
31. British Newspaper Archive, *Birmingham Mail* (Tuesday 8 February 1944).
32. British Newspaper Archive, *Liverpool Daily Post* (Thursday 1 February, 1945).
33. British Newspaper Archive, *Lancashire Evening Post*, Friday 5 October 1956).
34. British Newspaper Archive, *Mid Sussex Times* (Tuesday 11 February 1941).
35. British Newspaper Archive, *Eastbourne Herald* (Saturday 21 November 1942).
36. Roodhouse, M., *Black Market Britain 1939–1955* (OUP, Oxford. 2013).
37. Hicks, P., *Food and Rations* (Wayland, 2008).
38. Sitwell, W., *Eggs or Anarchy: The remarkable story of the man tasked with the impossible: to feed a nation at war* (Simon and Schuster, London, 2016).
39. Hughes, G., *The Lost Foods of England* (Derbyshire, 2017) 118.
40. British Newspaper Archive, *The Scotsman* (Monday 08 July, 1946).
41. Knight, K., *Spuds, Spam and Eating for Victory. Rationing in the Second World War.* Katherine (The History Press, 2011).
42. Robinson, J., *A Force to the Reckoned With: A History of the Women's Institute*2011, Hatchette UK, London, 2011).
43. British Newspaper Archive, *Ormskirk Advertiser* (22 February, 1940).
44. Food Education memo, no.3, *Good Fare in Wartime* (London, 1941).
45. British Newspaper Archive, *Yorkshire Evening Post* (Friday 3 May 1940).
46. Cauvain, S.P., Young, L.S., *The Chorleywood Bread Process* (Woodhead Publishing, 2006) 5.
47. Panayi, P., 'Sausages, Bakers and Waiters', In Manz, S, Schulte Beerbuhl, M, Davis, J.R., (ed.) *Migration and Transfer from Germany to Britain 160 to 1914* (K.G. Sauer, 2007).
48. Moey, S.C., Chinese Feasts and Festivals; a cookbook (Periplus Editions. Hong Kong, 2006).
49. Brinkhurst-Cuff, C., *Mother Country: Real Stories of the Windrush children* (Headline Publishing, 2018).
50. Lorren, K., *Caribbean Soul Cookbook* (Global LLC,2012) 35.
51. Hartley, J., *Bully Beef and Biscuits: Food in the Great War* (Pen and Sword Books, Yorkshire. 2015) 319.
52. Gregg, I., *Bread the Story of Greggs* (Ian Gregg, Corgi, London, 2013) 12.
53. *Punch, Vol.4–7* (punch Publications Limited, London, 1844) 12.
54. Shuman, C., *Favourite Dishes: A Columbian Autograph Souvenir Cookery Book* (Chicargo,1893) 50.
55. Reynolds, G., *The Household book of practical receipts, in the arts, manufactures and trades.* (John Dicks, London, 1871) 227.
56. British Newspaper Archive, *Berwickshire News and General Advertiser* (Tuesday 9 March 1954).
57. British Newspaper Archive, *Daily Mirror* (Friday 2 June 1967).
58. British Newspaper Archive, *Reading Evening Post* (Friday 21 July 1967).

59. Beaver, P., *A Taste of Tradition. The Story of the Samworth Family Business (1896–1996)* (The Athlone Press, London and the USA,1997) 100–109.
60. Ibid. 160–164.
61. British Newspaper Archive, *Portadown News* (Saturday 11 March 1905).
62. British Newspaper Archive, *Portadown Times* (Friday 23 December 1927).
63. British Newspaper Archive, *Portadown News* (Saturday 23 September 1933).
64. Dept of Agriculture Advisory Services *Agriculture in Northern Ireland, Volume 8* (1994).
65. Kinchin, P., *Taking Tea with Mackintosh: The Story of Miss Cranston's Tea Rooms* (Perilla Pomegranate, San Francisco, 1998) 14.
66. Brown, C., *Scottish Regional Recipes* (Molendinar Press, Glasgow, 1981) 38.
67. British Newspaper Archive, *Yorkshire Post and Leeds Intelligencer* (Monday 20 November 1950).
68. Library of Congress, U.S. Newspaper Directory, *Western Temperance Journal* (1841)
69. Yates, A., Welsh Traditional Recipes (Hermes House, London, 2006) 94.
70. Zweiniger-Bargielowska, I, *Austerity in Britain: Rationing, Controls and Consumption, 1939–1955* 38.

Bibliography

A Topographical Dictionary of England. (S Lewis, London, 1848).

Amr Hussein, M., *The Pharaoh's Kitchen: Recipes from Ancient Egypt's Enduring food Traditions* (American University in Cairo Press, Cairo and NY, 2010).

Amr Hussein, M., *The Pharaoh's Kitchen: Recipes from Ancient Egypt's Enduring Food Traditions* (American University in Cairo Press, Cairo and NY, 2010).

Amussen, S.D., *Caribbean Exchanges: Slavery and the Transformation of English Society, 1640–1700* (University of North Carolina Press, USA, 2009).

Andrews, C., *The Country Cooking of Ireland*, (Chronicle Books, California, 2012)

Askew, R., *The House of Everyone: the consumption of material culture in castles during the English Civil War, vol 1.*

Austin, T., (ed.) *Two fifteenth-century cookery-books*: Harleian MS. 279 (ab.1430) & Harl. MS. 4016 (ab.1450) with extracts from Ashmole MS. 1439, Laud MS. 553, & Douce MS. 55 (Oxford University Press, London, New York, Toronto,1996).

Bailey, N., *The Dictionarium Domesticum of 1736* (C. Hitch and C. Davis, London).

Bailey, N., *The New Universal Etymological English Dictionary* (W. Cavell, London, 1775).

Baldwin, H., *The Plays and Poems of William Shakespeare* (1790)

Banham, D., Faith, R., *Anglo-Saxon Farms and Farming* (Oxford University Press, Oxford, 2014)

Baugh, D.A., 'British Naval Administration in the Age of Walpole', *The Historical Journal*

Beadon, R.H., Col., *A History of Transport and Supply in the British Army, Vol. 2* (Cambridge).

Beaver, P., *A Taste of Tradition. The Story of the Samworth Family Business (1896–1996)* (The Athlone Press, London and the USA,1997)

Bennett, H.S., *A Study of Peasant Conditions 1150–1400*, in Coulton, G. G., (ed.) *Medieval Life and Thought* (Cambridge University Press, London,1938).

Biagini, E., Mulhall, D., *The Shaping of Modern Ireland: A Centenary Assessment* (Irish Academic Press, Ireland, 2016).

Braidwood, S.J., *Black Poor and White Philanthropists: London's Blacks and the Foundation of the Sierra Leone Settlement 1786–1791* (Liverpool University Press, 1994)

Brinkhurst-Cuff, C., *Mother Country: Real Stories of the Windrush children* (Headline Publishing, 2018).

British Newspaper Archive *Daily Mirror* (Saturday 1 September 1917).

British Newspaper Archive *London Evening Standard* (Saturday 1 March 1905).

British Newspaper Archive *The Suffragette* (Friday 27 March 1914)

British Newspaper Archive *Votes for Women* (Thursday 31 December 1908).
British Newspaper Archive, *Aberdeen Press and Journal* (Saturday 23 July 1881).
British Newspaper Archive, *Bath Chronicle and Weekly Gazette* (Thursday 8 Dec 1791).
British Newspaper Archive, *Berwickshire News and General Advertiser* (Tuesday 9 March 1954).
British Newspaper Archive, *Birmingham Mail* (Tuesday 8 February 1944).
British Newspaper Archive, *Brechin Advertiser* (Tuesday 24 December 1872).
British Newspaper Archive, *Bristol Mercury* (Saturday 18 April 1846).
British Newspaper Archive, *Daily Mirror* (Friday 2 June 1967).
British Newspaper Archive, *Derby Mercury* (Thursday 19 November 1789).
British Newspaper Archive, *Derbyshire Courier* (Tuesday 14 November, 1916).
British Newspaper Archive, *Dundee Courier* (Saturday 14 November 1885).
British Newspaper Archive, *Eastbourne Herald* (Saturday 21 November 1942).
British Newspaper Archive, *Evening Mail* (Monday 23 September 1822).
British Newspaper Archive, *Globe* (Wednesday 11 February 1920).
British Newspaper Archive, *Hastings and St Leonards Observer* (Saturday 24 November 1888).
British Newspaper Archive, *Hull and Eastern Counties Herald* (Thursday 27 May 1869).
British Newspaper Archive, *Hull Packet* (Friday 6 March 1874).
British Newspaper Archive, *Lancashire Evening Post*, Friday 5 October 1956).
British Newspaper Archive, *Landswoman* (Tuesday 1 January 1918).
British Newspaper Archive, *Liverpool Daily Post* (Thursday 1 February, 1945).
British Newspaper Archive, *London Daily News* (Thursday 12 November 1908).
British Newspaper Archive, *Mid Sussex Times* (Tuesday 11 February 1941).
British Newspaper Archive, *Newcastle Courant* (Saturday 13 June 1741).
British Newspaper Archive, *Newcastle Courant*, (Saturday 22 October 1743).
British Newspaper Archive, *Ormskirk Advertiser* (22 February 1940).
British Newspaper Archive, *Portadown News* (Saturday 11 March 1905).
British Newspaper Archive, *Portadown News* (Saturday 23 September 1933).
British Newspaper Archive, *Portadown Times* (Friday 23 December 1927).
British Newspaper Archive, *Reading Evening Post* (Friday 21 July 1967).
British Newspaper Archive, *Sheffield Independent* (Wednesday 2 June 1915).
British Newspaper Archive, *Sussex Advertiser* (Sunday 23 March 1746).
British Newspaper Archive, *The Scotsman* (Monday 8 July, 1946).
British Newspaper Archive, *The Sphere* (Saturday 13 October 1917).
British Newspaper Archive, *War Savings Campaign* (Thursday 17 Feb 1916).
British Newspaper Archive, *York Herald* (Saturday 25 August, 1866).
British Newspaper Archive, *York Herald* (Saturday 28 December 1872).
British Newspaper Archive, *Yorkshire Evening Post* (Friday 3 May 1940).
British Newspaper Archive, *Yorkshire Evening Post* (Friday 4 July 1930).
British Newspaper Archive, *Yorkshire Post and Leeds Intelligencer* (Monday 20 November 1950).
British Newspaper Archives *Belfast News Letter* (Monday 21 November 1904).
British Newspaper Archives *Bradford Daily Telegraph* (Monday 2 January 1899).
British Newspaper Archives *Daily Mirror* (Monday 13 July 1964).

British Newspaper Archives, *Bath Chronicle and Weekly Gazette* (Thursday 2 December 1869).

British Newspaper Archives, *Caledonian Mercury* (Tuesday 9 May 1758).

British Newspaper Archives, *Chester Courant* (Tuesday 17 March 1801).

British Newspaper Archives, *Daily Mirror* (Friday 24 July 1964).

British Newspaper Archives, *Darlington & Stockton Times, Ripon & Richmond Chronicle* (Saturday 24 June 1911).

British Newspaper Archives, *Hartlepool Northern Daily Mail*, (Thursday 13 February 1930).

British Newspaper Archives, *Hendon and Finchley Times* (Friday 23 June 1893).

British Newspaper Archives, *Ipswich Journal* (Saturday 4 December 1756).

British newspaper Archives, *Leeds Intelligencer* (Tuesday 21 February 1758).

British Newspaper Archives, *Leeds Mercury*, (Thursday 21 October 1858).

British Newspaper Archives, *Liverpool Echo* (Thursday 22 May 1890).

British Newspaper Archives, *Nelson Leader* (Friday 9 November 1934).

British Newspaper Archives, *Northern Whig* (Wednesday 19 April 1939).

British Newspaper Archives, *Waterford Mail* (Saturday 23 April 1853).

British Newspaper Archives, *West London Observer* (Friday 29 May 1931).

British Newspaper Archives, *Western Times* (Saturday 29 August 1846).

British Newspaper Archives, *Westmeath Independent* (Saturday 10 October 1846).

British Newspaper Library, *Kinross-shire Advertiser* (Saturday 21 October 1882).

British Newspaper Archives, *Nottinghamshire Guardian*, (Thursday 25 January 1855).

British Newspaper Archive *Bucks Herald* (13 May 1837).

British Newspaper Archive *Horefield and Bishopston Record and Montpelier & District Free Press*, (Saturday 20 January 1912).

British Newspaper Archive *Reading Mercury* (Saturday 3 February 1844).

British Newspaper Archive *Yorkshire Evening Post* (Tuesday 27 September 1927).

British Newspaper Archive, *Airdrie & Coatbridge Advertiser*, (Saturday 28 December, 1907).

British Newspaper Archive, *Bellshill Speaker* (Friday 24 March 1939).

British Newspaper Archive, *Bournemouth Daily Echo* (Thursday 10 April 1902).

British Newspaper Archive, *Dundee Evening Telegraph* (Saturday 10 June 1893).

British Newspaper Archive, *Illustrated London News* (Saturday 15 August 1846).

British Newspaper Archive, *London Evening Standard* (Monday 6 Oct 1845).

British Newspaper Archive, *Morning Post* (Wednesday 15 April 1857).

British Newspaper Archive, *Newcastle Evening Chronicle* (Thursday 3 August 1944).

British Newspaper Archive, *Sheffield Independent* (Tuesday 13 May, 1879).

British Newspaper Archive, *The Graphic*, (Saturday 6 January, 1894).

British Newspaper Archive, *The Leeds Mercury* (28 September 1923).The British

British Newspaper Archive, *Western Times* (Monday 24 March 1890).

British Newspaper Archive, *Western Times* (Monday 29 October 1917).

British Newspaper Archive, *Yorkshire Evening Post* (Wednesday 10 February 1915).

British Newspaper Archives, *Leeds Intelligencer* (Tuesday 8 January 1765).

British Newspaper Archives, *Derby Mercury* (Thursday 22 May 1740).

British Newspaper Archives, *London Evening Standard* (Saturday 26 August 1865).

Brown, C., *Classic Scots Cookery* (Neil Wilson Publishing, Scotland, 2011).

Brown, C., *Scottish Regional Recipes* (Molendinar Press, Glasgow, 1981)

Buchan, W., *Domestic Medicine: A Treatise on the prevention and cure of Diseases* (U.P. James,1838).

Bucholz,, R.O., *The Augustan Court: Queen Anne and the Decline of Court Culture* (Stanford university Press, California, 1993)

Calendar of Letter-Books of the City of London: B, 1275–1312. (Her Majesty's Stationery Office, London, 1900).

Calendar of the Manuscripts of the Dean and Chapter of Wells: Volume 2, (HM Staionery Office, London, 1914)

Carlton, C., *Going to the wars: The Experience of the British Civil Wars 1638–1651* (Routledge, London and New York, 2003)

Carraro, L.F., 'Susanna Centilivre', (The Literary Encyclopedia, 2001).

Cauvain, S.P., Young, L.S., *The Chorleywood Bread Process* (Woodhead Publishing, 2006)

Chansky, D., White, Ann, (ed.) *Food and Theatre on the World Stage*, (Routledge, New York, 2016).

Civitello, L., *Baking Powder Wars: The Cutthroat Food fight that Revolutionised cooking* (University of Illinois Press, USA, 2017).

Civitello, L., *Baking Powder Wars: The Cutthroat Food fight that Revolutionised cooking* (University of Illinois Press, USA, 2017).

Cockayne, T.O., *Leechdoms, Wortcunning and Starcraft of Early England*, Vol. 3. 1866, (Longmans, Green, Reader and Dyer,1866)

Cole, M.H., *The Portable Queen: Elizabeth I and the Politics of Ceremony* (University of Massachusetts Press, 1999, USA)

Coote, L.A., (ed.) *The Canterbury Tales*, Geoffrey Chaucer, (Wordsworth Poetry Library, Hertfordshire,2002)

Craighill, W.P., *The Army Officer's Pocket Companion: Principally designed for staff officers*. (D. Van Nostrand, New York, 1862).

Creighton, C., *A History of Epidemics in Britain, Volume 1* (C.J. Clay and Sons. Cambridge University Press, 1891)

Crossley, A., Chane, E., Colvin, C., Cooper, J., Day, C.J., Hassall, T.G., (ed.) *Early Modern Oxford*, in *A History of the County of Oxford: Volume 4, the City of Oxford*.

Cubberley, A.L., Lloyd, J.J., Roberts, P.C., 'Testa and Clibani: the Baking Covers of Classical Italy', *Papers of The British School at Rome,* vol. 56 (1988)

Darley, G., *John Evelyn: Living for Ingenuity*, (Yale University Press, New Haven and London, 2006).

Davies, H., *The Biscuit Girls* (Random House, 2014).

Dawson, T., *The Good Huswifes Jewell* (Edward White, London,1596).

Dawson, T., *The Good Huswifes Handmaide for the Kitchin*, (Richard Jones,London, 1594).

De Fonlanque, E.B., Treatsie on the Administration and Organization of the British Army (Longman, Brown, Green, Longmans, 1858)

Defoe, D., *A Journal of the Plague Year*, (1722)

Dept of Agriculture Advisory Services *Agriculture in Northern Ireland, Volume 8* (1994).

Dewing, H.B., (ed.) *The Wars of Justinian'*, *Procopius*, (Hackett Publishing Co. Inc Indianapolis/Cambridge 2014)

Digby Knight, K., *The Closet of Sir Kenelm Digby Knight Opened* (London, 1669)

Dommers Vehling, J., (ed.) *Apicius, Cookery and Dining in Imperial Rome, A Bibliography*, *Critical Review and Translation of the Ancient Book known as Apicius de re Coquinaria*, (Dover Publications, New York,1977).

Dommers Vehling, J., (ed.) *Apicius, Cookery and Dining in Imperial Rome, A Bibliography*, *Critical Review and Translation of the Ancient Book known as Apicius de re Coquinaria*, (Dover Publications, New York, 1977)

Draper, W., *The Morning Walk, or City Encompassed* (1751, London).

Dugdale, J., The New British Traveller, (J. Robins and Company, 1819, London)

Eaton, M., *The Cook and Housekeeper's Complete and Universal Dictionary* (J and R Childs, 1822)

Edwards, W.P., *The Science of Bakery Products* (Royal Society of Chemistry, Cambridge, 2007)

Elliot, P., *Food and Farming in Prehistoric Britain*, (Fonthill Media, 2017).

English and Foreign Mining Glossary, (London 1860)

Evelyn, J., *Acetaria: A Discourse of Sallets*, (Women's Auxilary, Brooklyn USA, 1937).

Ezzamel, M., *Accounting and Order*, (Routledge, New York, 2012).

Faas, P., *Around the Roman Table: Food and Feasting in Ancient Rome*, (University of Chicago,2005).

Farmer, F.M., *Boston Cooking-School Cook Book* Little Brown and Company, Boston, 1896)

Finn, M., Smith, K., (ed.) *East India Company at Home, 1757–1857* (UCL Press 2018, London)

Fisher, H.K., (ed.) *What Mrs Fisher Knows about Old Southern Cooking* (Bedford USA: Applewood Books, 1995) .

Fletcher Moore, G., *Diary of ten years eventful life of an early settler in western Australia; and also A descriptive vocabulary of the language of the aborigines*, (M. Walbrook, London,1884).

Food Education memo, no.3, *Good Fare in Wartime* (London, 1941).

Forsyth, H., *Butcher, Baker, Candlestick Maker: Surviving the Great Fire of London* (I.B. Tauris, London and New York, 2016)

Francatelli, C.E., *The Modern Cook*, (R. Bentley, London, 1846)

Francois Massialot, *The Court and Country Cook* (A&J Churchill, M. Gillyflower, London, 1702)

Frere, C., (ed.) *A Propre New Booke of Cokery*, 1545 (W. Heffer & Sons, London, 1913).

Gairdner, J., Brodie, R.H., (ed.) *Letter from Marillac to Francis I, 1541 Letters and papers, Foreign and Domestic, Henry VIII, Volume 16, 1540–1541*, (Her Majesty's Stationery Office, London, 1898).

Gautier, A *Cooking and Cuisine in late Anglo-Saxon England*, in Anglo-Saxon England Vol. 41, (2013)

September 1995).

Giguere, J., *Plymouth Revisited* (Arcadia Publishing, S.Carolina., 2011)

Gimpel, J., (1977) *The Medieval Machine: The Industrial Revolution of the Middle Ages*, (Penguin, London,1977).

Gisslen, W., *Professional Baking*, fifth edition, (John Wiley & sons: New Jersey and Canada, 2008)

Glasse, H,. *The Art of Cookery made plain and easy*. (A. Millar, London, 1763)

Gonzalez-Wippler, M., *The Complete Book of Spells, Ceremonies and Magic* (Llewellyn Publications, Minnesota, 1978)

Gouffe, J., *The Book of Preserves* (S. Low, Son and Marston, London, 1871)

Gouldman, F., *A Copius Dictionary in Three Parts*, (John Hayes, London 1674).

Green, O., *Everyday Deserts* (G.P. Putnam and Sons, New York,1911).

Gregg, P., *King Charles I*, (University of California Press, 1984, USA)

Gregg, I., *Bread the Story of Greggs* (Ian Gregg, Corgi, London,2013)

Hagan, A., *A Handbook of Anglo Saxon Food* (Anglo Saxon Books, 1992) 9.

Hagan, A., *A Handbook of Anglo Saxon Food* (Anglo Saxon Books, 1992)

Hammerton, J.A., *Harmsworth's Household encyclopaedia: G–MED* (Harmsworth Encyclopaedia, 1920)

Hanson, N., *The Custom of the Sea* (Corgi, 2009) 60.

Harrison, S., *The House-keeper's pocket-book; And complete Family cook*, (R.Ware,1739)

Hartley, J., *Bully Beef & Biscuits: Food in the Great War* (Pen and Sword, 2015 Yorkshire).

Hawes, D., *Who's who in Dickens*. (Routledge, London, 2006).

Hensperger, B., *The Bread Lover's Bread Machine Cookbook* (Harvard Common Press, USA)

Hicks, P., *Food and Rations* (Wayland, 2008).

Hindley, C., *A History of the cries of London*, (Reeves and Turner, London,1881) 217

Hinke, V., *The Last Night on the Titanic: Unsinkable Drinking, Dining and Style* (Simon & Schuster, USA, 2019).

Holman, H., *The Trench Cookbook 1917* (Amberley Publishing, Stroud).

Holme, R., *The Third Chapter of the Book of the Academy of Armory and Blazon, Chap. VII Academy of Armory*, (Chester, 1688)

Houghton, J., John Evelyn, *Panificium*, 1666, in *A Collection Of Letters For the Improvement Of Husbandry And Trade* (Woodman and Lyon, London, 1728).

Hughes, G., *The Lost Foods of England* (Derbyshire, 2017)

Hughes, R., *The Fatal Shore*, 2003 (Vintage Books, London, 2003)

Jacob, E., *Physicall and Chyrurgicall Receipts. Cookery and preserves* (1654–1685). Wellcome Trust Archive, Ref: MS3009.

Jeake, S., *Arithmetick surveyed and reviewed: in four books, etc*. (1696).

Jenks, J., *The Complete cook: Teaching the Art of cookery in all its Branches* (J. Potts and J. Williams. Dublin, 1769)

Jennings, J., *Observations on some of the dialects in the West of England* (Baldwick, Craddock and Joy, London,1825)

Jolly, K., *Witchcraft and Magic in Europe. Vol 3: The Middle Ages*, (Athlone Press,2002)

Jones, M., *These obstreperous lassies: a history of the IWWU* (Gill and Macmillan, Ireland, 1988)

Journal of Taste, volume 16 (1909).

Kaufman, H., *Black Tudors: The Untold Story* (Oneworld Publications, 2017)

Kay, E., *Dining with the Victorians*, (Amberley, Gloucestershire, 2015).

Kidder, E., 'Receipts of pastry and cookery: for the use of his scholars', Edward Kidder (London, 1720).

Kieckhefer, R., *Magic in the Middle Ages*, (Cambridge University Press, 2014)

Kinchin, P., *Taking Tea with Mackintosh: The Story of Miss Cranston's Tea Rooms* (Perilla Pomegranate, San Francisco, 1998)

Knight, K., *Spuds, Spam and Eating for Victory. Rationing in the Second World War.* Katherine (The History Press, 2011).

Knight, R., *A discourse on the worship of Priapus and its connection with the mystic theology of the ancients* (London,1865)

Ladies Home Journal Volume 29, (Philadelphia, 1912)

Ladye Katherine by one hole night wherin she dyet in the morning.(University of Pennsylvania, 2007).

Lamb, A.L., Evans, J.E., Buckley, R., 'Multi-isotope analysis demonstrates significant lifestyle changes in King Richard III', *Journal of Archaeological Science*,Vol 50, (2014)

Langland, W., *Piers Plowman: A New Translation of the B-text* (Oxford University Press, Oxford) 1992.

Letters and Papers, Foreign and Domestic, Henry VIII, Volume 4, 1524–1530. (Her Majesty's Stationery Office, London, 1875).

Lewis, C.P., Thacker, A.T., *Early modern Chester 1550–1762: Economy and society, 1550–1642* in *A History of the County of Chester: Volume 5 Part 1, the City of Chester: General History and Topography.* Originally published by (Victoria County History, London, 2003)

Lewis, S., (ed.) *A Topographical Dictionary of England*, (Samuel Lewis, 1848)

Lewis, M., *Social History of the Navy* (London,1961).

Library of Congress, US Newspaper Directory, *Western Temperance Journal* (1841)

Lilwall, J., *Bondage in the bakehouse; or, the case of the journeyman Baker* (Kent & Co, London,1859).

Lorren, K., *Caribbean Soul Cookbook* (Global LLC, 2012)

MacVeigh, J., *International Cuisine* (Cengage Learning, 2006, USA).

Macdonald, J., *Feeding Nelson's Navy: The True Story of Food at Sea in the Georgian Era* (Frontline Books, Yorkshire, 2014).

Macdonald, J., *The British Navy's Victualling Board, 1793–1815* (Boydell and Brewer, Suffolk, 2010)

Macdonell, A., (ed.) *The Closet of Sir Kenelm Digby Knight Opened* (Philip Lee Warner, London, 1910)

Machyn, H., *The Diary of Henry Machyn*, (Camden Society, Longmans, London, 1838).

Magazine of Domestic Economy and Family Review 1838–1842 (W.S. Orr & Co., London, 1838).

Maitland, W., *The Court-Baron Pub* (Selden Society, 1891)

Major, A.P., *The Book of Seaweed*, (Gordon & Cremonesi,1977).

Makepeace, M, *The East India Company's London Workers: Management of the Warehouse Labourers* (Boydell & Brewer, Suffolk, 2010)

Markham, G., *The English Huswife* (Hannah Sawbridge, London, 1615)

Markham, G., *The English Huswife, extracted from the original work published in 1653*, (Grosvenor Library, London, 1908)

Markham, G., *Country Contentments, or The English Huswife*, 1623 R. Jackson, London, 1623) 231.

Mason, C., *The Lady's Assistant*, Charlotte Mason (J. Walter, London, 1777) 348.

Matossian, M., *Poisons of the Past: Molds, Epidemics and History* (Yale University Press, 1989)

May, R., *Accomplisht Cook*, (Obadiah Blagrove, London, 1685).

Mayerne, Sir Theodore, *Archimagirus Anglo-Gallicus; or, excellent and approved receipts and experiments in cookery. Together with the best way of preserving. As also, rare formes of sugar works; according to the French mode and English manner* (Bedell & T.Collins, London, 1658).

Mayhew, H., *The Criminal Prisons of London and Scenes of Prison Life*, (Griffin, Bohn and Company, London, 1862)

Mayhew, H., *London Labour and the London Poor. Vol 1* (New York, 2009), 179.

McCavour, T., *Killed by Fire* (Friesen Press, Canada, 2017)

Mest, M.R., (ed.) *The English Housewife*, (McGill-Queens University Press, Canada, 1986)

Moey, S.C., Chinese Feasts and Festivals; a cookbook (Periplus Editions. Hong Kong, 2006).

Monk, M., Sheehan, J., (ed.) *Early Medieval Munster: Archaeology, History and Society*, (Cork University Press, 1999)

Morris, R., (ed.) *Liber Cure Cocorum*, (Philological Society, Berline, 1862)

Mottershead, B., Woods, L., *Food Technology* (Heinemann, Oxford,2003)

Mrs Frazer, *The Practice of Cookery, Pastry, Pickling, Preserving &c*, (Dublin, 1791).

Mulvihill, M., *Ingenious Ireland: A County-by-County Exploration of the mysteries and Marvels of the ingenious Irish* (Town House, Dublin, 2003)

Myers, D., (ed.) *The commonplace book of Countess Katherine Seymour Hertford (1567)*

Naidoo, J., Wills, J., (ed.) *Health Studies: An Introduction* (Macmillan International Higher Education, London, 2015)

Napier, A., (ed.) *A Noble boke off cookry ffor a prynce houssolde or eny other estately houssolde: reprinted verbatim from a rare ms. in the Holkham collection* (Elliot Stock, London, 1882).

National Library of Australia, *Australian Town and Country Journal* (Saturday, 1 December 1900).

National Library of Australia, *Yass Evening Tribune*, (Thursday 10 May, 1900).

Naval and Military Gazette and Weekly Chronicle of the united service (Wednesday 25 September, 1878

Norfolk Island, 1846 the accounts of Robert Pringle (Stuart and Thomas Beagley Naylor, Sullivan's Cove, 1979)

Notes and Queries, (Oxford University Press, 1878)

Notices and Anecdotes Illustrative of the Incidents, Charcters and Scenery Described in the Novels and Romances of Sir Walter Scott (Baudry's European Library, Paris, 1833).

Observations by Master George Percy, 1607 (Wisconsin Historical Society, 2003).

Orwell, George, as quoted in: Popham, P., 'The Great Escape,' *The Independent* (Friday, 22

Page, C., *The Guitar in Stuart England: A Social and musical history* (Cambridge University Press, 2017)

Page, W., (ed.) *Letters of Denization and Acts of Naturalization for Aliens in England, 1509–1603* (Huguenot Society of London, London, 1893)

Page, W., A History of the County of Northampton: Volume 3. (Victoria County History, London, 1930)

Panayi, P., (ed.) *Germans in Britain since 1500*, (Hambleton Press, London and Rio Grande, 1996)

Panayi, P., 'Sausages, Bakers and Waiters', In Manz, S., Schulte Beerbuhl, M., Davis, J.R., (ed.) *Migration and Transfer from Germany to Britain 160 to 1914* (K.G. Sauer, 2007).

Patten. M., *Century of British Cooking* (Grub Street Cookery, London, 2015).

Peak Frean & Co, *1857–1957, A hundred years of biscuit making by Peek, Frean and Company Limited*, (Peek Frean and Co. 1957)

Pepys, S,. The Diary of Samuel Pepys, (B&R Samizdat Express, 2018).

Petersen, C., Jenkins, A., *Bread and the British Economy, 1770–1870* (Routledge, London, 1995)

Petersen, C., Jenkins, A., (ed.) *Bread and the British economy, 1770–1870* (Routledge Oxford and New York, 2017)

Pilkington, M.C., *Bristol*, (University of Toronto Press, Canada, 1997).

Plat, H., *Delightes for Ladies* (London, 1609).

Punch, Vol.4–7 (Punch Publications Limited, London, 1844)

Reynolds, G., *The Household book of practical receipts, in the arts, manfactures and trades.* (John Dicks, London, 1871)

Riley, T.H., *Memorials of London and London Life in the 13th, 14th and 15th centuries*, (Longmans, Green, London, 1868)

Robinson, J., *A Force to the Reckoned With: A History of the Women's Institute* (Hatchette UK, London, 2011).

Roodhouse, M., *Black Market Britain 1939–1955* (OUP, Oxford. 2013).

Rorer, S.T., *Bread and bread-making; how to make many varieties easily and with the best results* (Arnold and Company, Philadelphia, 1899).

Roud, S., London Lore: The Legends and Traditions of the World's Most Vibrant City (Random House, London, 2008)

Rundell, M., *A New System of Domestic Cookery* (John Murray, London, 1832)

Rundell, M.E., *A New System of Domestic Cookery* (John Murray, London and Edinburgh, 1808)

Russell, J., *The Boke of Nurture*, c.*1460–70*, (J. Childs and Son, London, 1867) 33.

Ruth Cowen, *Relish: The Extraordinary Life of Alexis Soyer, Victorian Celebrity Chef*, Phoenix, 2010.

Shakespeare, W., *Troilus and Cressida*, (Cambridge University Press, 2005) 95

Shakespeare, W., Uyl, A., (ed.) *Titus Andronicus The Tragedy of Titus Andronicus* (Devoted publishing, Canada, 2016)

Shields, N., *Comfort and Spice: Recipes for Modern Living* (Rowman & Littlefield, USA, 2012)

Shuman, C., *Favourite Dishes: A Columbian Autograph Souvenir Cookery Book* (Chicargo, 1893)

Sitwell, W., *Eggs or Anarchy: The remarkable story of the man tasked with the impossible: to feed a nation at war* (Simon and Schuster, London, 2016).

Slater, H., *A Book of pagan Rituals*, 1978 (Weiser Books, Boston USA, 1978)

Smith, E., *The Compleat Housewife: Or Accomplished Gentlewoman's Companion* (J. Pembertton, London)

Smith, R., *Court Cookery, or the Compleat English Cook*, (T. Wooton, London, 1725)

Soyer, A., *The Modern Housewife or Menagere* (Simpkin and Marshall, London, 1850)

Spalinger, A.J., *War in Ancient Egypt: The New Kingdom* (Blackwell Publishing, USA, 2008)

Table Talk, Volume 24 number 12. (London, 1909)

Taylor, J., *The great eater, of Kent, or Part of the admirable teeth and stomacks exploits of Nicholas Wood, of Harrisom in the county of Kent His excessiue manner of eating without manners, in strange and true manner described, by Iohn Taylor* (1610)

The Agrarian History of England and Wales, Vol VII, (ed.) Edward John T. Collins, Joan Thirsk, (Cambridge University Press, Cambridge, New York, Melbourne, 2000)

The Old Bailey, ref: tl6910114–28.

The Old Bailey, ref: t16850429–56.

The Old Bailey, ref: t17220228–66

The Old Bailey, Ref: t18981212–85, The case of Johann Schneider and Richard Mandelkow 12 December, 1898.

The Whole Duty of a Woman (T. Reed. London,1737)

The Gentleman's Magazine, Volume 64, (E. Cave. London,1794)

The Manual of Military Cooking (HMSO, Mackie, London 1910)

Tschirky, O., *The Cook Book of Oscar Tschirky* (The Saalfield Publishing Co., Cchicargo, 1896)

Vermont Cookery as practiced in 1899 by the women of the first Congregational Church of Bellows Falls, Vermont 1899 (Argus and Patriot Press, USA)

W.M., *The Compleat Cook* (Nath Brook, London,1658)

Wallace, E., *Kitchener's Army* (George Newnes Ltd, London 1915)

Warner, R., *Antiquitates Culinarie. Or Curious Tracts Relating to the Culinary Affairs of the Old English* (Blamire, London,1791).

Warr, P., *Sheffield in the Great War* Pen and Sword, 2015, Yorkshire).

Wellcome Library, Ref: MS4047, Recipe Book Manuscripts.

Whelan, F., *The Making of Manners and Morals in Twelfth-Century England: The Book of the Civilised Man* (Routledge, London and New York, 2017) 164.

Whelan, F., Petrizzo, F., Spenser, O., (ed.) *The Book of the Civilised Man: An English Translation of the Urbanus magnus of Daniel of Beccles* (Routledge, London,2019)

White, F., *Good Things in England* (J. Cape, London, 1936)

White, P., *King: Charles I, Traitor, Murdere, Martyr Leanda de Lisle*, (Random House, 2018).

White, J., *A Treatise on the Art of Baking*, (Anderson and Bryce, Edinburgh, 1828)

Williams, T., *The Accomplished Housekeeper and Universal Cook* (J. Scratcherd, London,1717)

Williamson, T.P., *The Colonial Baker* (A.G. Brander and Son, Yass, 1900)

Wilson, C.A., *Food and Drink in Britain* (Cookery Book Club, London,1973)

Winsham, W., *England's Witchcraft Trials* (Pen and Sword, Yorkshire, 2018)

Wolseley, G.J. Sir., *The soldier's pocket-book for field service* (Macmillan and Co. London and New York, 1871)

Women workers; papers read at the conference held in London Oct 4 to 7, 1915 (National Union of Women Workers (Great Britain) Westminster, London).

Worth, V., *Crone's Book of Magical Words* (Llewellyn Publications, Minnesota, 2004)

Yates, A., Welsh Traditional Recipes (Hermes House, London, 2006) 94.

Yetman, N.R., (ed.) *Voices from Slavery* (Dover publications, USA, 2012)

Zweiniger-Bargielowska, I., *Austerity in Britain: Rationing, Controls and Co* Vol. 9, No. 3 (1966

Websites References

'Powering a Giant', *National Geographic*, 02 August 2015, (accessed on 7 August 2019) https://www.nationalgeographic.com.au/engineering/powering-a-giant.aspx

'Testimony of Charles Joughin' *Titanic Inquiry Project , British Wreck Commissioner's Inquiry* (accessed on 7 August 2019). .https://www.titanicinquiry.org/BOTInq/BOTInq06Joughin03.php

Austin, T (ed.) *Two fifteenth-century cookery-books*: Harleian MS. 279 (ab. 1430) & Harl. MS. 4016 (ab. 1450) with extracts from Ashmole MS. 1439, Laud MS. 553, & Douce MS. 55 (Oxford University Press, London, New York, Toronto,1996) 47

Benton, J.T., 'Roman Baking' (2016)

Brander, G., (ed.) *Forme of Curye, 1390,* (1780) 29 https://archive.org/stream/theformeofcury08102gut/7cury10.txt (accessed on 12 September, 2019).

Cobb, H.S., 'Petty Custom Account 1480–1: Imports, Oct – Dec 1480 (nos 1–55)', in *The Overseas Trade of London: Exchequer Customs Accounts, 1480–1*, (ed.) H S Cobb (London, 1990) 1–19. *British History Online* http://www.british-history.ac.uk/london-record-soc/vol27/19 (accessed 17 September 2019).

Cox, D.C., Edwards, J.R., Hill, R.C., Kettle, A.J., Perren, R., Rowley, T., Stamper, P.A,. 'Domesday Book: 1540–1750', in *A History of the County of Shropshire: Volume 4, Agriculture,* (ed.) G C Baugh and C R Elrington (London, 1989) 119–168. *British History Online* http://www.british-history.ac.uk/vch/salop/vol4/119-168 (accessed 27 February 2019).

Cox, N., Dannehl, K., 'Apaveris – Apulia oil', in *Dictionary of Traded Goods and Commodities 1550–1820* (Wolverhampton, 2007) *British History Online* http://www.british-history.ac.uk/no-series/traded-goods-dictionary/1550-1820/apaveris-apulia-oil (accessed 24 September 2019).

Crittall, E., (ed.) 'Salisbury: Trade companies since 1612', in *A History of the County of Wiltshire: Volume 6* (London, 1962) 136–138. *British History Online* http://www.british-history.ac.uk/vch/wilts/vol6/pp136-138 (accessed 28 February 2019).

Croot, P.E.C., (ed.) 'Social history: Social and cultural activites', in *A History of the County of Middlesex: Volume 12, Chelsea,* (London, 2004) 166–176. *British History Online* http://www.british-history.ac.uk/vch/middx/vol12/ 166–176 (accessed 12 March 2019).

Digital Panopticon, Tracing London Convicts in Britain & Australia 1780–1925 https://www.digitalpanopticon.org/search?from=40&e0.type.t.t=root&e0._all.s.s=baker&e0.surname.s.s=&e0.given.s.s= (accessed 30 March 2019).

Farrell, T., *Strange But True: Meredith Drew*, (2015) online at http://letslookagain.com/2015/11/strange-but-true-meredith-drew/(accessed 8 Aug 2019).

Farrer, W., Brownbill, J., 'Townships: Manchester (part 2 of 2)', in *A History of the County of Lancaster: Volume 4*, (ed.) William Farrer and J. Brownbill (London, 1911) 230–251. *British History Online* http://www.british-history.ac.uk/vch/lancs/vol4/pp230-251 (accessed 27 February 2019).

'House of Lords Journal Volume 7: 2 April 1645', in *Journal of the House of Lords: Volume 7, 1644* (London, 1767–1830) pp. 299–301. *British History Online* http://www.british-history.ac.uk/lords-jrnl/vol7/pp299-301 (accessed 28 February 2019).

J.S. Barrow, J.D. Herson, A.H. Lawes, P.J. Riden and M.V.J. Seaborne, 'Economic infrastructure and institutions: Craft guilds', in *A History of the County of Chester: Volume 5 Part 2, the City of Chester: Culture, Buildings, Institutions,* (ed.) A.T. Thacker and C.P. Lewis (London, 2005) pp. 114–124. *British History Online* http://www.british-history.ac.uk/vch/ches/vol5/pt2/pp114-124 (accessed 21 September 2019).

Knapton, S., 'World's oldest bread shows hunter-gatherers were baking 4,000 years before birth of farming', *The Daily Telegraph* 16 July 2018 https://www.telegraph.co.uk/science/2018/07/16/worlds-oldest-bread-shows-hunter-gathers-baking-4000-years-birth/. (accessed 12 March 2019).

Lewis, S., (ed.) 'Orby – Ormskirk', in *A Topographical Dictionary of England*, (London, 1848) 479–483. *British History Online* http://www.british-history.ac.uk/topographical-dict/england/479-483 (accessed 19 September 2019).

Lilian J. Redstone, 'The history of All Hallows Church: To c.1548', in *Survey of London: Volume 12, the Parish of All Hallows Barking, Part I: the Church of All Hallows* (London, 1929) pp. 1–20. *British History Online* http://www.british-history.ac.uk/survey-london/vol12/pt1/pp1–20 (accessed 13 September 2019).

'London tradesmen and their creditors: (G. Unwin)', in *Finance and Trade Under Edward III the London Lay Subsidy of 1332*, (ed.) George Unwin (Manchester, 1918) pp. 19–34. *British History Online* http://www.british-history.ac.uk/manchester-uni/london-lay-subsidy/1332/pp19-34 (accessed 14 September 2019).

Mackman, J., Stevens, M., 'CP40/585: Easter term 1407', in *Court of Common Pleas: the National Archives, Cp40 1399–1500* (London, 2010) *British History Online* http://www.british-history.ac.uk/no-series/common-pleas/1399-1500/easter-term-1407 (accessed 24 September 2019).

Malden, H.E., (ed.) *A History of the County of Surrey: Volume 3* (London, 1911) 560–570. *British History Online* http://www.british-history.ac.uk/vch/surrey/vol3/pp560-570 (accessed 27 February 2019).

Martha Ballard's Diary Online http://dohistory.org/diary/(accessed 13 March 2019).

Maxwell Lyte, H.C., (ed.) 'Close Rolls, Edward II: July 1317', in *Calendar of Close Rolls, Edward II: Volume 2, 1313–1318,* (London, 1893) pp. 556–560. *British History Online*. http://www.british-history.ac.uk/cal-close-rolls/edw2/vol2/pp556-560   (accessed 14 September 2019).

McKinley, R.A, (ed.) 'The City of Leicester: Political and administrative history, 1509–1660', in *A History of the County of Leicester: Volume 4, the City of Leicester*, (London, 1958) 55–75. *British History Online* http://www.british-history.ac.uk/vch/leics/vol4/pp55-75 (accessed 27 February 2019).

Morgan, H, 'Bakers and the Baking Trade in the Roman Empire' (2015) http://www.academia.edu/13319823/Bakers_and_the_Baking_Trade_in_the_Roman_Empire_Social_and_Political_Responses_from_the_Principate_to_Late_Antiquity (accessed 12 March 2019).

'Prebendaries: Moreton Parva', in *Fasti Ecclesiae Anglicanae 1066–1300: Volume 8, Hereford*, (ed.) J.S. Barrow (London, 2002) pp. 50–51. *British History Online* http://www.british-history.ac.uk/fasti-ecclesiae/1066-1300/vol8/pp50–51 (accessed 14 September 2019).

Rabbi Susser, B., *The Jews of South-West England* (2003) Jewish Communities and records. Online at https://www.jewishgen.org/jcr-uk/susser/thesis/thesisacknowledgements.htm (accessed 27 February, 2018).

Raimer, C., Ancient Roman Recipes', (2000) https://www.pbs.org/wgbh/nova/article/roman-recipes/ (accessed 4 April 2019).

Riley, H.T., (ed.) 'Memorials: 1417', in *Memorials of London and London Life in the 13th, 14th and 15th Centuries*, (ed.) H.T. Riley (London, 1868) pp. 644–660. *British History Online* http://www.british-history.ac.uk/no-series/memorials-london-life/pp644-660 (accessed 14 September 2019).

Sharpe, R., (ed.) 'Folios xci – xcix: Sept 1378 -', in *Calendar of Letter-Books of the City of London: H, 1375–1399*, (London, 1907) pp. 97–111. *British History Online* http://www.british-history.ac.uk/london-letter-books/volh/pp97-111 (accessed 21 September 2019).

Sharpe, R., (ed.) 'Folios xli – l: 1315', in *Calendar of Letter-Books of the City of London: E, 1314–1337* (London, 1903) 53–66. *British History Online* http://www.british-history.ac.uk/london-letter-books/vole/53-66 (accessed 19 September 2019).

Styles, P., (ed.) 'The borough of Stratford-upon-Avon: Historical account', in *A History of the County of Warwick: Volume 3, Barlichway Hundred*, (London, 1945) pp. 234–244. *British History Online* http://www.british-history.ac.uk/vch/warks/vol3/pp234-244 (accessed 27 February 2019).

Taken from John Strype's *A Survey of the City of London* https://www.dhi.ac.uk/strype/TransformServlet?page=book2_022&display=normal&highlight=+Bakers (accessed 2 April 2019)

The Forme of Cury, 1390, by the Master-Cooks of King Richard II, available online. Samuel Pegge (ed.) 2013. http://www.gutenberg.org/cache/epub/8102/pg8102-images.html (accessed 21 September 2019).

*The Huntley & Palmers Collection.*Reading Biscuit town online at http://www.huntleyandpalmers.org.uk/ixbin/hixclient.exe?a=query&p=huntley&f=generic_theme.htm&_IXFIRST_=1&_IXMAXHITS_=1&t=rm-rm-biscuits_content1&%3dtheme_record_id=rm-rm-biscuits_content12&s=FHzVByQxOiH (accessed 20 May, 2019).

The Original Journals of Captains Meriwether Lewis and William Clark. The Journals Proper, vol 5 (1804–6) 127 http://content.wisconsinhistory.org/cdm/search/

collection/aj/searchterm/baking/field/all/mode/all/conn/and/order/extra5/ad/asc/cosuppress/0 (accessed 12 April 2019).

Thornbury,W., 'Holborn: To Chancery Lane', in *Old and New London: Volume 2* (London, 1878) 526–542. *British History Online* http://www.british-history.ac.uk/old-new-london/vol2/526-542 (accessed 1 October 2019).

'Upton St Leonards', in *Ancient and Historical Monuments in the County of Gloucester Iron Age and Romano-British Monuments in the Gloucestershire Cotswolds* (London, 1976)123. *British History Online* http://www.british-history.ac.uk/rchme/ancient-glos/p123a (accessed 2 March 2019).

'Vickery TV', Laverbread bread, https://vickery.tv/phil-vickerys-recipes/this-morning/item/laverbread-bread (accessed 13 September 2019).

Walford, E., 'Chelsea', in *Old and New London: Volume 5* (London, 1878) 50–70. *British History Online* http://www.british-history.ac.uk/old-new-london/vol5/50-70 (accessed 12 March 2019).

Walford, J., *Chairman of Brace's Bakery dies aged 96* (Wales online, 15 February, 2018, https://www.walesonline.co.uk/business/business-news/chairman-braces-bakery-dies-aged-14291879 accessed, 24/09/2019.

Watkins, A.E., (ed.) *Ælfric's Colloquy*, http://www.kentarchaeology.ac/authors/016.pdf(accessed 15 September, 2019).